SUPERMAN
ACTION COMICS
VOL. 2 LEVIATHAN RISING

SUPERMAN
ACTION COMICS
VOL. 2 LEVIATHAN RISING

BRIAN MICHAEL BENDIS
writer

STEVE EPTING
YANICK PAQUETTE
artists

BRAD ANDERSON
NATHAN FAIRBAIRN
colorists

JOSH REED
ROB LEIGH
DAVE SHARPE
ALW'S TROY PETERI
letterers

STEVE EPTING
collection cover artist

SUPERMAN created by **JERRY SIEGEL** and **JOE SHUSTER**
By special arrangement with the Jerry Siegel family

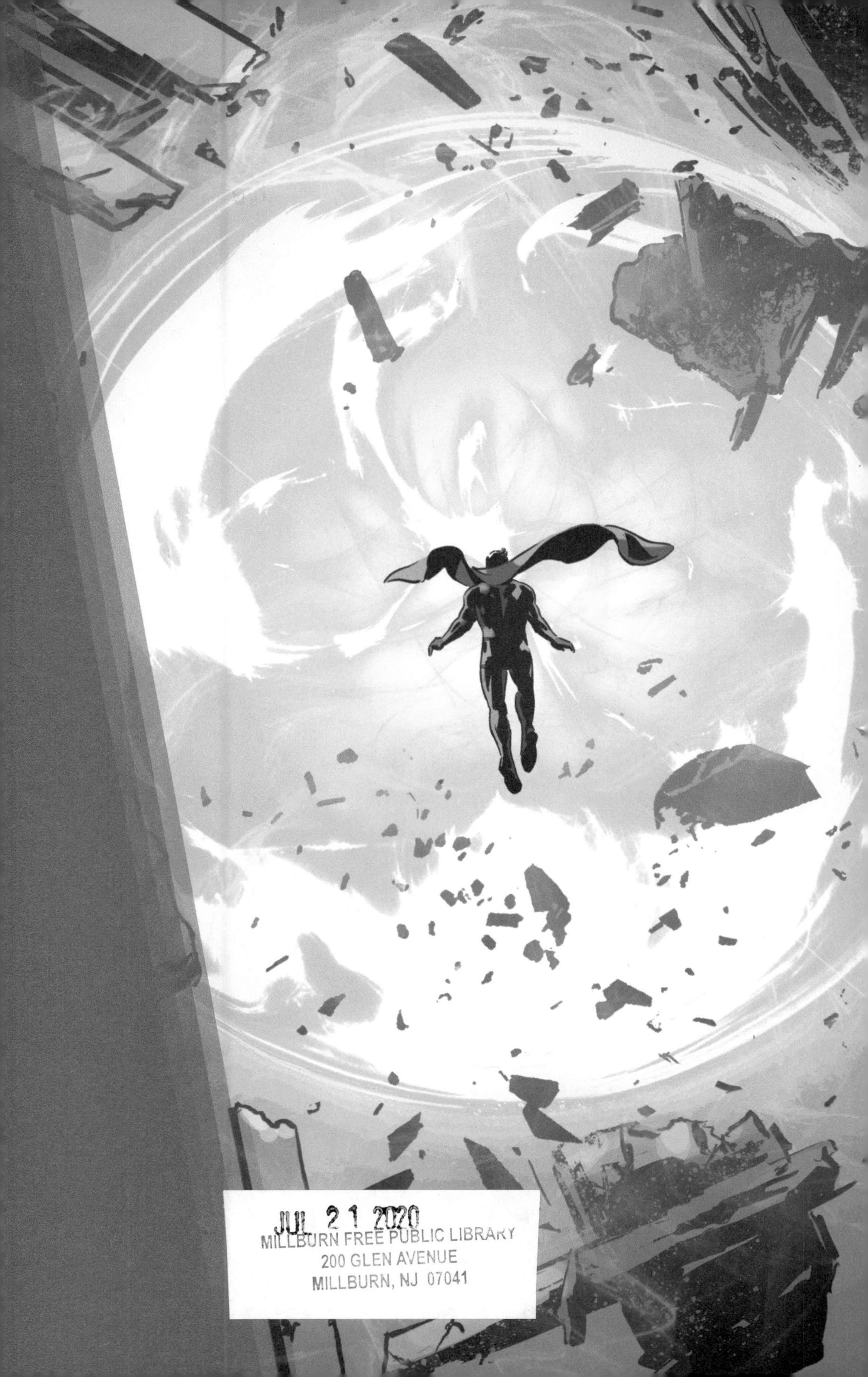

MIKE COTTON Editor – Original Series
JESSICA CHEN Associate Editor – Original Series
JEB WOODARD Group Editor – Collected Editions
ROBIN WILDMAN Editor – Collected Edition
STEVE COOK Design Director – Books
MONIQUE NARBONETA Publication Design
CHRISTY SAWYER Publication Production

BOB HARRAS Senior VP – Editor-in-Chief, DC Comics
PAT McCALLUM Executive Editor, DC Comics

DAN DiDIO Publisher
JIM LEE Publisher & Chief Creative Officer
BOBBIE CHASE VP – New Publishing Initiatives & Talent Development
DON FALLETTI VP – Manufacturing Operations & Workflow Management
LAWRENCE GANEM VP – Talent Services
ALISON GILL Senior VP – Manufacturing & Operations
HANK KANALZ Senior VP – Publishing Strategy & Support Services
DAN MIRON VP – Publishing Operations
NICK J. NAPOLITANO VP – Manufacturing Administration & Design
NANCY SPEARS VP – Sales
MICHELE R. WELLS VP & Executive Editor, Young Reader

SUPERMAN: ACTION COMICS VOL. 2: LEVIATHAN RISING

Published by DC Comics. Compilation and all new material Copyright © 2020 DC Comics. All Rights
Reserved. Originally published in single magazine form in ACTION COMICS 1007-1011 and SUPERMAN:
LEVIATHAN RISING SPECIAL 1. Copyright © 2019 DC Comics. All Rights Reserved. All characters, their
distinctive likenesses and related elements featured in this publication are trademarks of DC Comics. The
stories, characters and incidents featured in this publication are entirely fictional. DC Comics does not read
or accept unsolicited submissions of ideas, stories or artwork. DC – a WarnerMedia Company.

DC Comics, 2900 West Alameda Ave., Burbank, CA 91505
Printed by LSC Communications, Owensville, MO, USA. 4/3/20. First Printing.
ISBN: 978-1-77950-004-5

Library of Congress Cataloging-in-Publication Data is available.

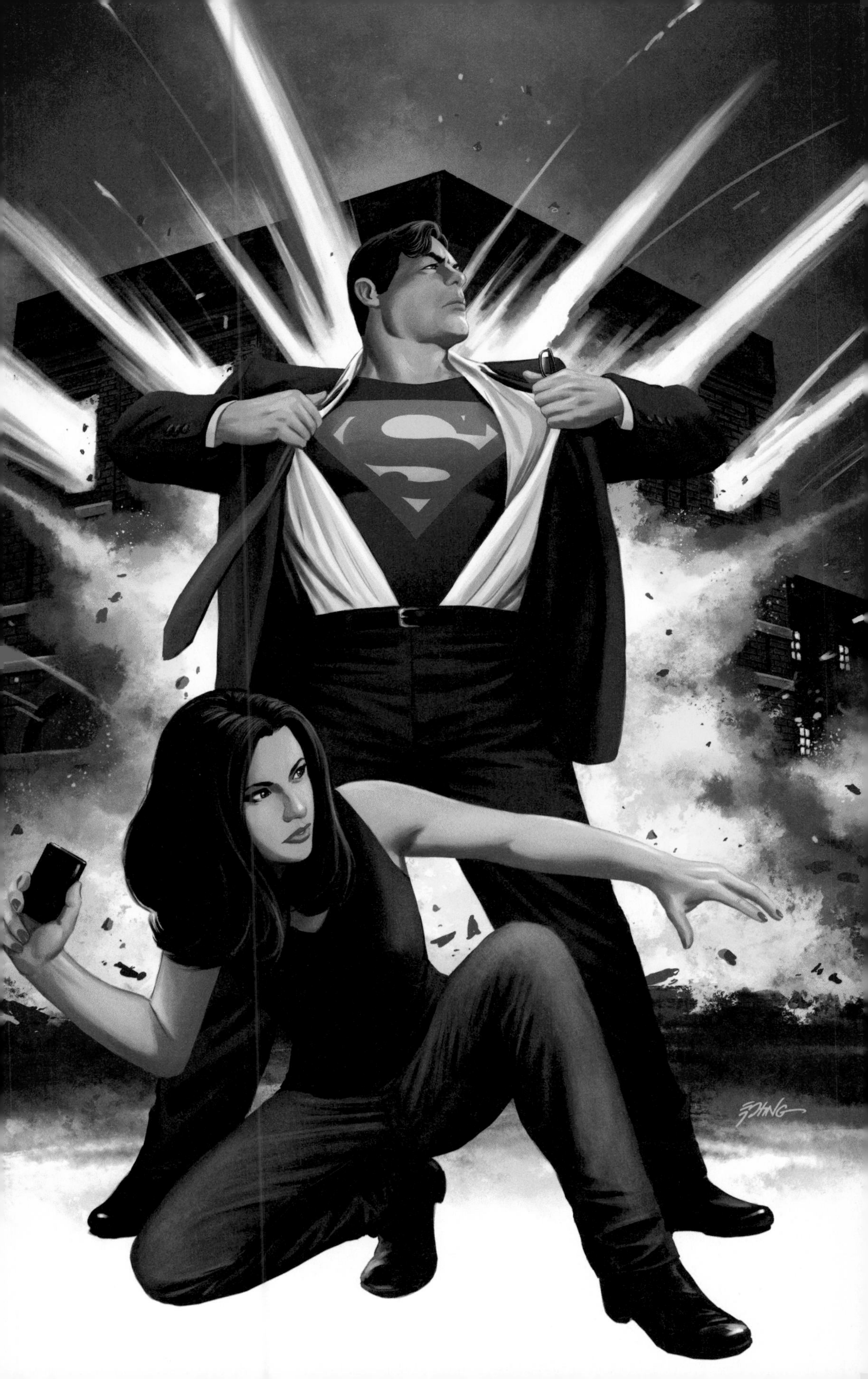

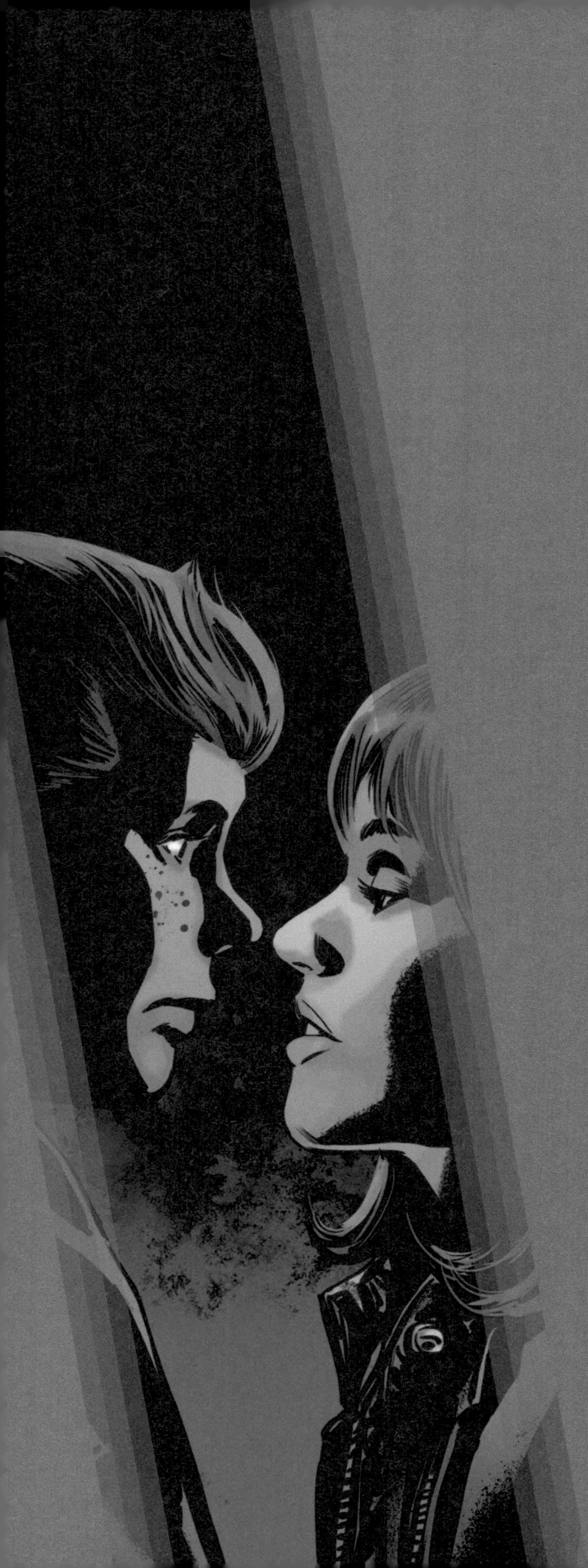

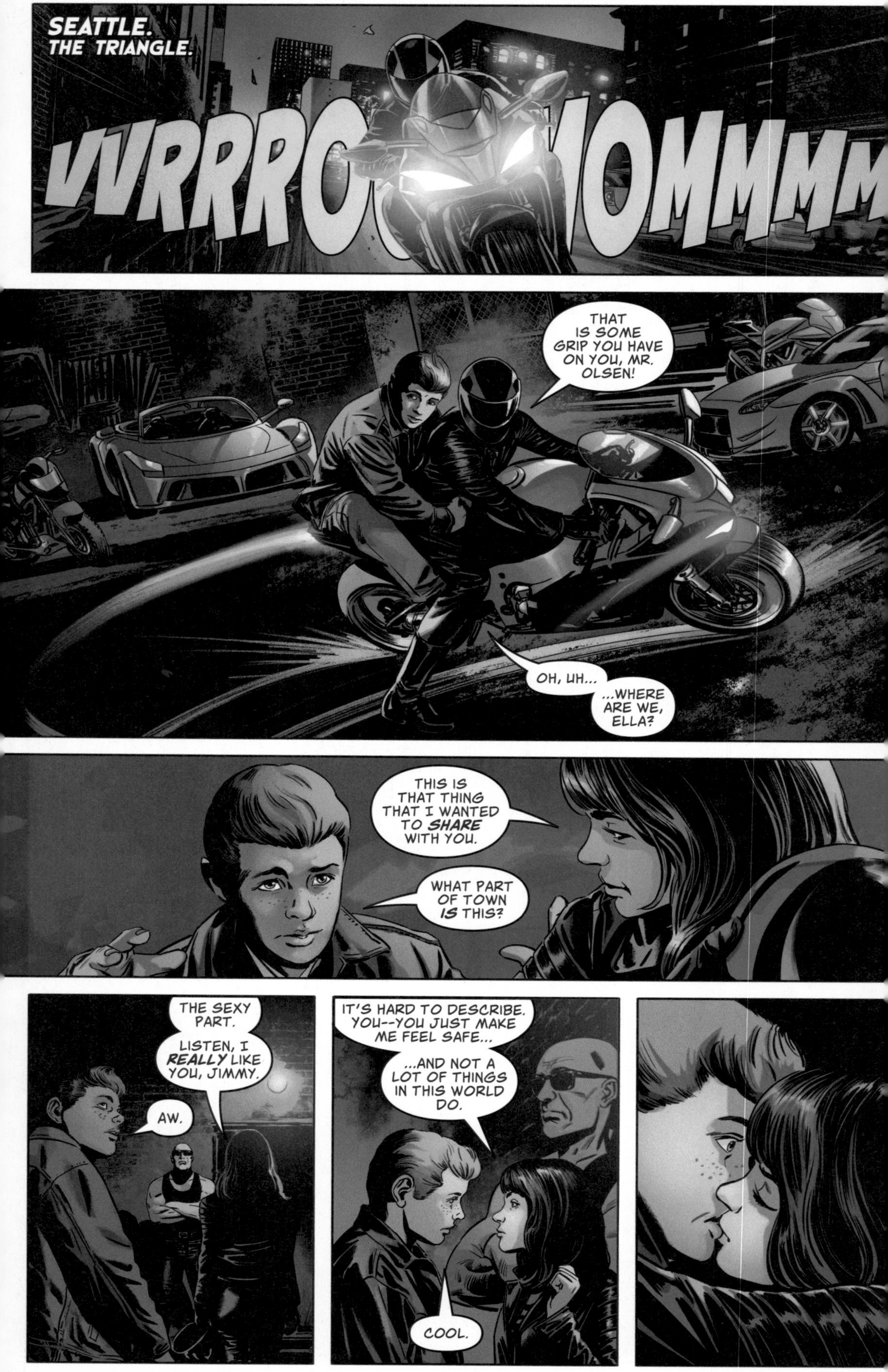
SEATTLE.
THE TRIANGLE.
VVRRROOOOMMMMM
THAT IS SOME GRIP YOU HAVE ON YOU, MR. OLSEN!
OH, UH...
...WHERE ARE WE, ELLA?
THIS IS THAT THING THAT I WANTED TO SHARE WITH YOU.
WHAT PART OF TOWN IS THIS?
THE SEXY PART.
LISTEN, I REALLY LIKE YOU, JIMMY.
AW.
IT'S HARD TO DESCRIBE. YOU--YOU JUST MAKE ME FEEL SAFE...
...AND NOT A LOT OF THINGS IN THIS WORLD DO.
COOL.

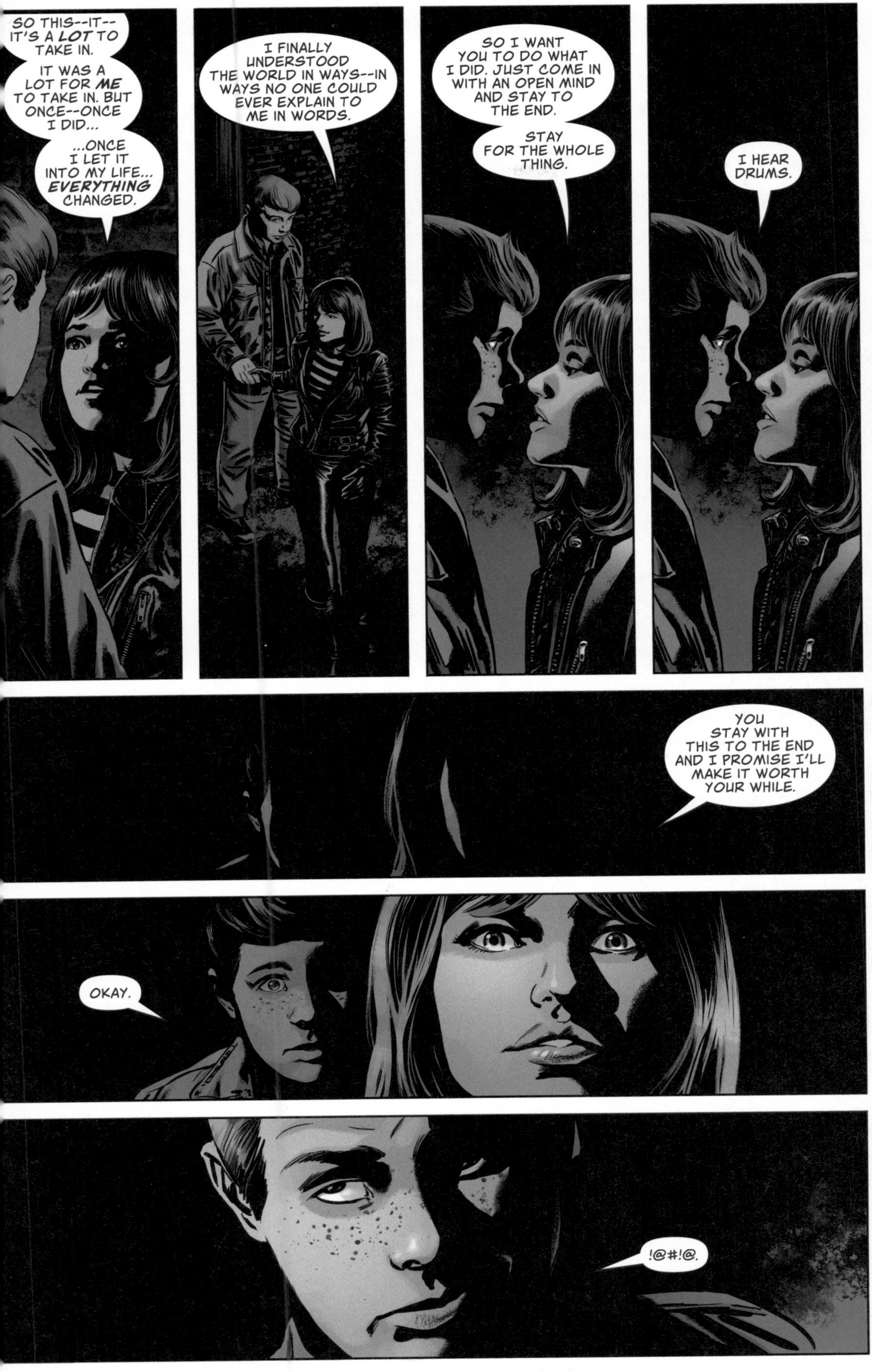
SO THIS--IT--IT'S A LOT TO TAKE IN.
IT WAS A LOT FOR ME TO TAKE IN. BUT ONCE--ONCE I DID...
...ONCE I LET IT INTO MY LIFE... EVERYTHING CHANGED.
I FINALLY UNDERSTOOD THE WORLD IN WAYS--IN WAYS NO ONE COULD EVER EXPLAIN TO ME IN WORDS.
SO I WANT YOU TO DO WHAT I DID. JUST COME IN WITH AN OPEN MIND AND STAY TO THE END.
STAY FOR THE WHOLE THING.
I HEAR DRUMS.
YOU STAY WITH THIS TO THE END AND I PROMISE I'LL MAKE IT WORTH YOUR WHILE.
OKAY.
!@#!@.

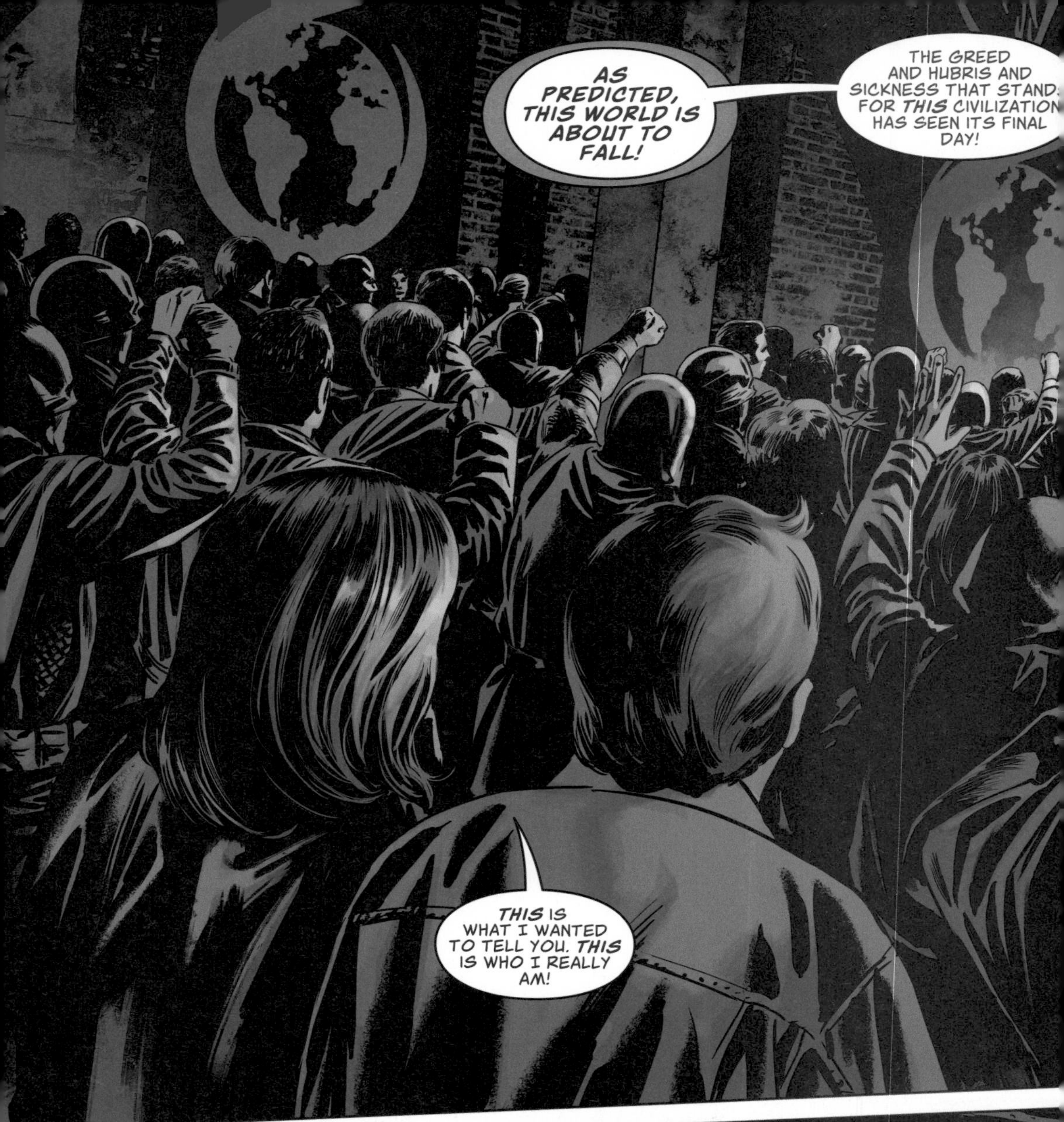
AS PREDICTED, THIS WORLD IS ABOUT TO FALL!
THE GREED AND HUBRIS AND SICKNESS THAT STAND FOR THIS CIVILIZATION HAS SEEN ITS FINAL DAY!
THIS IS WHAT I WANTED TO TELL YOU. THIS IS WHO I REALLY AM!

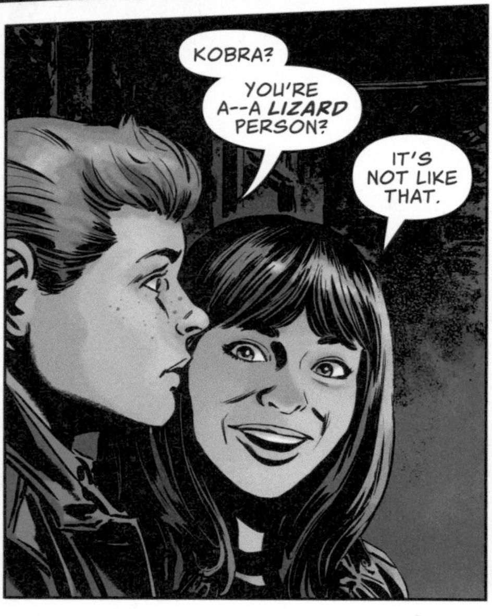
KOBRA?
YOU'RE A--A LIZARD PERSON?
IT'S NOT LIKE THAT.

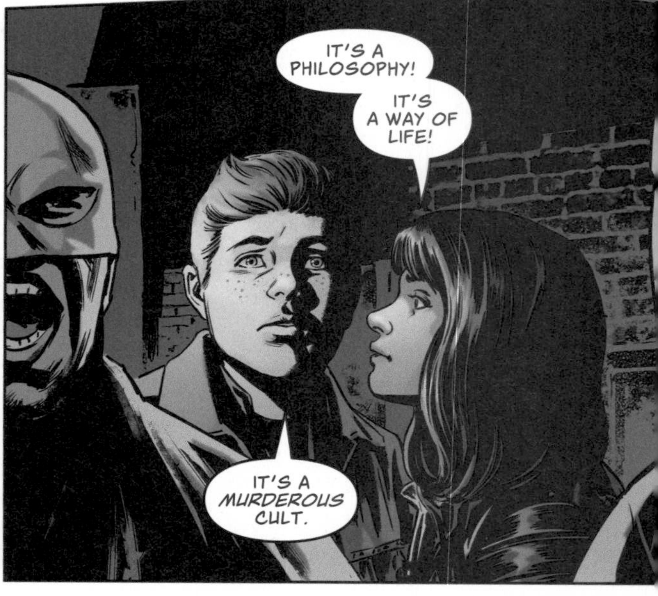
IT'S A PHILOSOPHY!
IT'S A WAY OF LIFE!
IT'S A MURDEROUS CULT.

WE ARE **KOBRA!**

FAITH TO KALI YUGA!

WE ARE THE FUTURE!

DC COMICS PROUDLY PRESENTS *Action* COMICS

BRIAN MICHAEL BENDIS Script

STEVE EPTING Art & Cover

BRAD ANDERSON Colors

JOSH REED Letters

JESSICA CHEN Associate Editor

MIKE COTTON Editor

BRIAN CUNNINGHAM Group Editor

LEVIATHAN RISES

part 1

THAT'S THE DISRUPTIVE MEDIA SELLING *THEIR OWN* CULT AGENDA.

THEY ARE THE CULT. *WE* ARE THE FUTURE OF THE SPECIES FREE OF *THEIR* POISON!

FAITH TO KALI YUGA!!

FAITH TO KALI YUGA!!

FAITH TO KALI YUGA!!

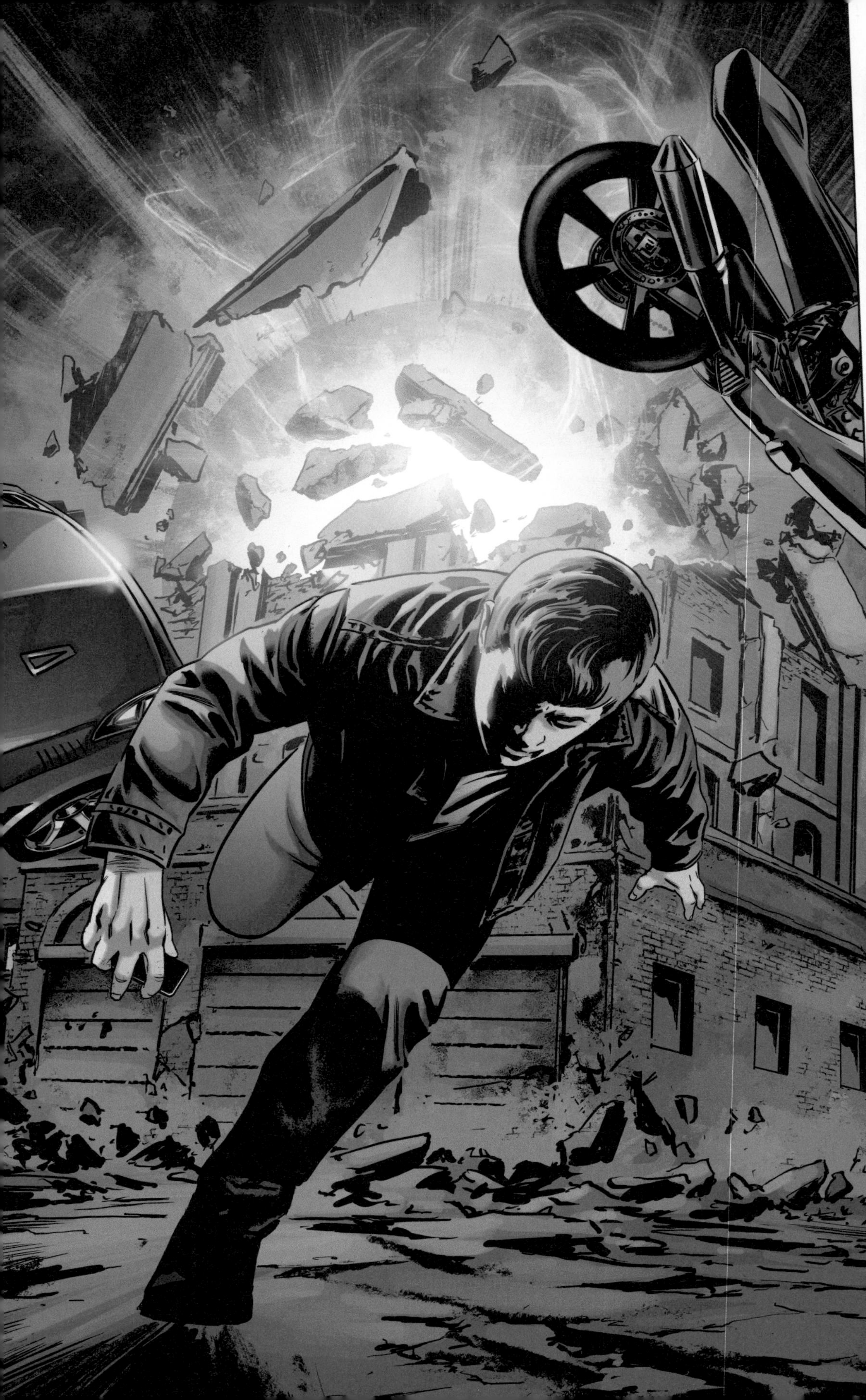

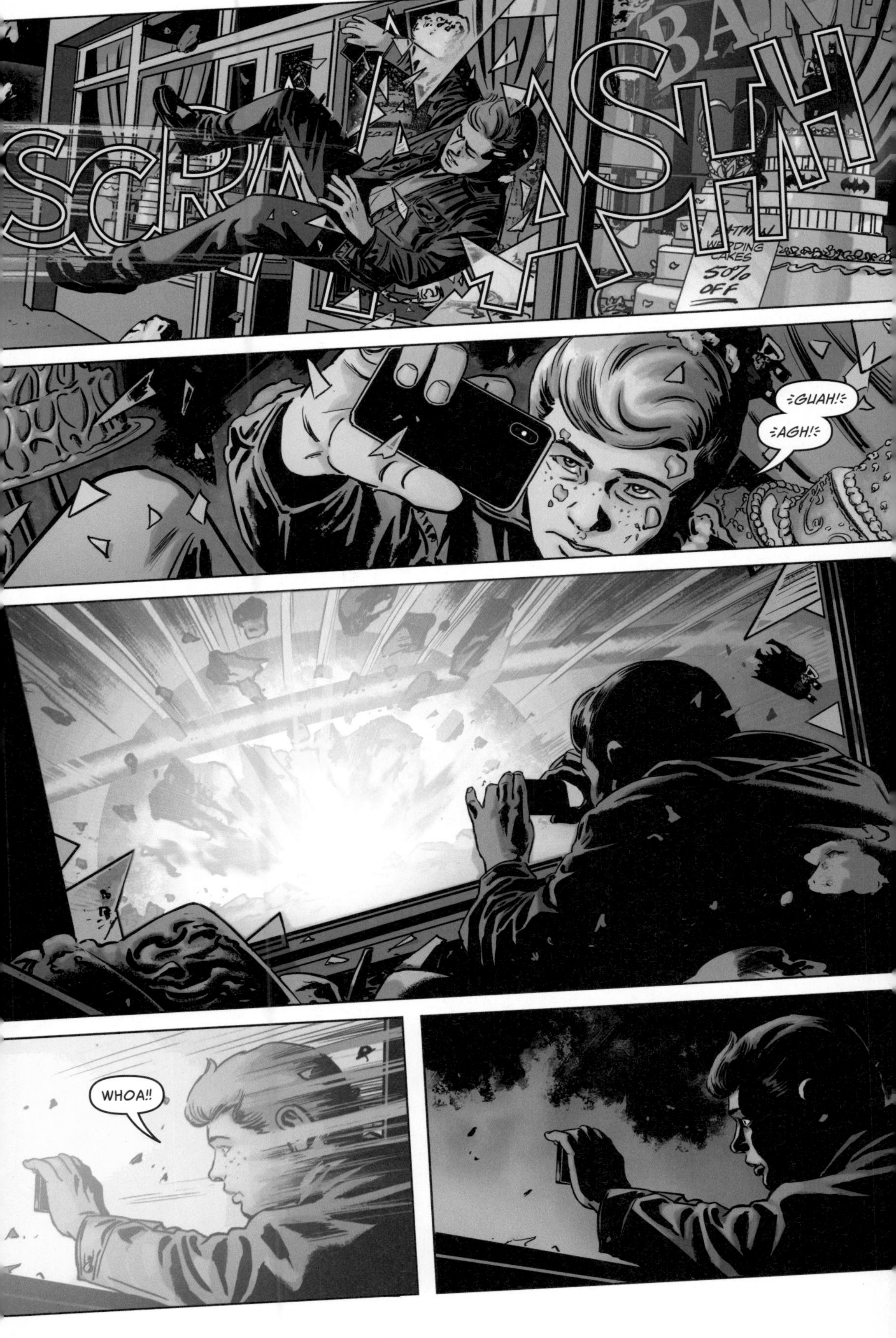
SCRAAASHH
BAKE
BATMAN WEDDING CAKES 50% OFF
GUAH!
AGH!
WHOA!!

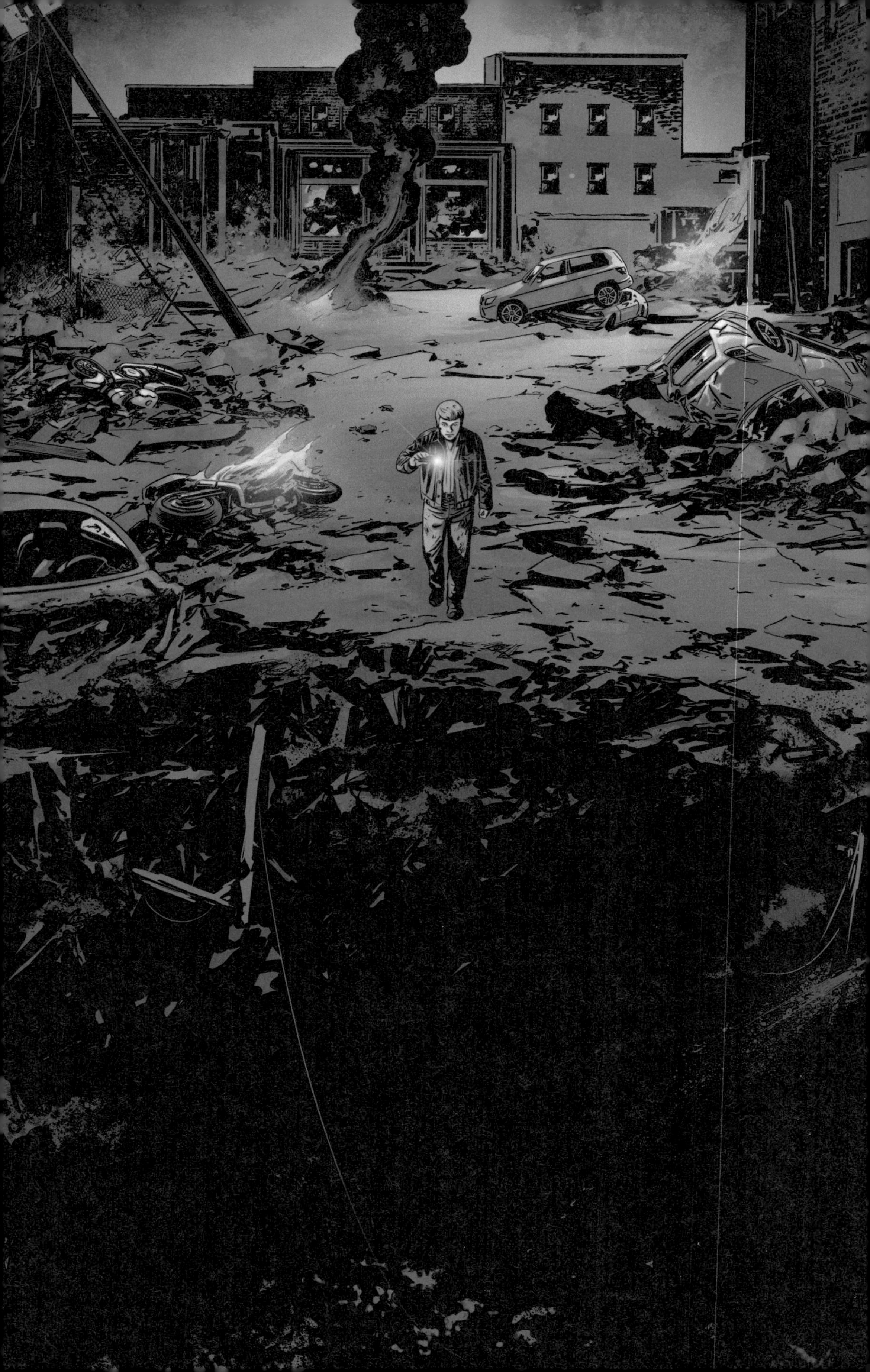

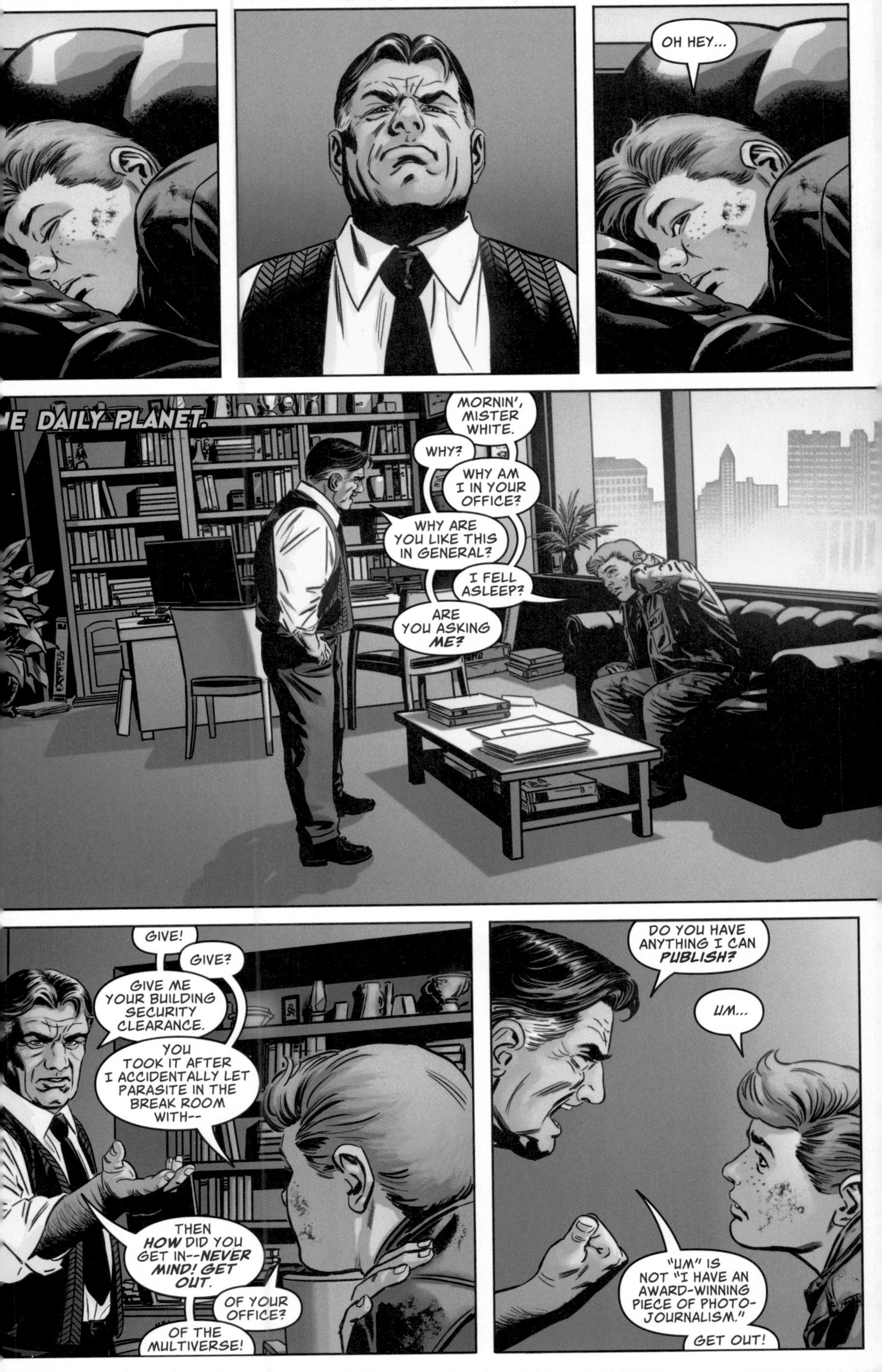
OH HEY...
E DAILY PLANET.
MORNIN', MISTER WHITE.
WHY?
WHY AM I IN YOUR OFFICE?
WHY ARE YOU LIKE THIS IN GENERAL?
I FELL ASLEEP?
ARE YOU ASKING ME?
GIVE!
GIVE?
GIVE ME YOUR BUILDING SECURITY CLEARANCE.
YOU TOOK IT AFTER I ACCIDENTALLY LET PARASITE IN THE BREAK ROOM WITH--
THEN HOW DID YOU GET IN--NEVER MIND! GET OUT.
OF YOUR OFFICE?
OF THE MULTIVERSE!
DO YOU HAVE ANYTHING I CAN PUBLISH?
UM...
"UM" IS NOT "I HAVE AN AWARD-WINNING PIECE OF PHOTO-JOURNALISM."
GET OUT!

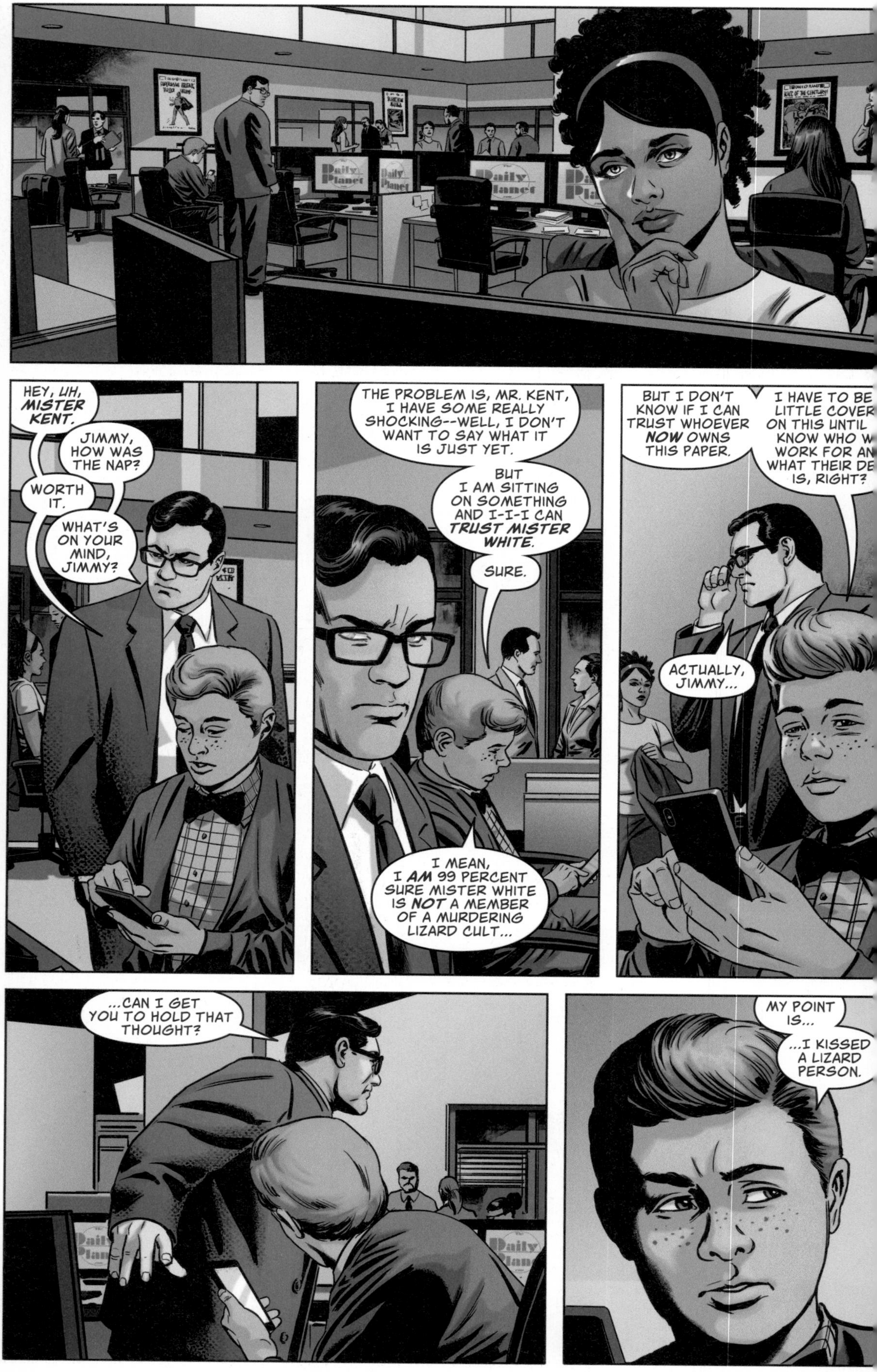
HEY, UH, *MISTER KENT.*
JIMMY, HOW WAS THE NAP?
WORTH IT.
WHAT'S ON YOUR MIND, JIMMY?
THE PROBLEM IS, MR. KENT, I HAVE SOME REALLY SHOCKING--WELL, I DON'T WANT TO SAY WHAT IT IS JUST YET.
BUT I AM SITTING ON SOMETHING AND I-I-I CAN *TRUST MISTER WHITE.*
SURE.
I MEAN, I *AM* 99 PERCENT SURE MISTER WHITE IS *NOT* A MEMBER OF A MURDERING LIZARD CULT...
BUT I DON'T KNOW IF I CAN TRUST WHOEVER *NOW* OWNS THIS PAPER.
I HAVE TO BE LITTLE COVER ON THIS UNTIL KNOW WHO W WORK FOR AN WHAT THEIR DE IS, RIGHT?
ACTUALLY, JIMMY...
...CAN I GET YOU TO HOLD THAT THOUGHT?
MY POINT IS...
...I KISSED A LIZARD PERSON.

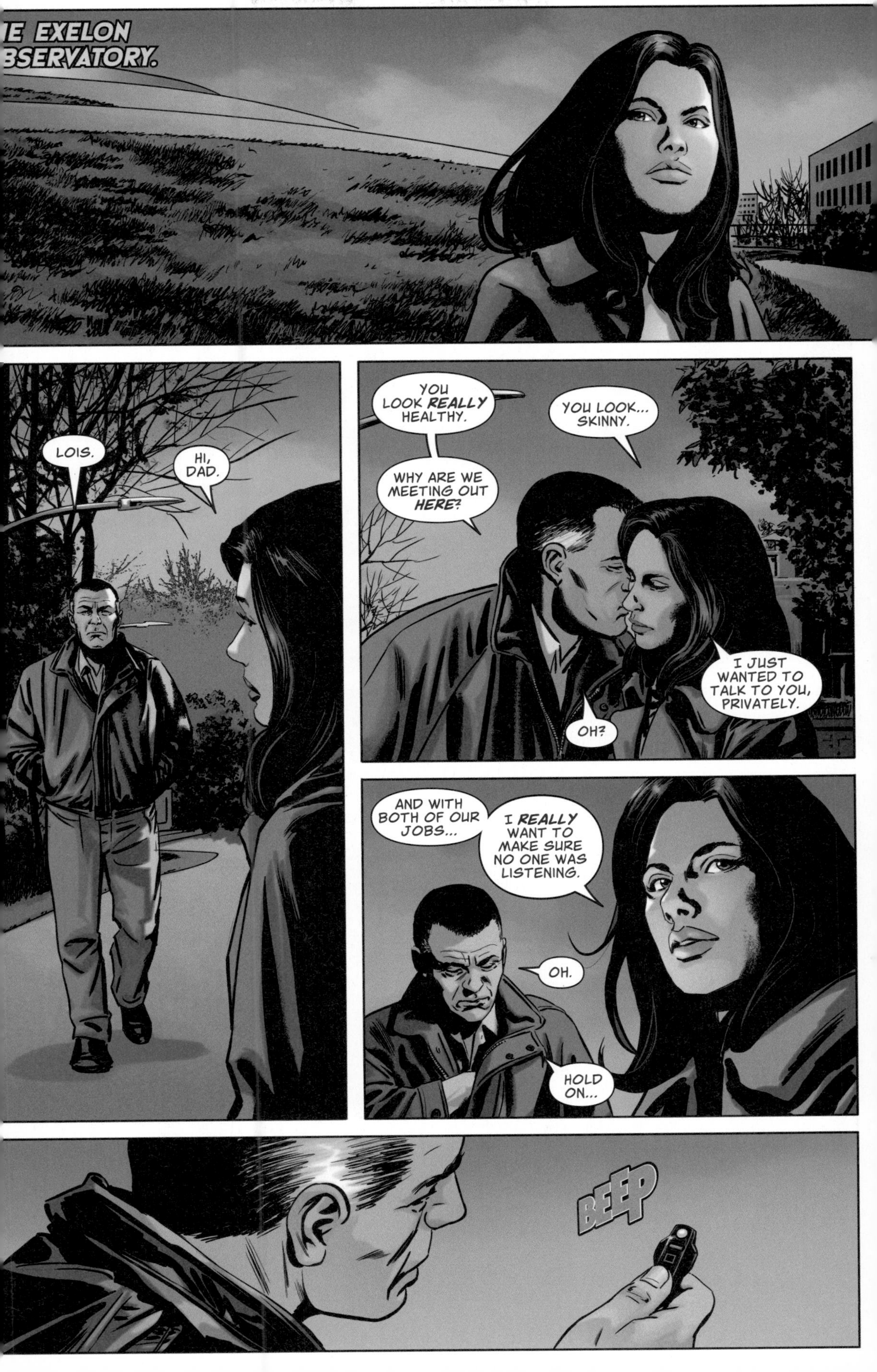

...E EXELON
...BSERVATORY.
LOIS.
HI, DAD.
YOU LOOK REALLY HEALTHY.
YOU LOOK... SKINNY.
WHY ARE WE MEETING OUT HERE?
I JUST WANTED TO TALK TO YOU, PRIVATELY.
OH?
AND WITH BOTH OF OUR JOBS...
I REALLY WANT TO MAKE SURE NO ONE WAS LISTENING.
OH.
HOLD ON...
BEEP

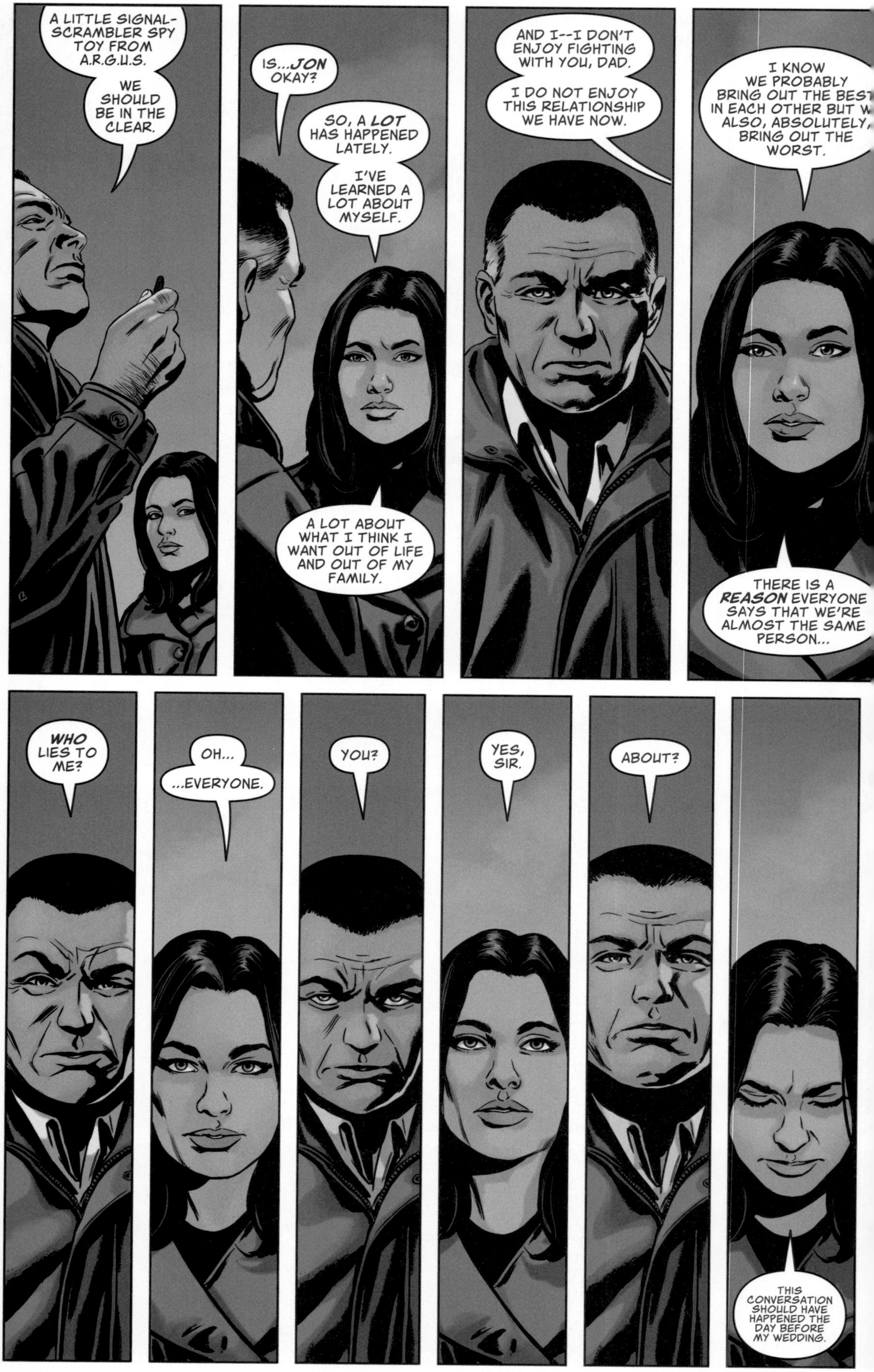
A LITTLE SIGNAL-SCRAMBLER SPY TOY FROM A.R.G.U.S.
WE SHOULD BE IN THE CLEAR.
IS...JON OKAY?
SO, A LOT HAS HAPPENED LATELY.
I'VE LEARNED A LOT ABOUT MYSELF.
A LOT ABOUT WHAT I THINK I WANT OUT OF LIFE AND OUT OF MY FAMILY.
AND I--I DON'T ENJOY FIGHTING WITH YOU, DAD.
I DO NOT ENJOY THIS RELATIONSHIP WE HAVE NOW.
I KNOW WE PROBABLY BRING OUT THE BEST IN EACH OTHER BUT WE ALSO, ABSOLUTELY, BRING OUT THE WORST.
THERE IS A REASON EVERYONE SAYS THAT WE'RE ALMOST THE SAME PERSON...
WHO LIES TO ME?
OH... ...EVERYONE.
YOU?
YES, SIR.
ABOUT?
THIS CONVERSATION SHOULD HAVE HAPPENED THE DAY BEFORE MY WEDDING.

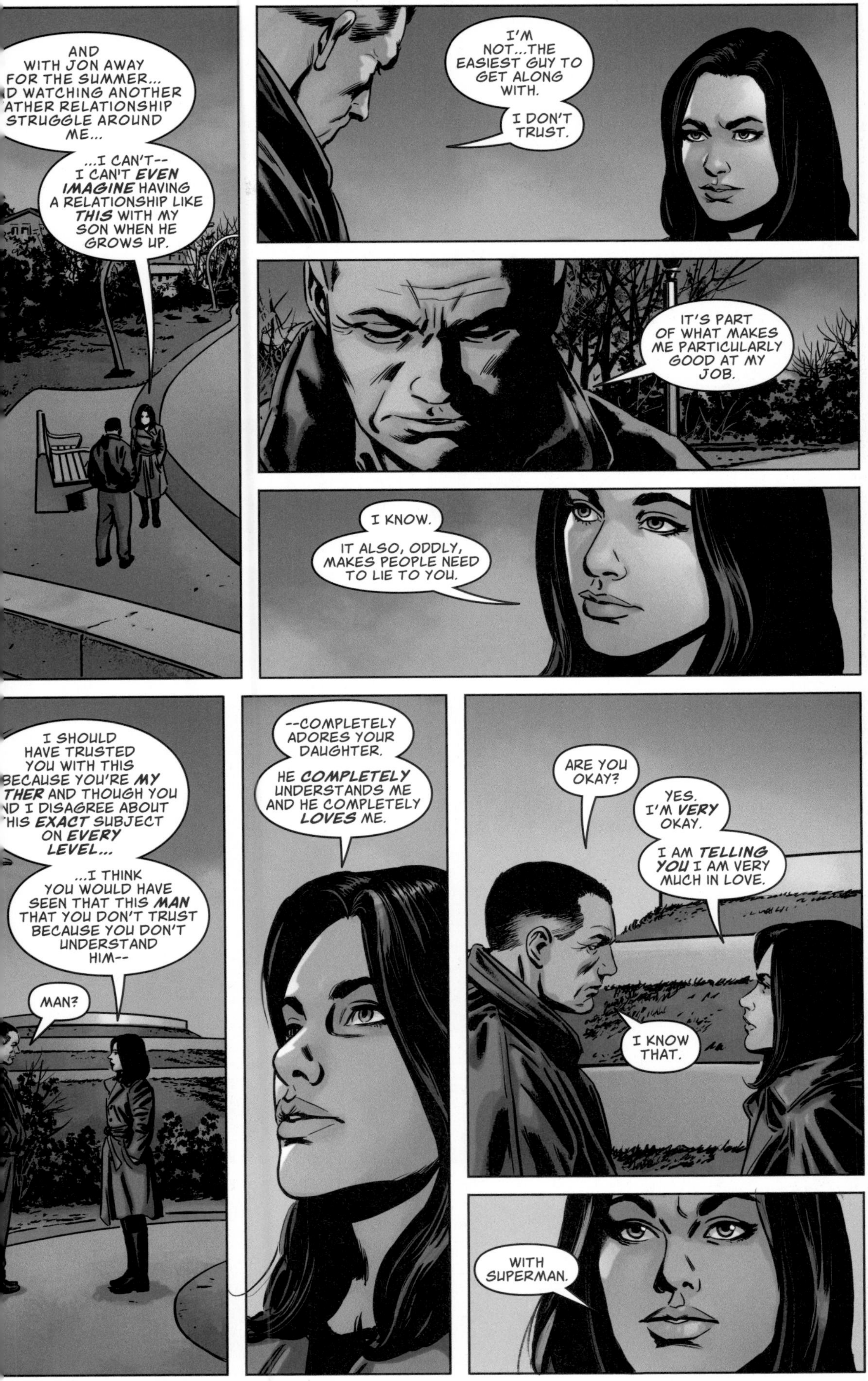
AND WITH JON AWAY FOR THE SUMMER... D WATCHING ANOTHER ATHER RELATIONSHIP STRUGGLE AROUND ME...
...I CAN'T-- I CAN'T EVEN IMAGINE HAVING A RELATIONSHIP LIKE THIS WITH MY SON WHEN HE GROWS UP.
I'M NOT...THE EASIEST GUY TO GET ALONG WITH.
I DON'T TRUST.
IT'S PART OF WHAT MAKES ME PARTICULARLY GOOD AT MY JOB.
I KNOW.
IT ALSO, ODDLY, MAKES PEOPLE NEED TO LIE TO YOU.
I SHOULD HAVE TRUSTED YOU WITH THIS BECAUSE YOU'RE MY THER AND THOUGH YOU ND I DISAGREE ABOUT THIS EXACT SUBJECT ON EVERY LEVEL...
...I THINK YOU WOULD HAVE SEEN THAT THIS MAN THAT YOU DON'T TRUST BECAUSE YOU DON'T UNDERSTAND HIM--
MAN?
--COMPLETELY ADORES YOUR DAUGHTER.
HE COMPLETELY UNDERSTANDS ME AND HE COMPLETELY LOVES ME.
ARE YOU OKAY?
YES. I'M VERY OKAY.
I AM TELLING YOU I AM VERY MUCH IN LOVE.
I KNOW THAT.
WITH SUPERMAN.

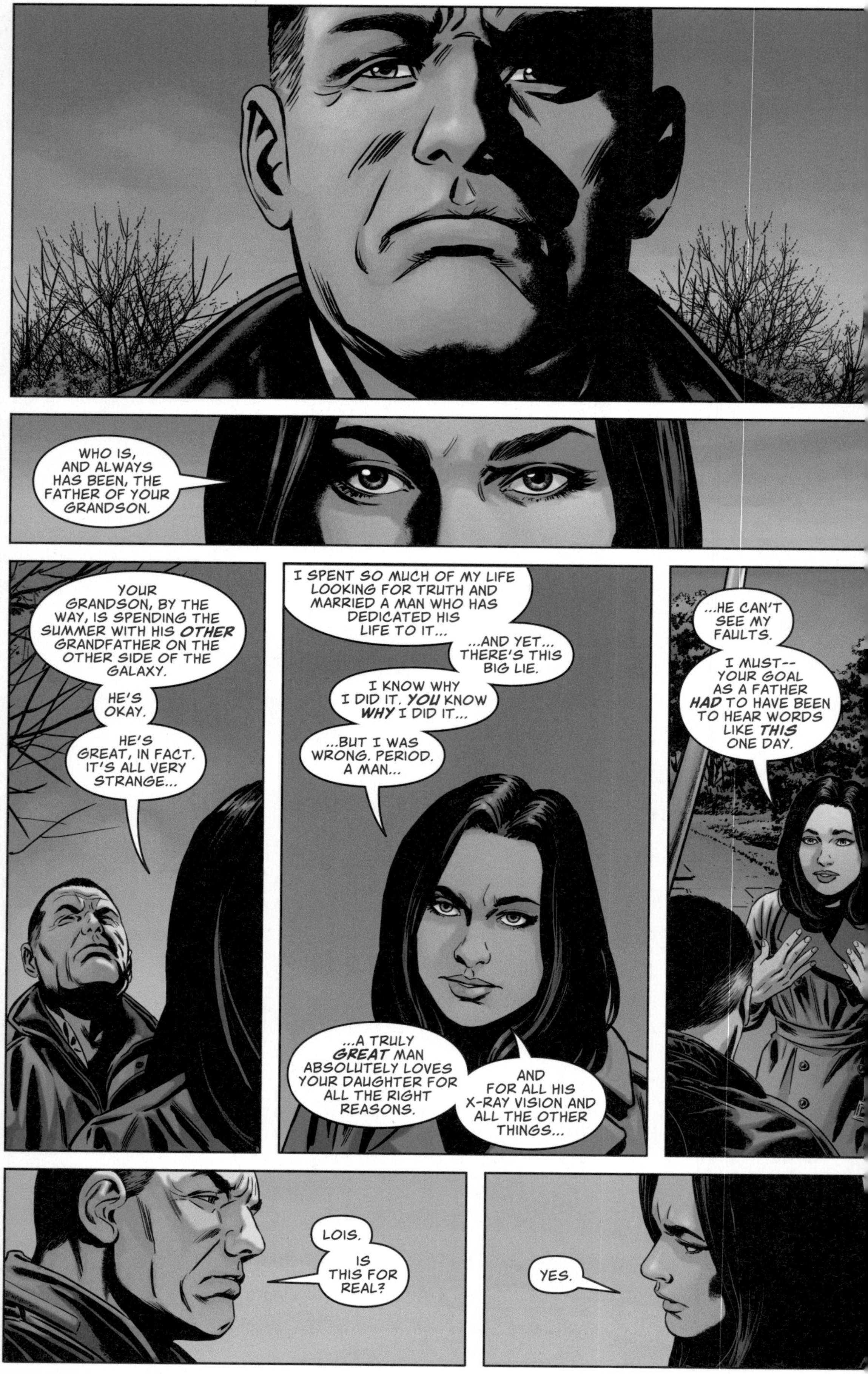
WHO IS, AND ALWAYS HAS BEEN, THE FATHER OF YOUR GRANDSON.
YOUR GRANDSON, BY THE WAY, IS SPENDING THE SUMMER WITH HIS OTHER GRANDFATHER ON THE OTHER SIDE OF THE GALAXY.
HE'S OKAY.
HE'S GREAT, IN FACT. IT'S ALL VERY STRANGE...
I SPENT SO MUCH OF MY LIFE LOOKING FOR TRUTH AND MARRIED A MAN WHO HAS DEDICATED HIS LIFE TO IT...
...AND YET... THERE'S THIS BIG LIE.
I KNOW WHY I DID IT. YOU KNOW WHY I DID IT...
...BUT I WAS WRONG. PERIOD. A MAN...
...A TRULY GREAT MAN ABSOLUTELY LOVES YOUR DAUGHTER FOR ALL THE RIGHT REASONS.
AND FOR ALL HIS X-RAY VISION AND ALL THE OTHER THINGS...
...HE CAN'T SEE MY FAULTS.
I MUST-- YOUR GOAL AS A FATHER HAD TO HAVE BEEN TO HEAR WORDS LIKE THIS ONE DAY.
LOIS.
IS THIS FOR REAL?
YES.

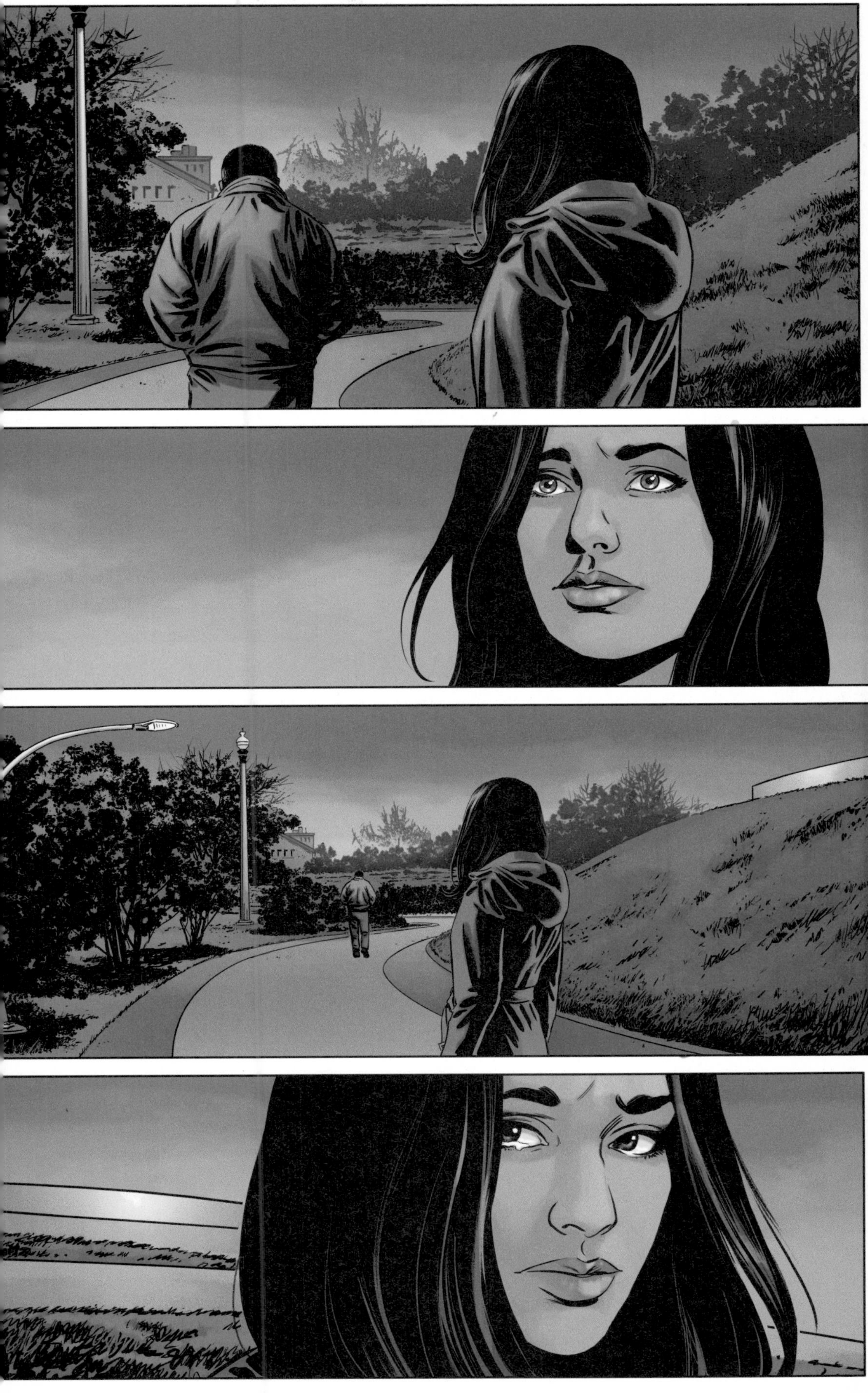

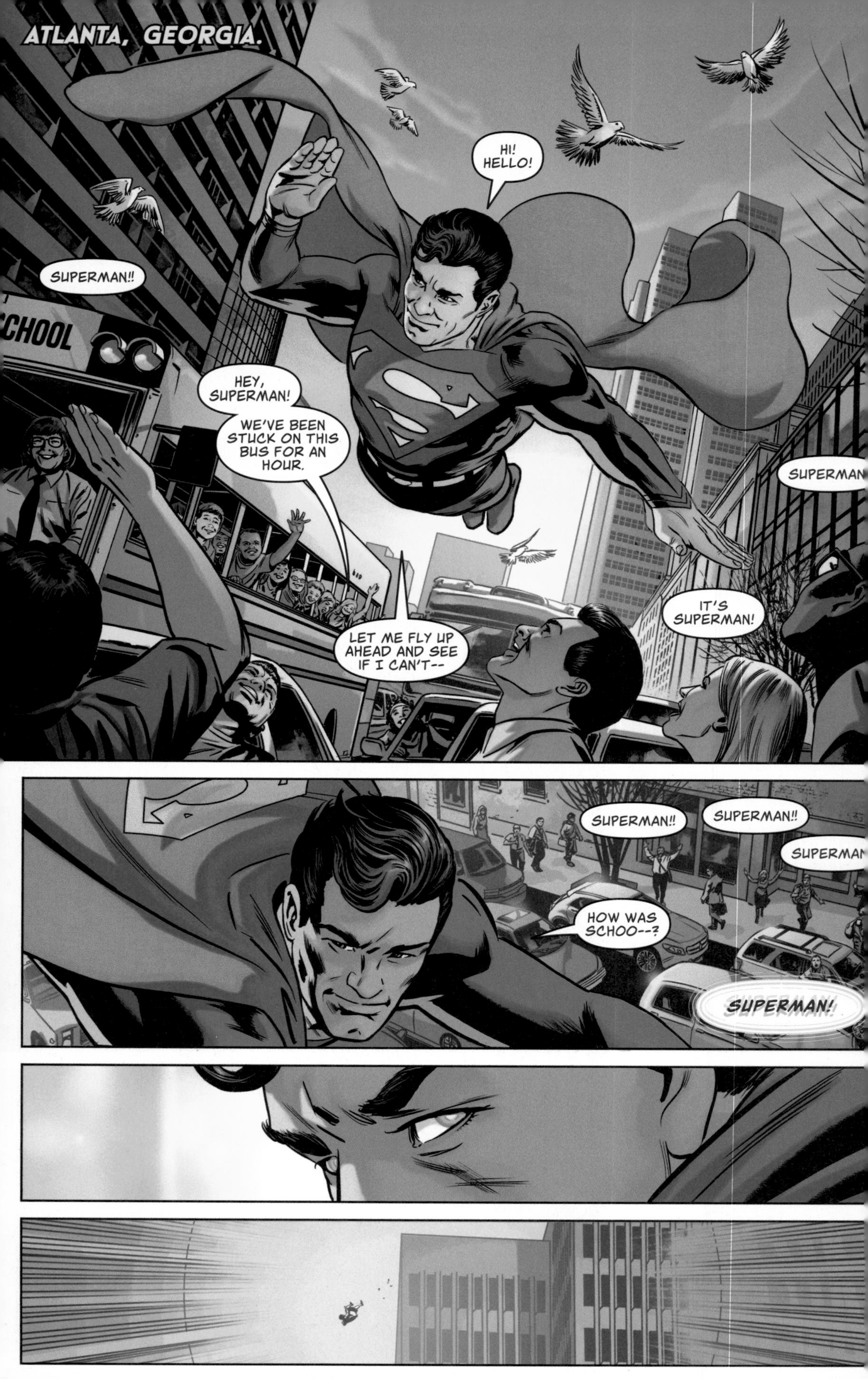
ATLANTA, GEORGIA.
HI! HELLO!
SUPERMAN!!
HEY, SUPERMAN!
WE'VE BEEN STUCK ON THIS BUS FOR AN HOUR.
LET ME FLY UP AHEAD AND SEE IF I CAN'T--
IT'S SUPERMAN!
SUPERMAN!!
SUPERMAN!!
HOW WAS SCHOO--?
SUPERMAN!

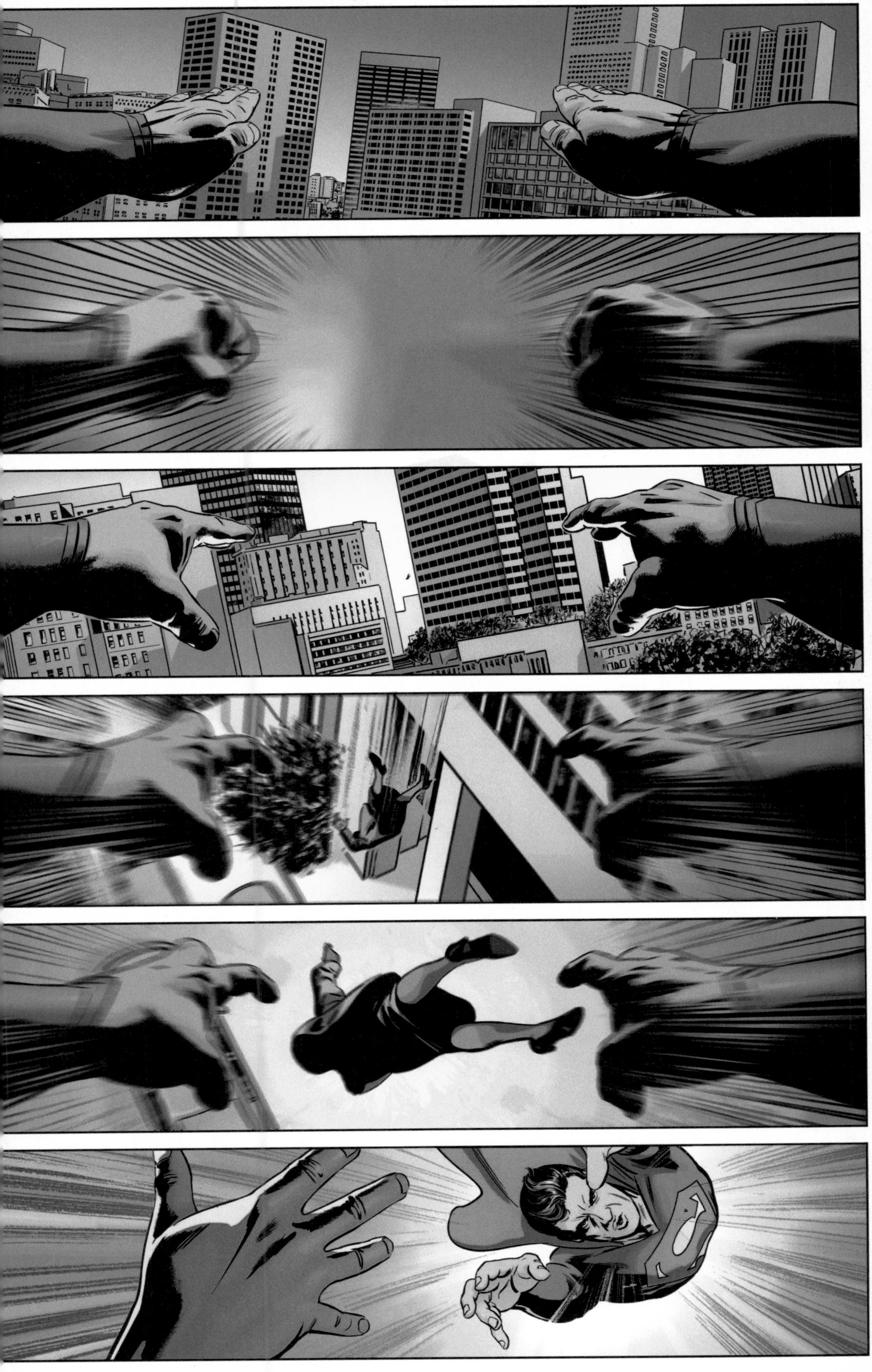

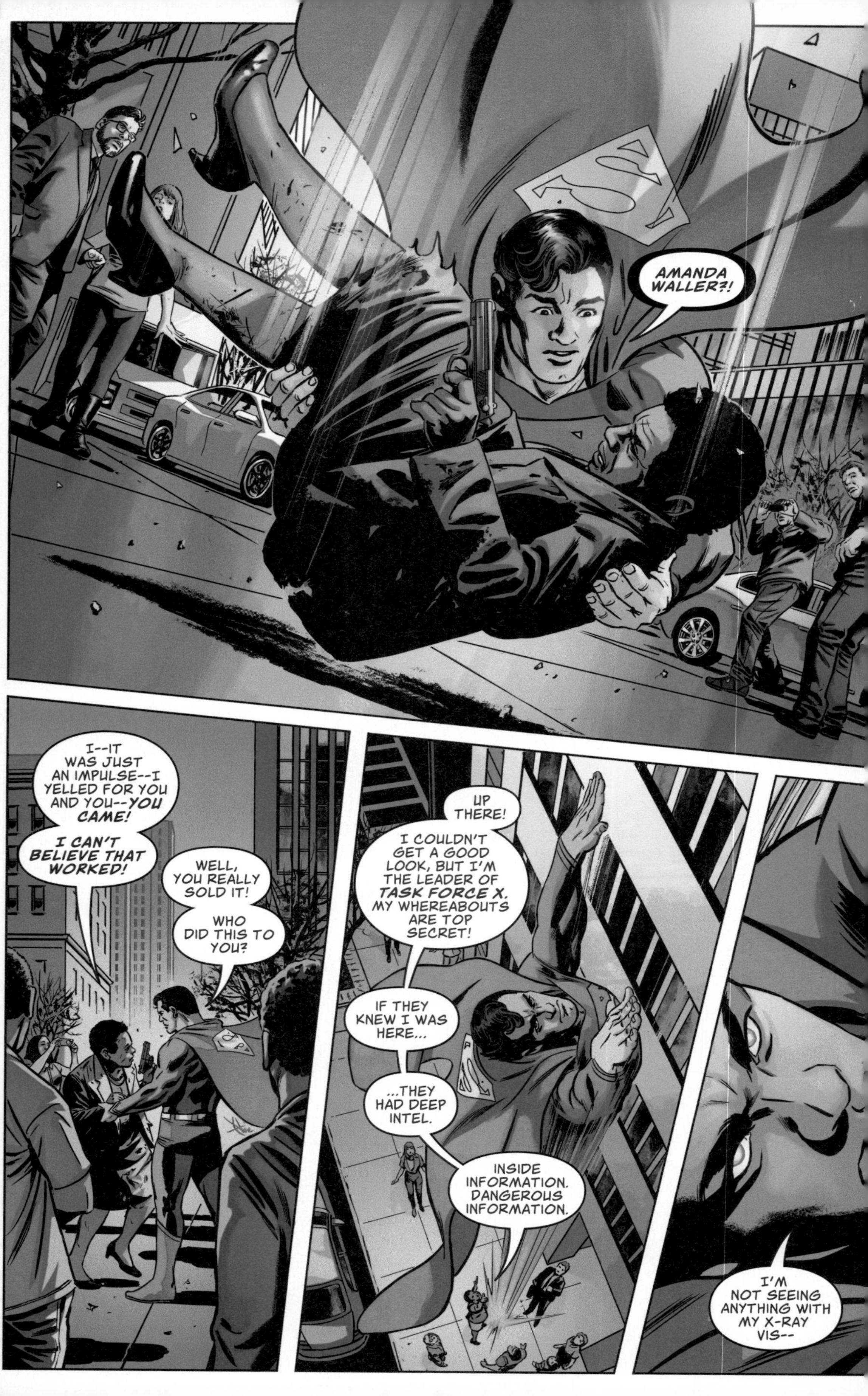
AMANDA WALLER?!
I--IT WAS JUST AN IMPULSE--I YELLED FOR YOU AND YOU--YOU CAME!
I CAN'T BELIEVE THAT WORKED!
WELL, YOU REALLY SOLD IT!
WHO DID THIS TO YOU?
UP THERE!
I COULDN'T GET A GOOD LOOK, BUT I'M THE LEADER OF TASK FORCE X. MY WHEREABOUTS ARE TOP SECRET!
IF THEY KNEW I WAS HERE...
...THEY HAD DEEP INTEL.
INSIDE INFORMATION. DANGEROUS INFORMATION.
I'M NOT SEEING ANYTHING WITH MY X-RAY VIS--

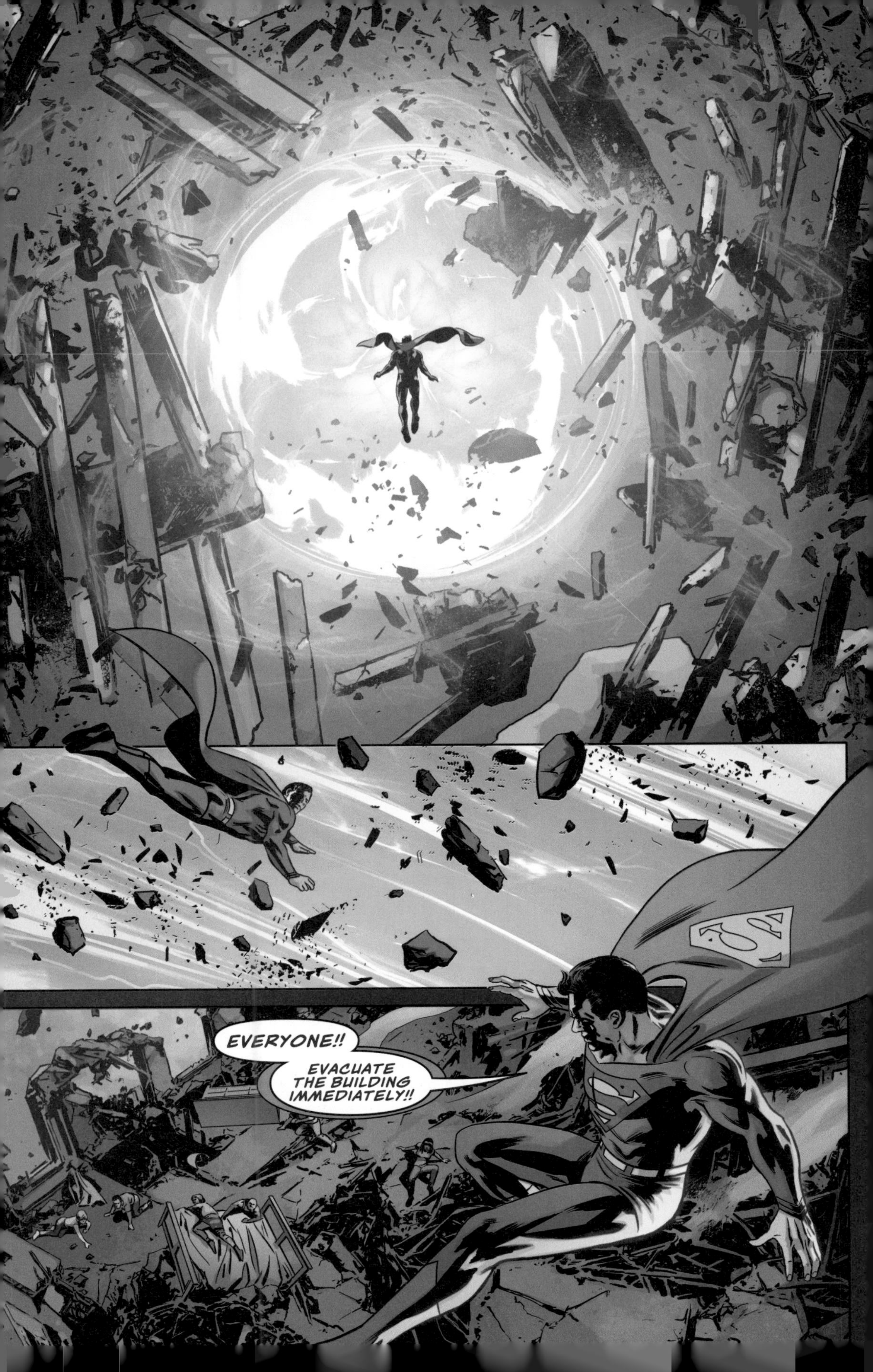
EVERYONE!!
EVACUATE THE BUILDING IMMEDIATELY!!

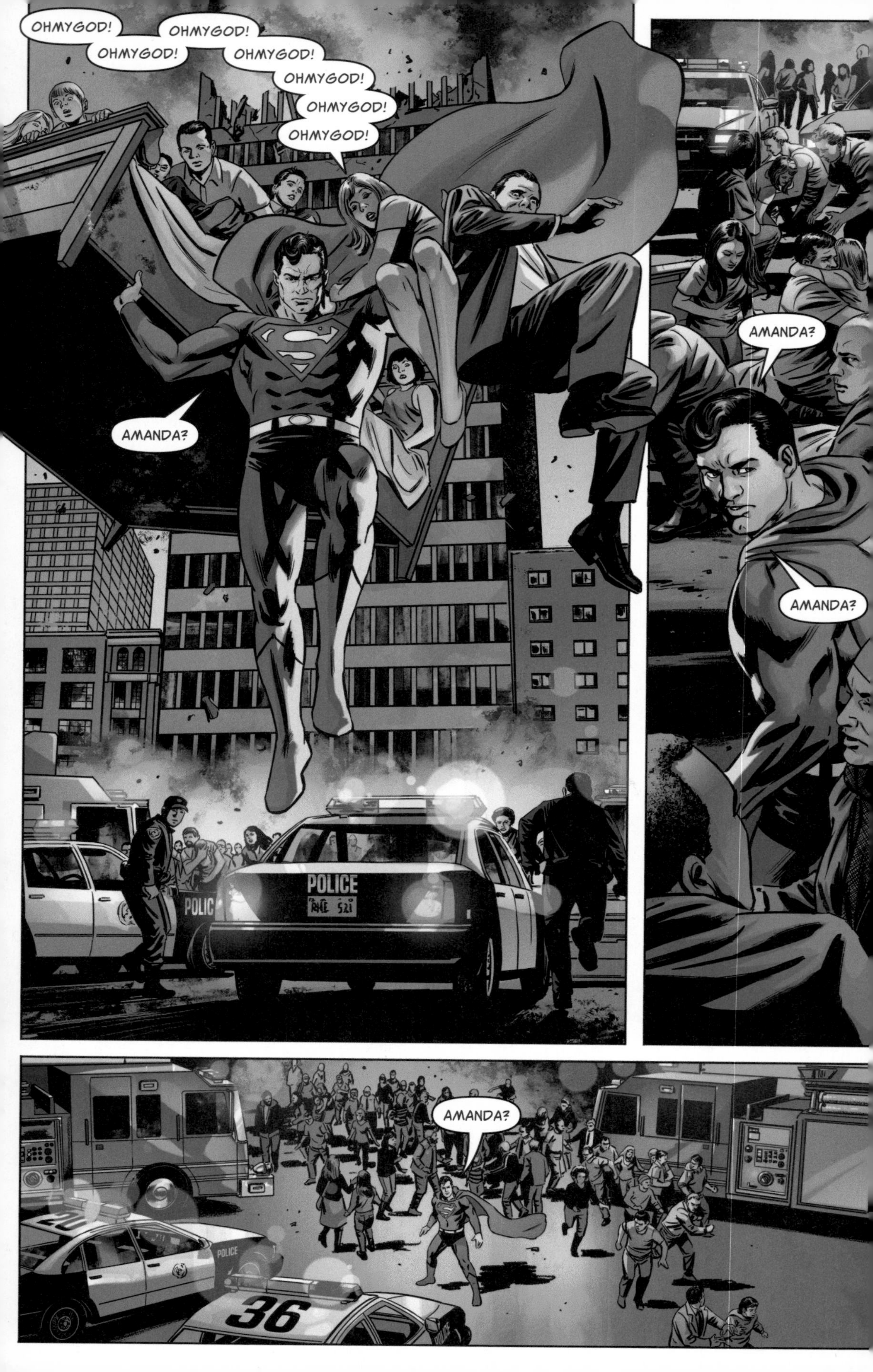
OHMYGOD!
OHMYGOD!
OHMYGOD!
OHMYGOD!
OHMYGOD!
OHMYGOD!
OHMYGOD!
AMANDA?
POLICE
POLIC
AMANDA?
AMANDA?
AMANDA?
POLICE
36

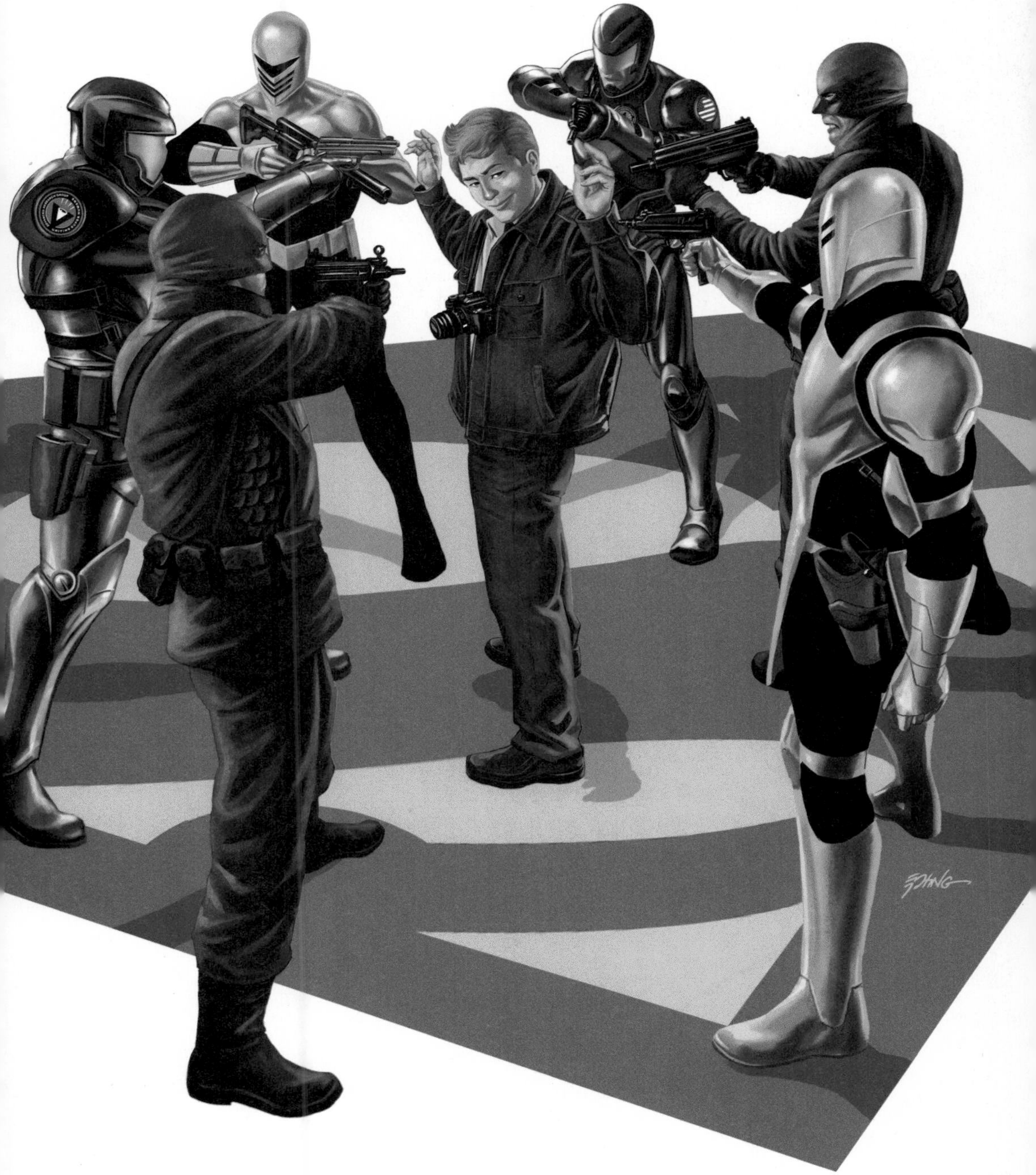

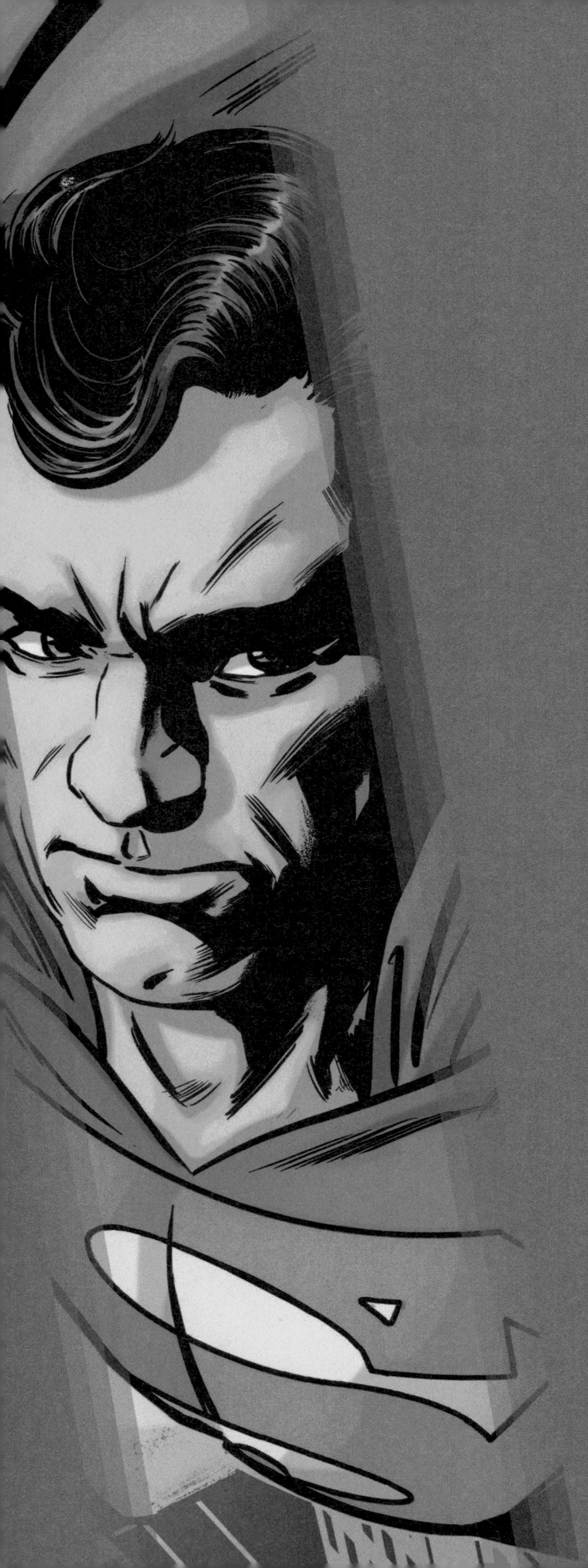

DEPARTMENT OF EXTRANORMAL OPERATIONS.

HE'S HERE.

ADAM STRANGE, REPORTING FOR DUTY.

I'M BONES.

I'M ACTING DIRECTOR OF T DEPARTMENT O EXTRANORMA OPERATIONS.

WE'VE MET.

I REMEMBER.

DO PEOPLE FORGET MEETING YOU?

OF COURSE NOT.

I WAS BEING CHEEKY.

THE PITCH: WITH SUPERGIRL OFF PLANET, WE NEED SOMEONE WITH A SPECIFIC SKILL SET AND KNOWLEDGE THAT--

OH, WAIT, ARE YOU OFFERING ME A GIG? HERE?

I WAS BUILDING UP TO IT.

WOW. WELL, I ACTUALLY DO HAVE A BUNCH OF IDEAS...

...ABOUT DRAGGING EARTH FORWARD INTO THE REAL GALACTIC CONVERSATION, BUT--

--FIRST I NEED TO TALK TO YOU ABOUT THE KRYPTONIAN GENERAL ZOD.

WHAT HAPPENED TO ZOD?

C I H YC

IT'S NOT "WHAT HAPPENED," BUT SOMETHING I DEFINITELY--

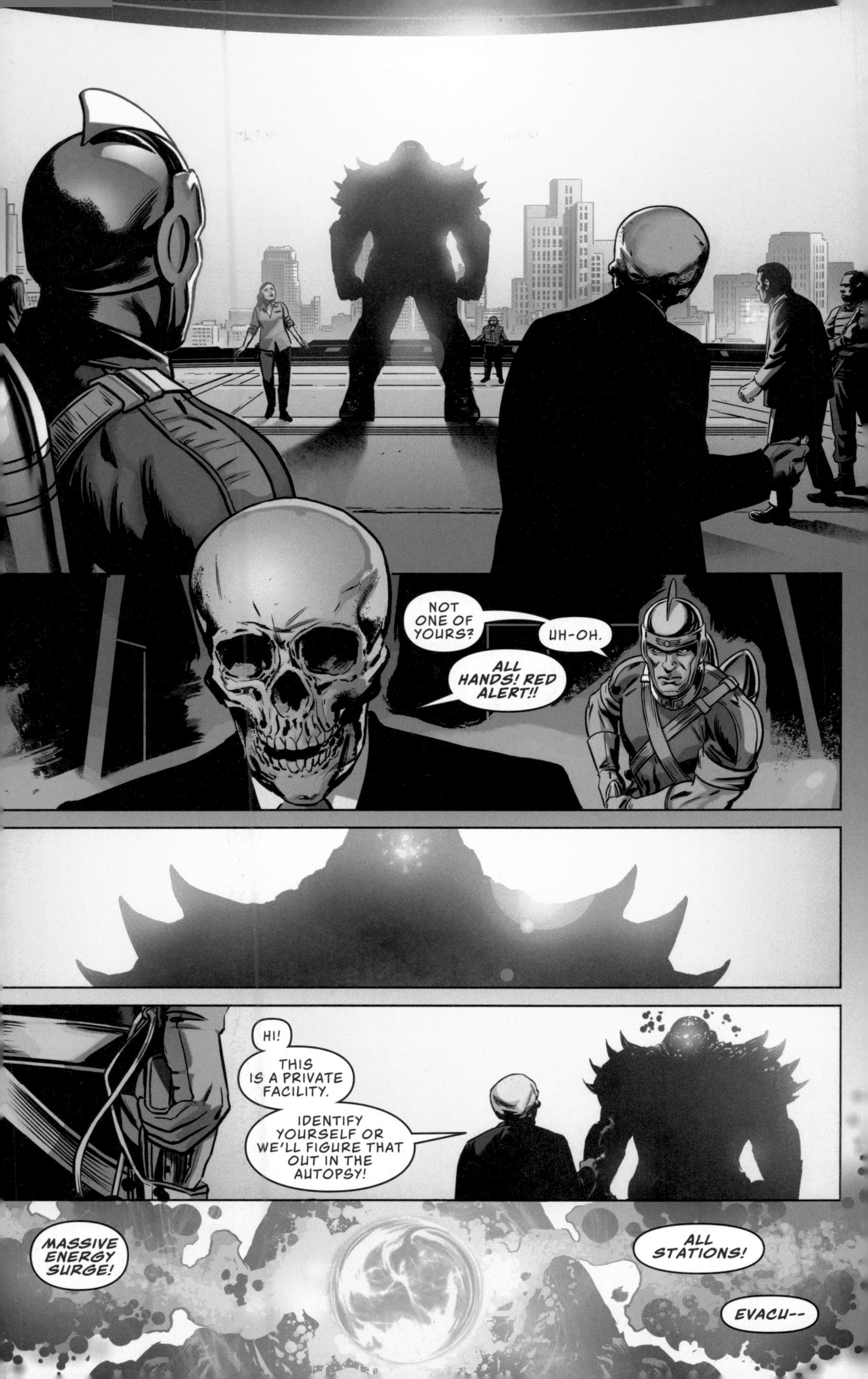
NOT ONE OF YOURS?
UH-OH.
ALL HANDS! RED ALERT!!
HI!
THIS IS A PRIVATE FACILITY.
IDENTIFY YOURSELF OR WE'LL FIGURE THAT OUT IN THE AUTOPSY!
MASSIVE ENERGY SURGE!
ALL STATIONS!
EVACU--

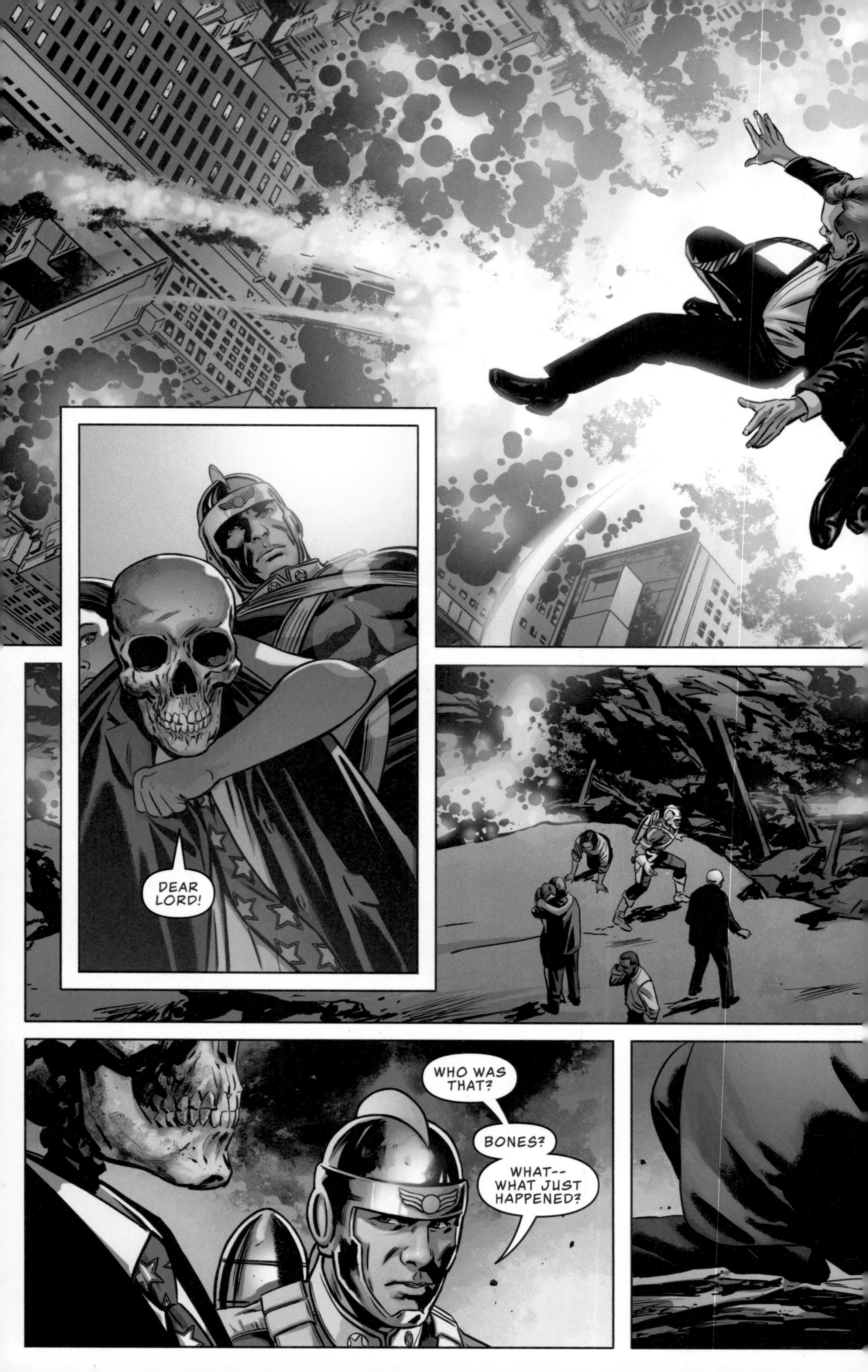
DEAR LORD!
WHO WAS THAT?
BONES?
WHAT-- WHAT JUST HAPPENED?

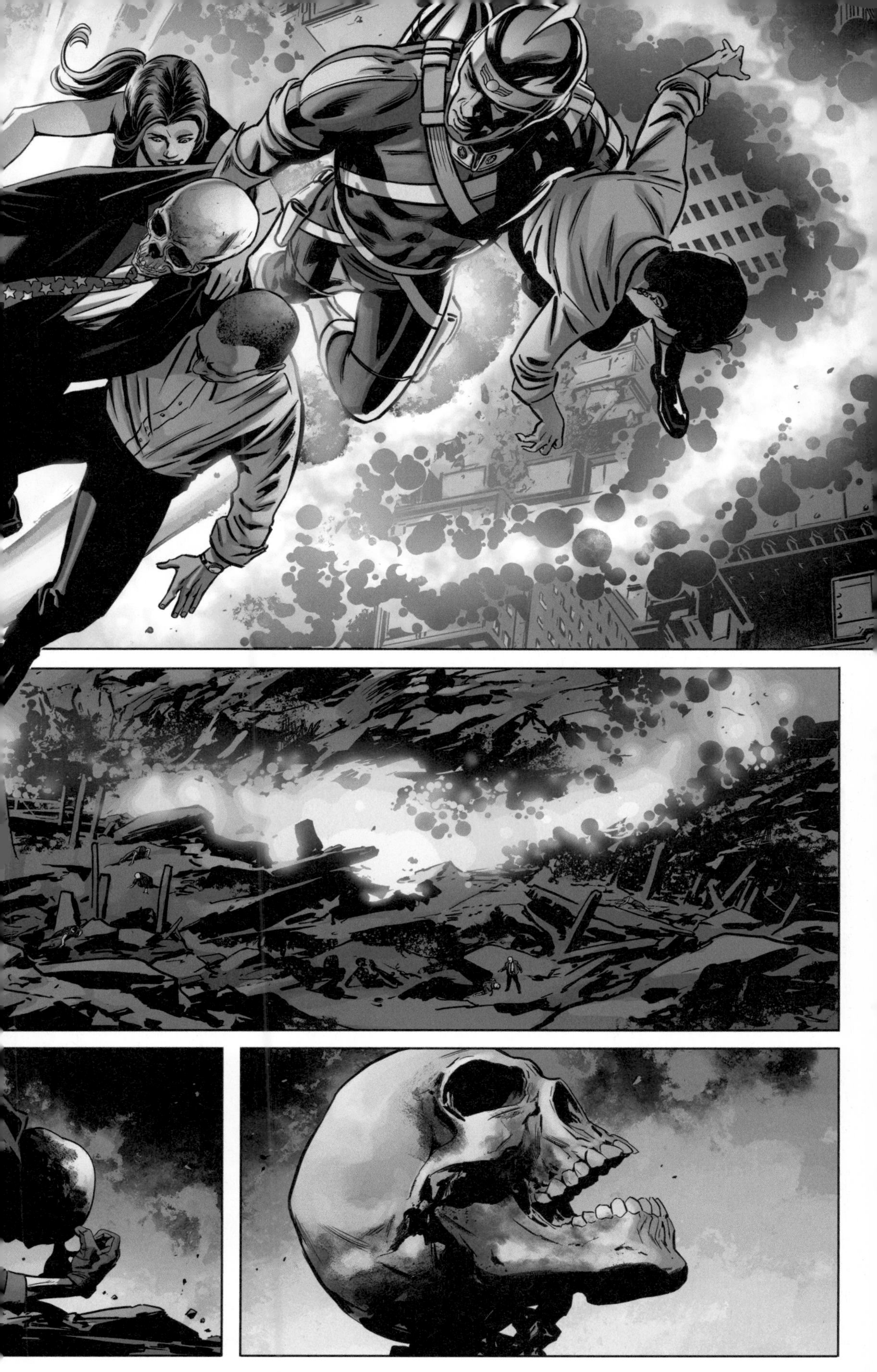

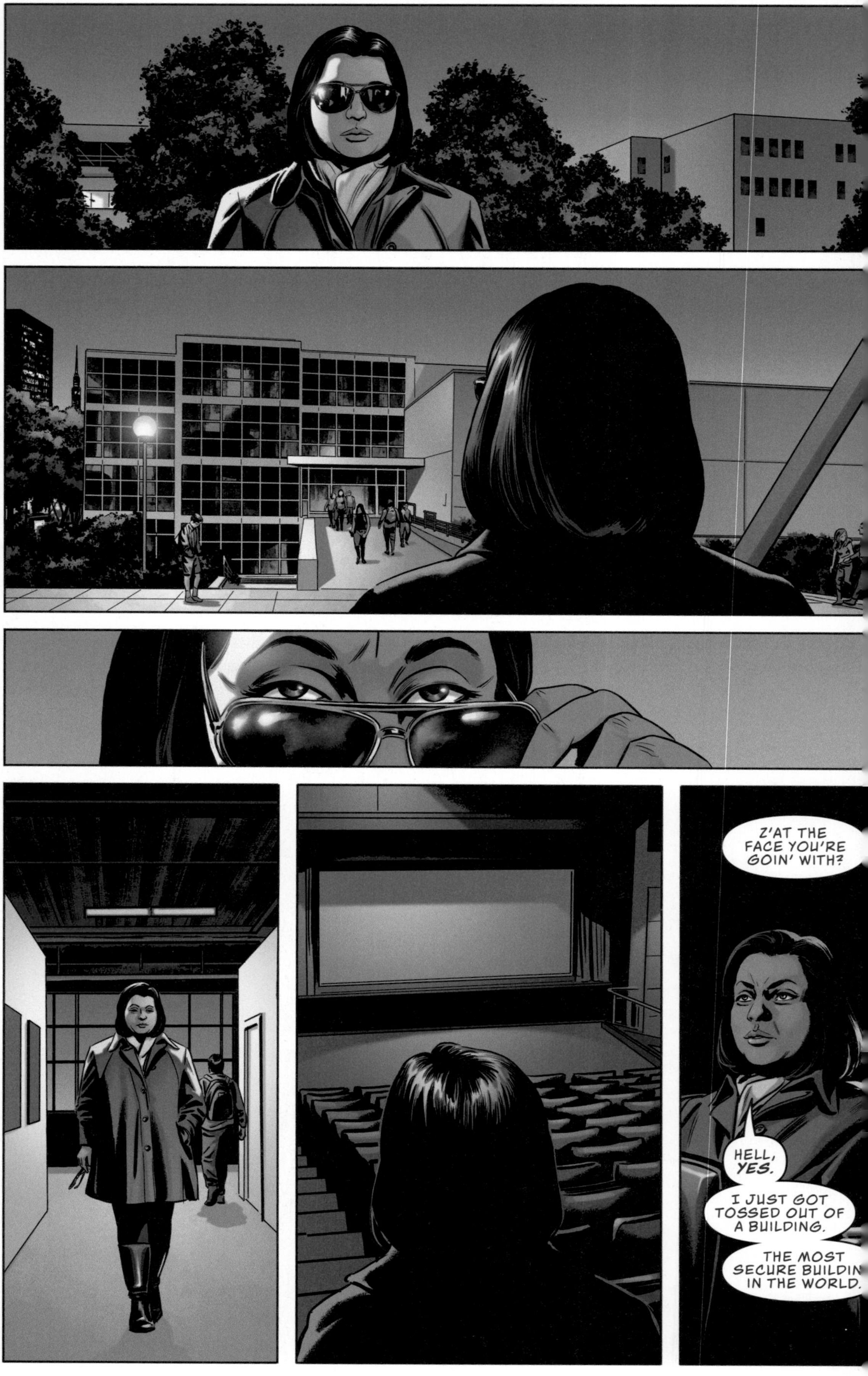
Z'AT THE FACE YOU'RE GOIN' WITH?
HELL, *YES.*
I JUST GOT TOSSED OUT OF A BUILDING.
THE MOST SECURE BUILDIN IN THE WORLD.

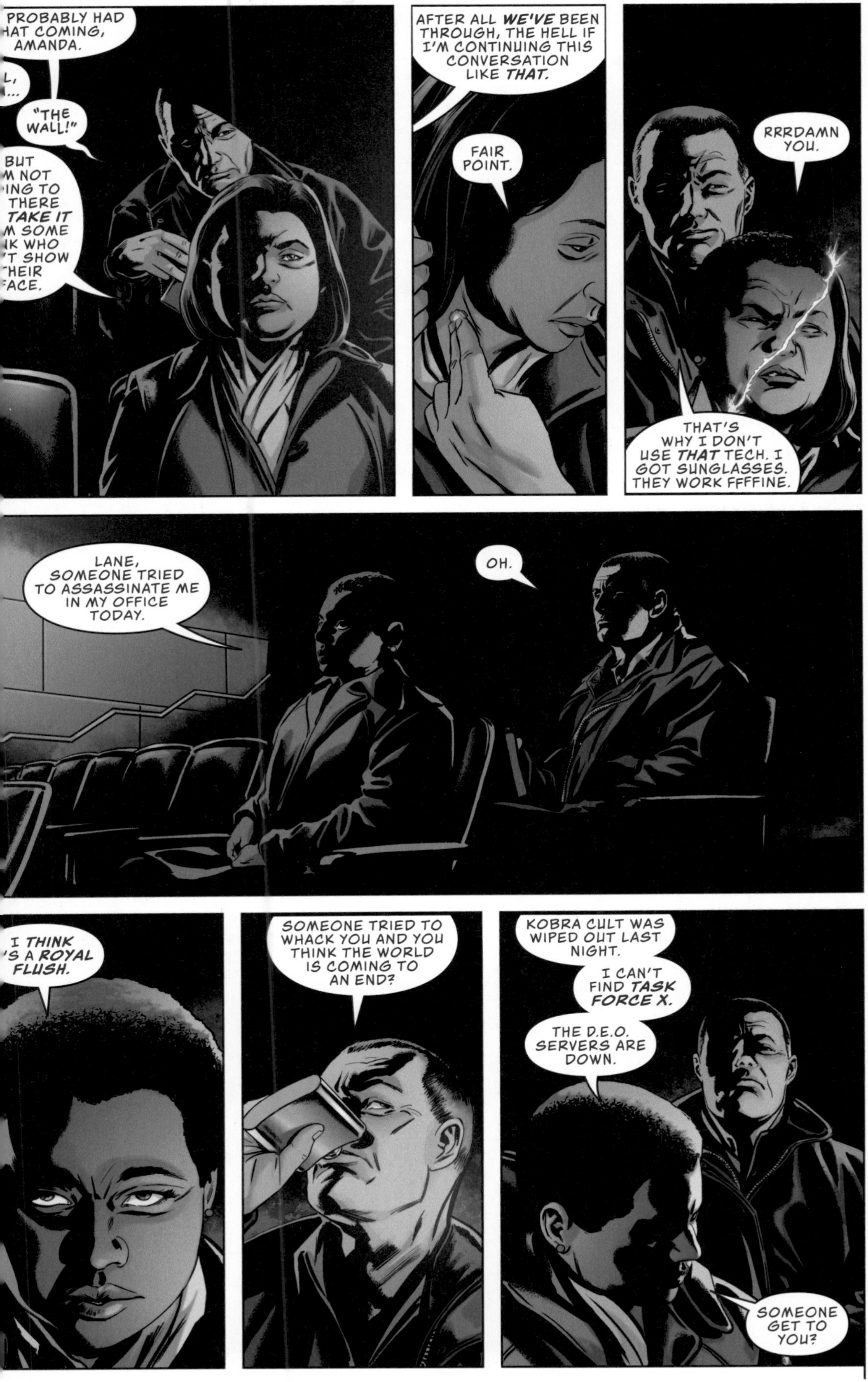
PROBABLY HAD HAT COMING, AMANDA.
L, ...
"THE WALL!"
BUT M NOT ING TO THERE TAKE IT M SOME IK WHO 'T SHOW THEIR FACE.
AFTER ALL WE'VE BEEN THROUGH, THE HELL IF I'M CONTINUING THIS CONVERSATION LIKE THAT.
FAIR POINT.
RRRDAMN YOU.
THAT'S WHY I DON'T USE THAT TECH. I GOT SUNGLASSES. THEY WORK FFFFINE.
LANE, SOMEONE TRIED TO ASSASSINATE ME IN MY OFFICE TODAY.
OH.
I THINK 'S A ROYAL FLUSH.
SOMEONE TRIED TO WHACK YOU AND YOU THINK THE WORLD IS COMING TO AN END?
KOBRA CULT WAS WIPED OUT LAST NIGHT.
I CAN'T FIND TASK FORCE X.
THE D.E.O. SERVERS ARE DOWN.
SOMEONE GET TO YOU?

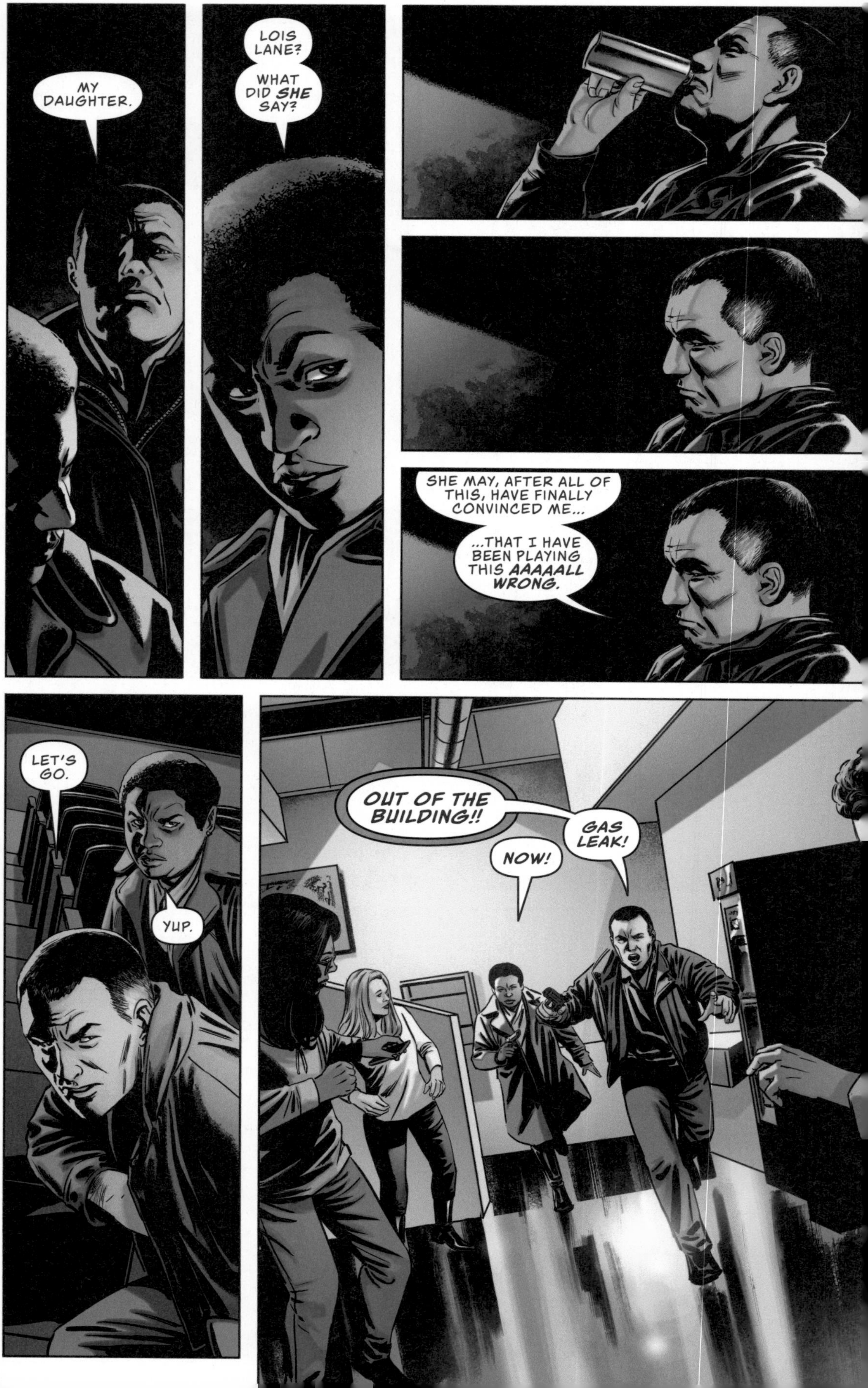
MY DAUGHTER.
LOIS LANE?
WHAT DID SHE SAY?
SHE MAY, AFTER ALL OF THIS, HAVE FINALLY CONVINCED ME...
...THAT I HAVE BEEN PLAYING THIS AAAAALL WRONG.
LET'S GO.
YUP.
OUT OF THE BUILDING!!
GAS LEAK!
NOW!

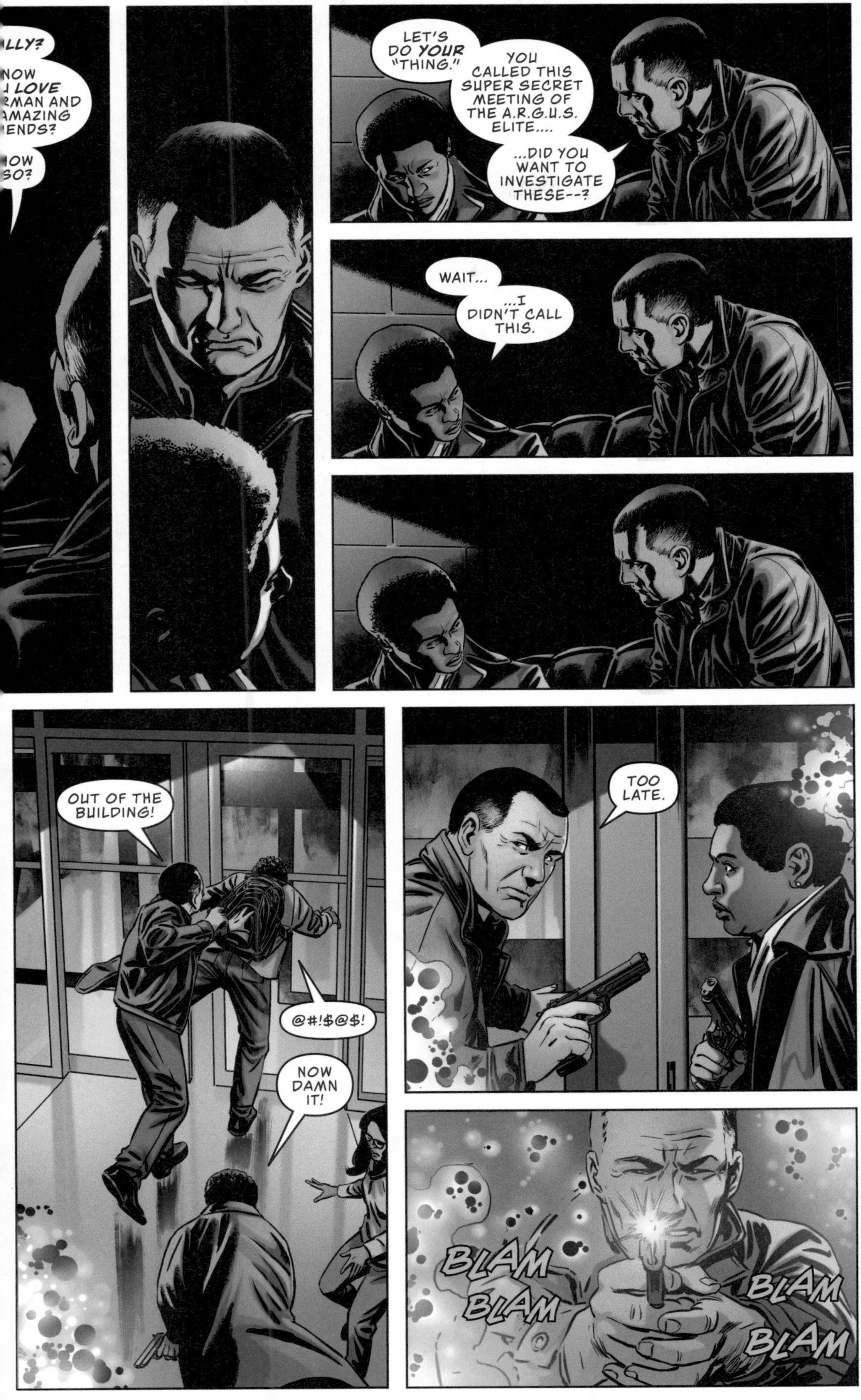
LLY?
NOW
LOVE
RMAN AND
AMAZING
IENDS?
HOW
SO?
LET'S DO *YOUR* "THING."
YOU CALLED THIS SUPER SECRET MEETING OF THE A.R.G.U.S. ELITE....
...DID YOU WANT TO INVESTIGATE THESE--?
WAIT...
...I DIDN'T CALL THIS.
OUT OF THE BUILDING!
@#!$@$!
NOW DAMN IT!
TOO LATE.
BLAM
BLAM
BLAM
BLAM

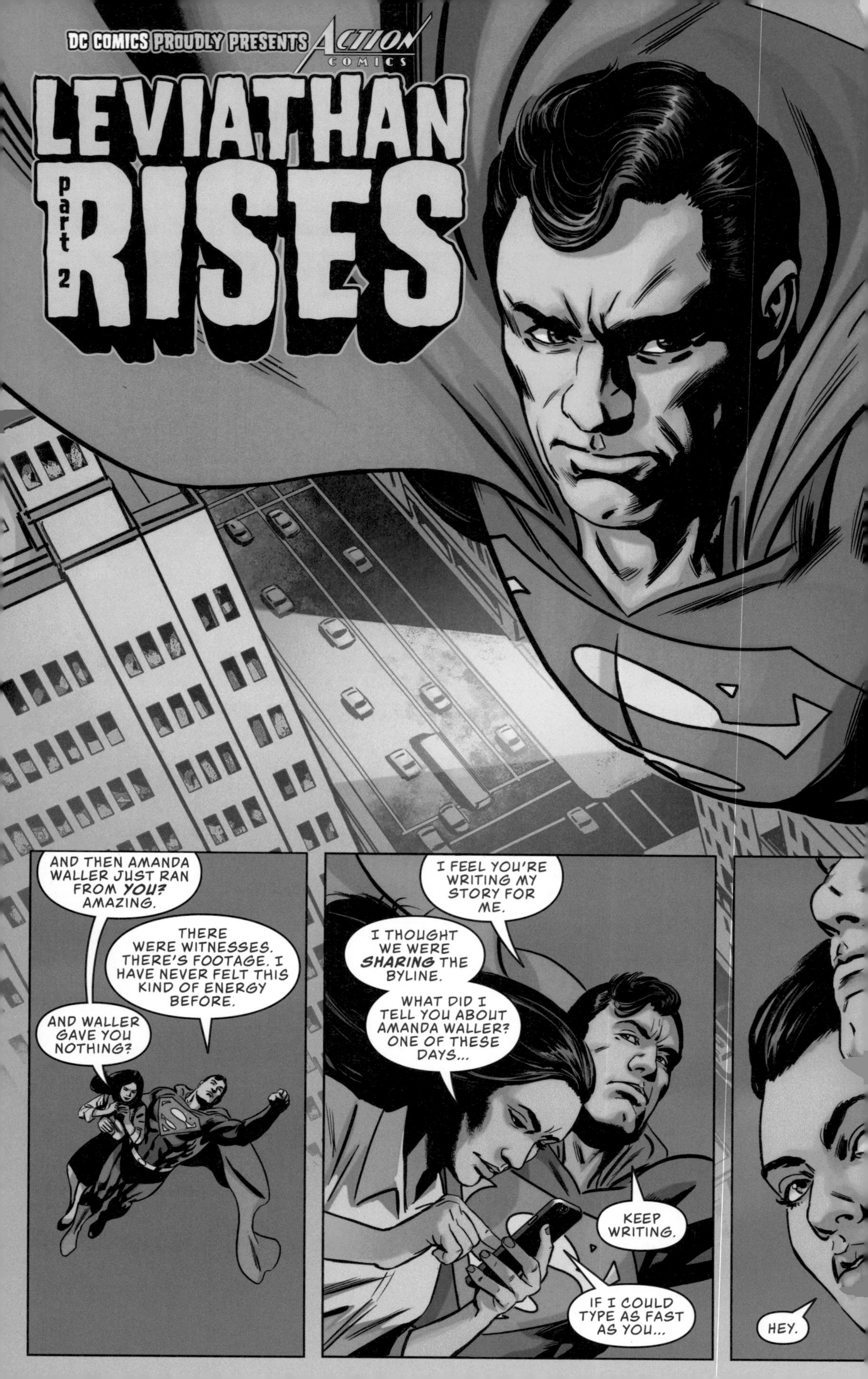
DC COMICS PROUDLY PRESENTS ACTION COMICS
LEVIATHAN RISES part 2
AND THEN AMANDA WALLER JUST RAN FROM *YOU?* AMAZING.
THERE WERE WITNESSES. THERE'S FOOTAGE. I HAVE NEVER FELT THIS KIND OF ENERGY BEFORE.
AND WALLER GAVE YOU NOTHING?
I FEEL YOU'RE WRITING MY STORY FOR ME.
I THOUGHT WE WERE ***SHARING*** THE BYLINE.
WHAT DID I TELL YOU ABOUT AMANDA WALLER? ONE OF THESE DAYS...
KEEP WRITING.
IF I COULD TYPE AS FAST AS YOU...
HEY.

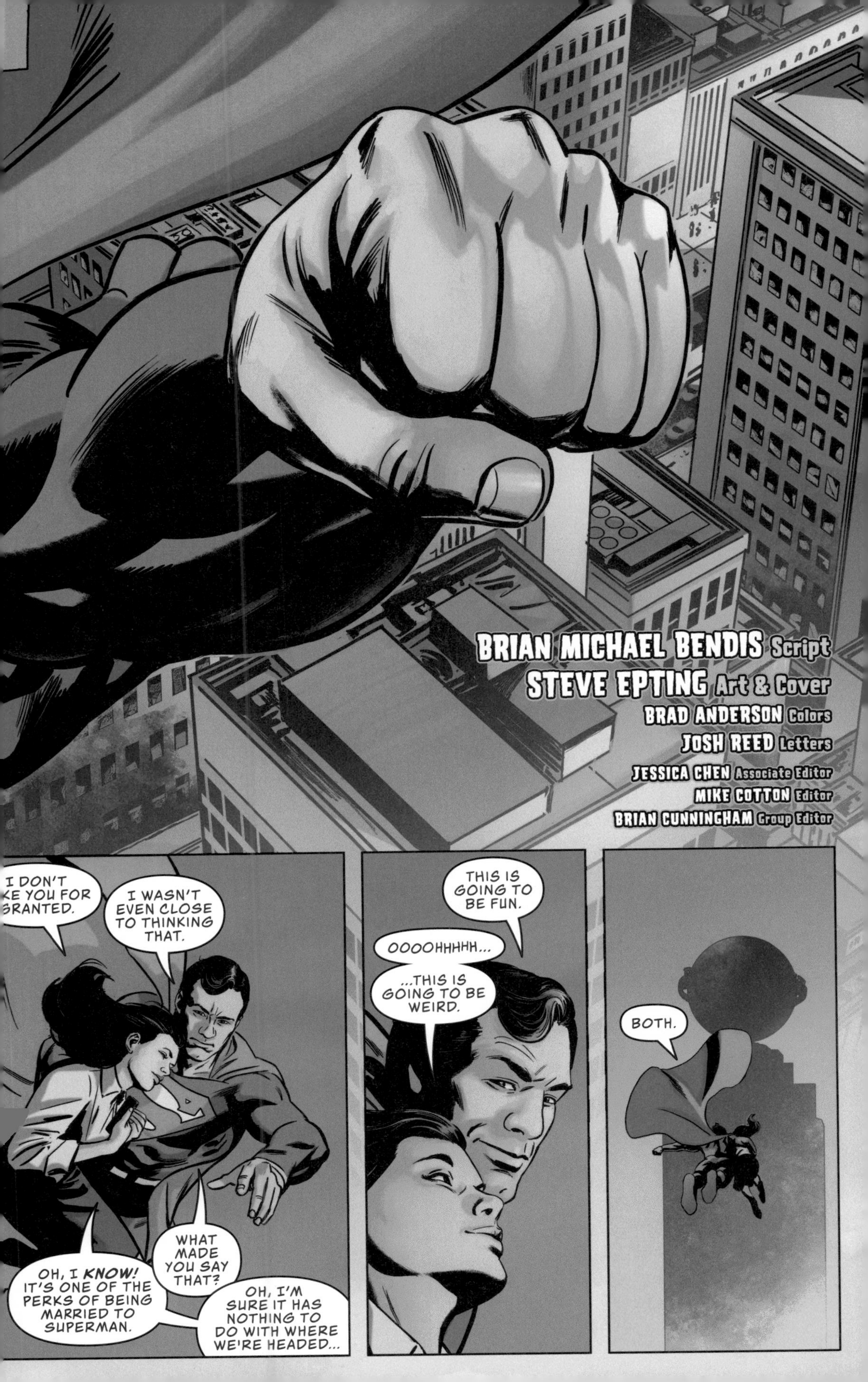
BRIAN MICHAEL BENDIS Script
STEVE EPTING Art & Cover
BRAD ANDERSON Colors
JOSH REED Letters
JESSICA CHEN Associate Editor
MIKE COTTON Editor
BRIAN CUNNINGHAM Group Editor
I DON'T
KE YOU FOR
GRANTED.
I WASN'T EVEN CLOSE TO THINKING THAT.
OH, I KNOW! IT'S ONE OF THE PERKS OF BEING MARRIED TO SUPERMAN.
WHAT MADE YOU SAY THAT?
OH, I'M SURE IT HAS NOTHING TO DO WITH WHERE WE'RE HEADED...
THIS IS GOING TO BE FUN.
OOOOHHHHH...
...THIS IS GOING TO BE WEIRD.
BOTH.

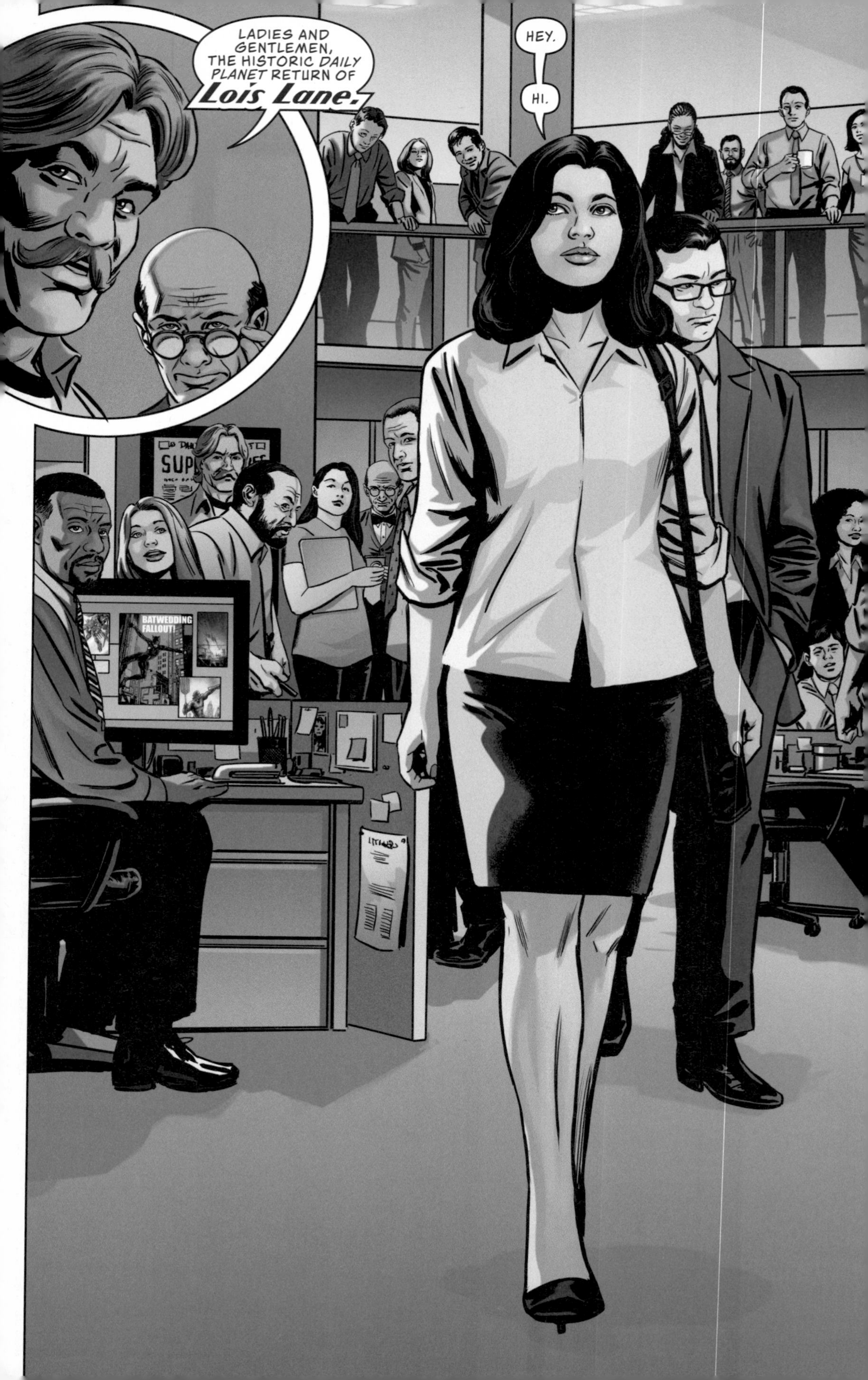

LADIES AND GENTLEMEN, THE HISTORIC DAILY PLANET RETURN OF Lois Lane.
HEY.
HI.
BATWEDDING FALLOUT!

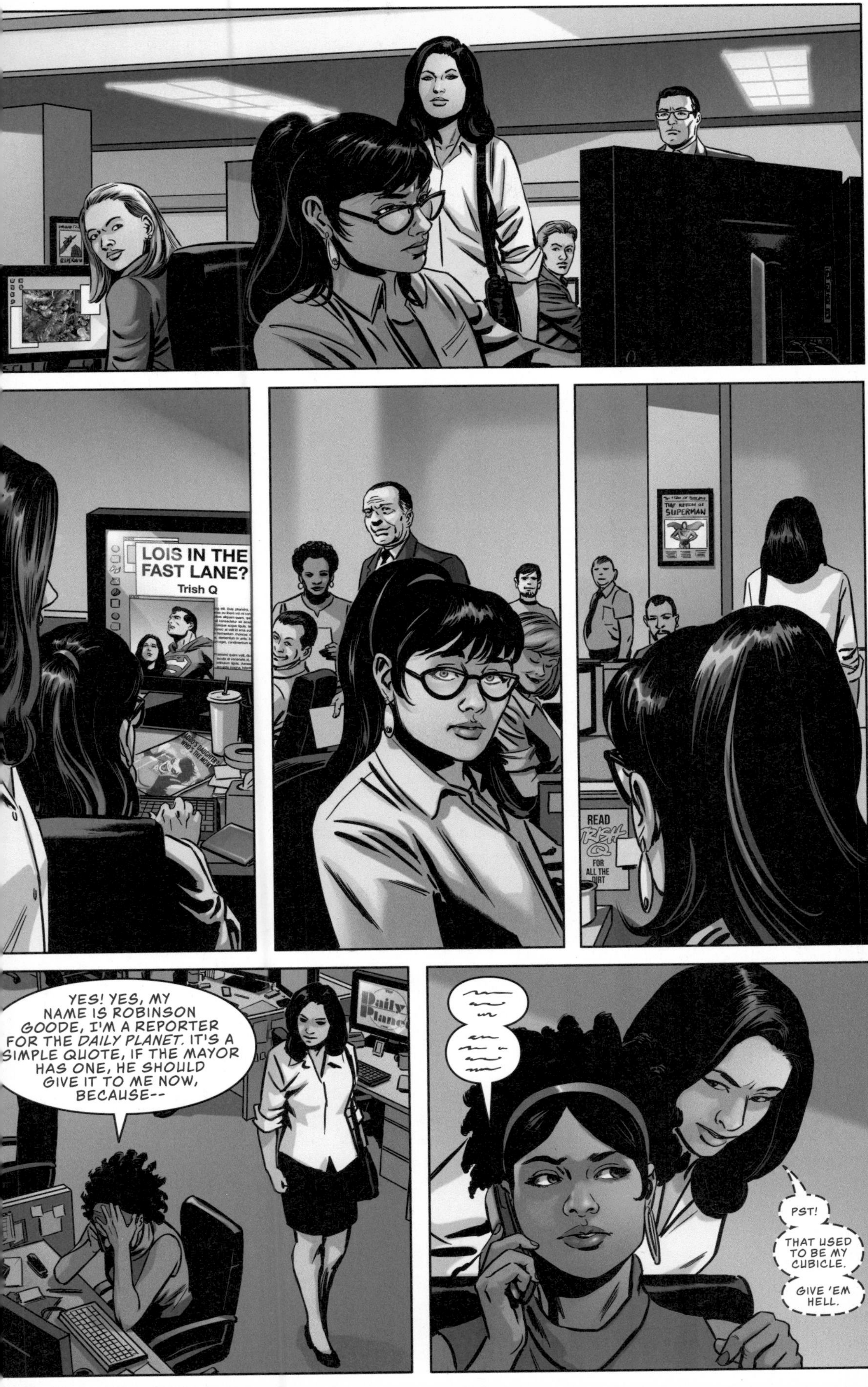
LOIS IN THE FAST LANE?
Trish Q
SUPERMAN
READ TRISH Q FOR ALL THE DIRT
Daily Planet
YES! YES, MY NAME IS ROBINSON GOODE, I'M A REPORTER FOR THE *DAILY PLANET*. IT'S A SIMPLE QUOTE, IF THE MAYOR HAS ONE, HE SHOULD GIVE IT TO ME NOW, BECAUSE--
PST!
THAT USED TO BE MY CUBICLE.
GIVE 'EM HELL.

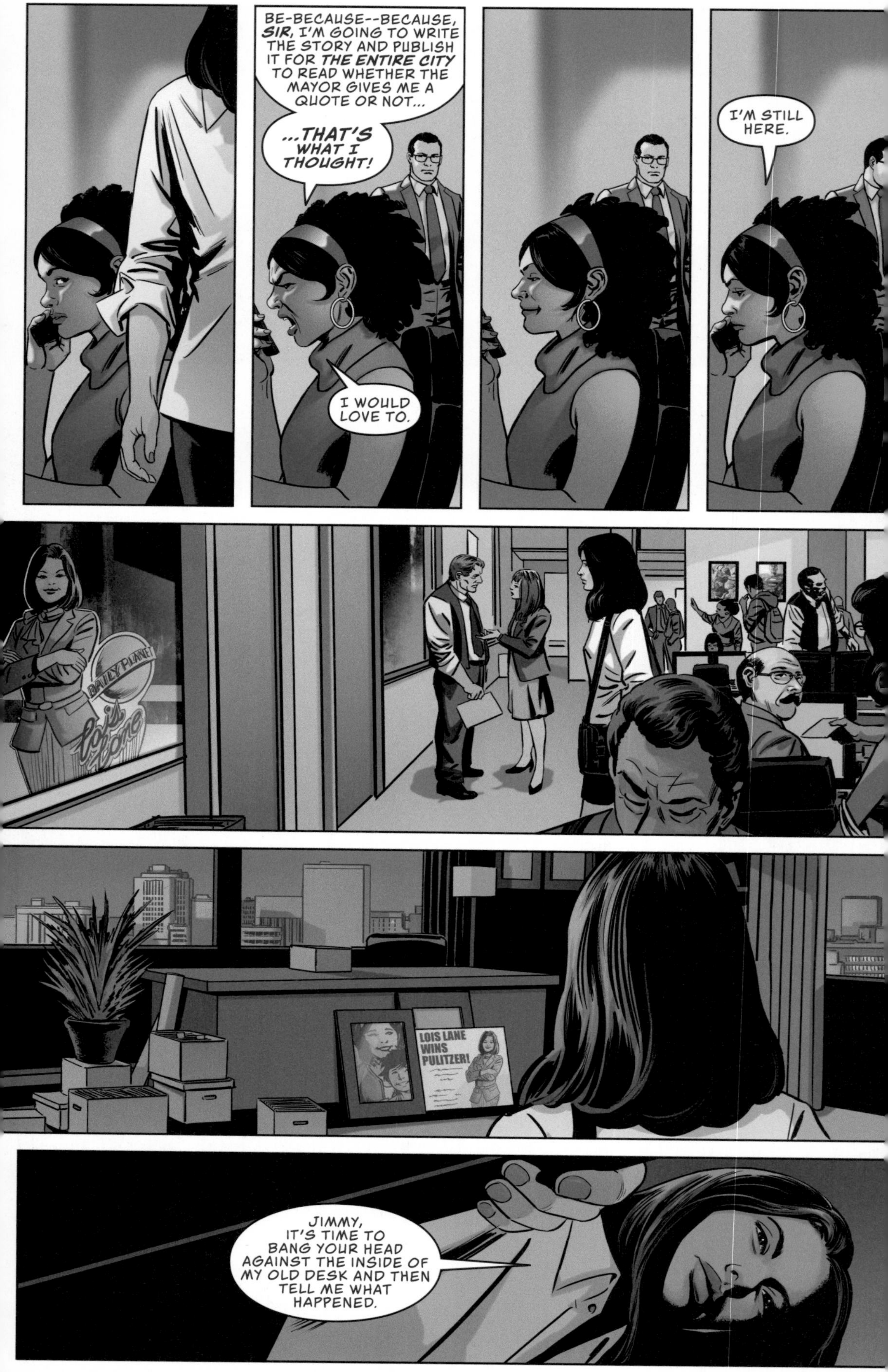
BE-BECAUSE--BECAUSE, SIR, I'M GOING TO WRITE THE STORY AND PUBLISH IT FOR THE ENTIRE CITY TO READ WHETHER THE MAYOR GIVES ME A QUOTE OR NOT...
...THAT'S WHAT I THOUGHT!
I WOULD LOVE TO.
I'M STILL HERE.
DAILY PLANET
LOIS LANE
LOIS LANE WINS PULITZER!
JIMMY, IT'S TIME TO BANG YOUR HEAD AGAINST THE INSIDE OF MY OLD DESK AND THEN TELL ME WHAT HAPPENED.

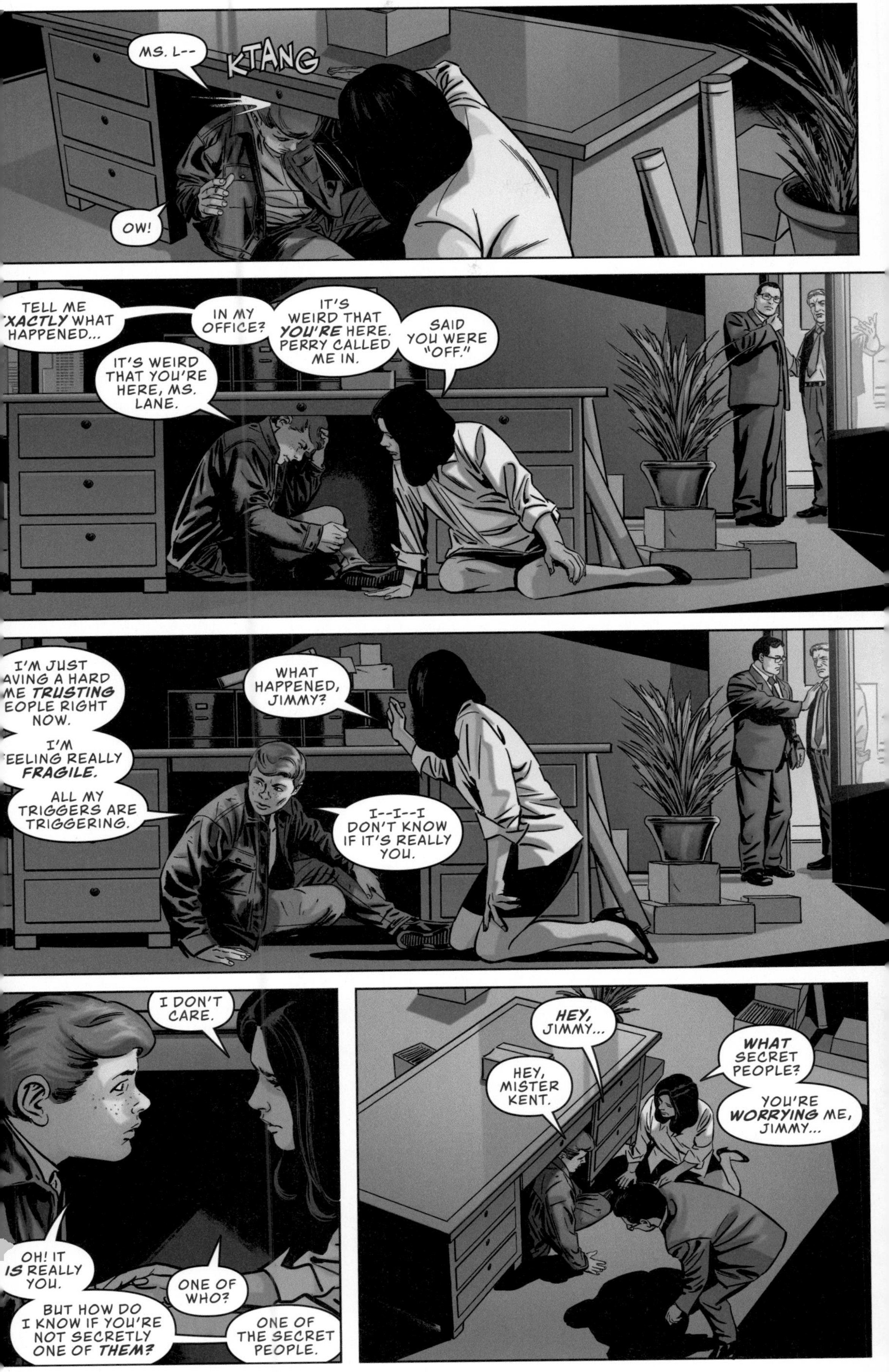
MS. L--
KTANG
OW!
TELL ME XACTLY WHAT HAPPENED...
IN MY OFFICE?
IT'S WEIRD THAT YOU'RE HERE, MS. LANE.
IT'S WEIRD THAT **YOU'RE** HERE. PERRY CALLED ME IN.
SAID YOU WERE "OFF."
WHAT HAPPENED, JIMMY?
I--I--I DON'T KNOW IF IT'S REALLY YOU.
I'M JUST AVING A HARD ME **TRUSTING** EOPLE RIGHT NOW.
I'M EELING REALLY **FRAGILE.**
ALL MY TRIGGERS ARE TRIGGERING.
I DON'T CARE.
OH! IT **IS** REALLY YOU.
BUT HOW DO I KNOW IF YOU'RE NOT SECRETLY ONE OF **THEM?**
ONE OF WHO?
ONE OF THE SECRET PEOPLE.
HEY, JIMMY...
HEY, MISTER KENT.
WHAT SECRET PEOPLE?
YOU'RE **WORRYING** ME, JIMMY...

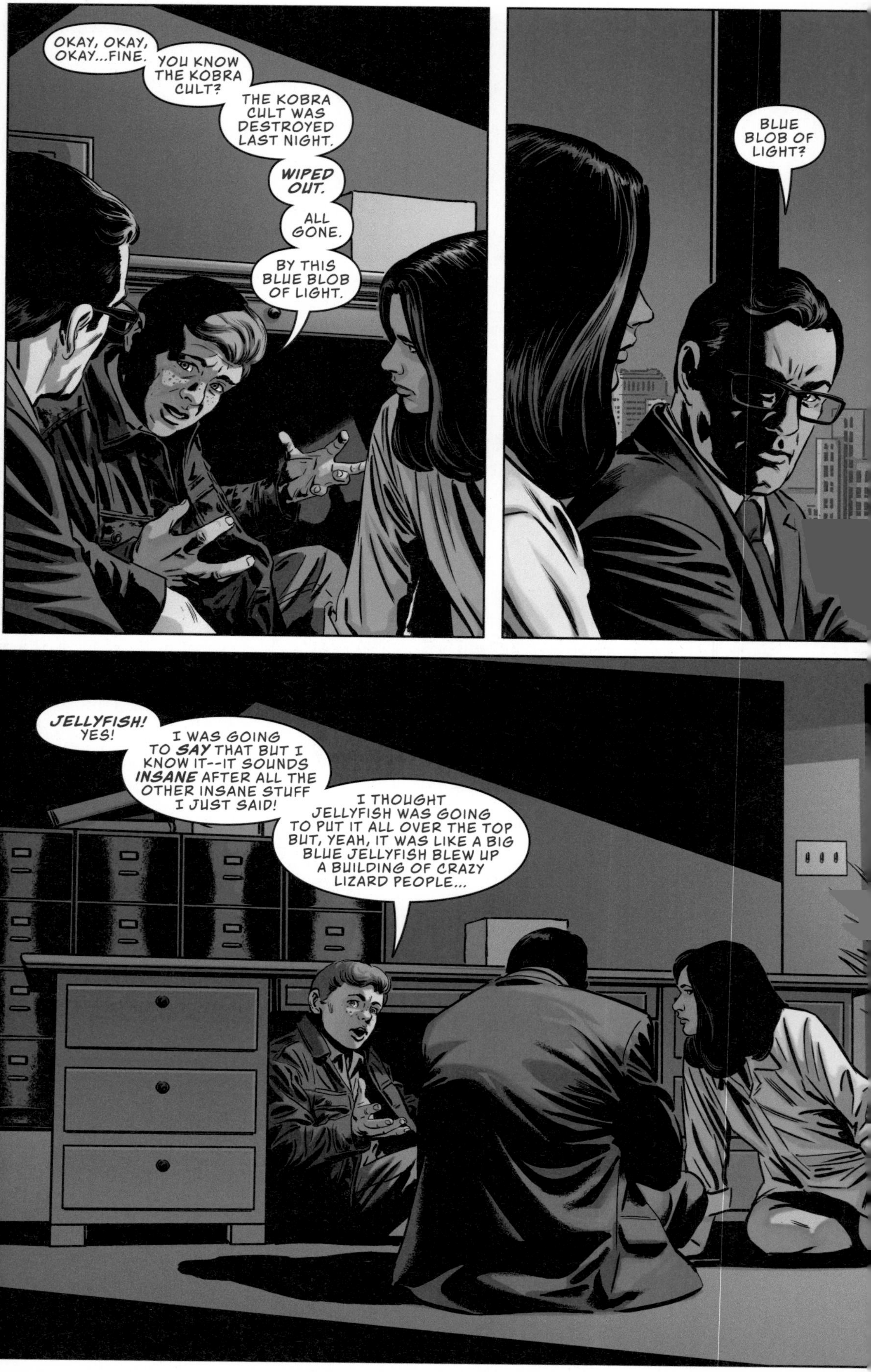
OKAY, OKAY, OKAY...FINE.
YOU KNOW THE KOBRA CULT?
THE KOBRA CULT WAS DESTROYED LAST NIGHT.
WIPED OUT.
ALL GONE.
BY THIS BLUE BLOB OF LIGHT.
BLUE BLOB OF LIGHT?
JELLYFISH! YES!
I WAS GOING TO SAY THAT BUT I KNOW IT--IT SOUNDS INSANE AFTER ALL THE OTHER INSANE STUFF I JUST SAID!
I THOUGHT JELLYFISH WAS GOING TO PUT IT ALL OVER THE TOP BUT, YEAH, IT WAS LIKE A BIG BLUE JELLYFISH BLEW UP A BUILDING OF CRAZY LIZARD PEOPLE...

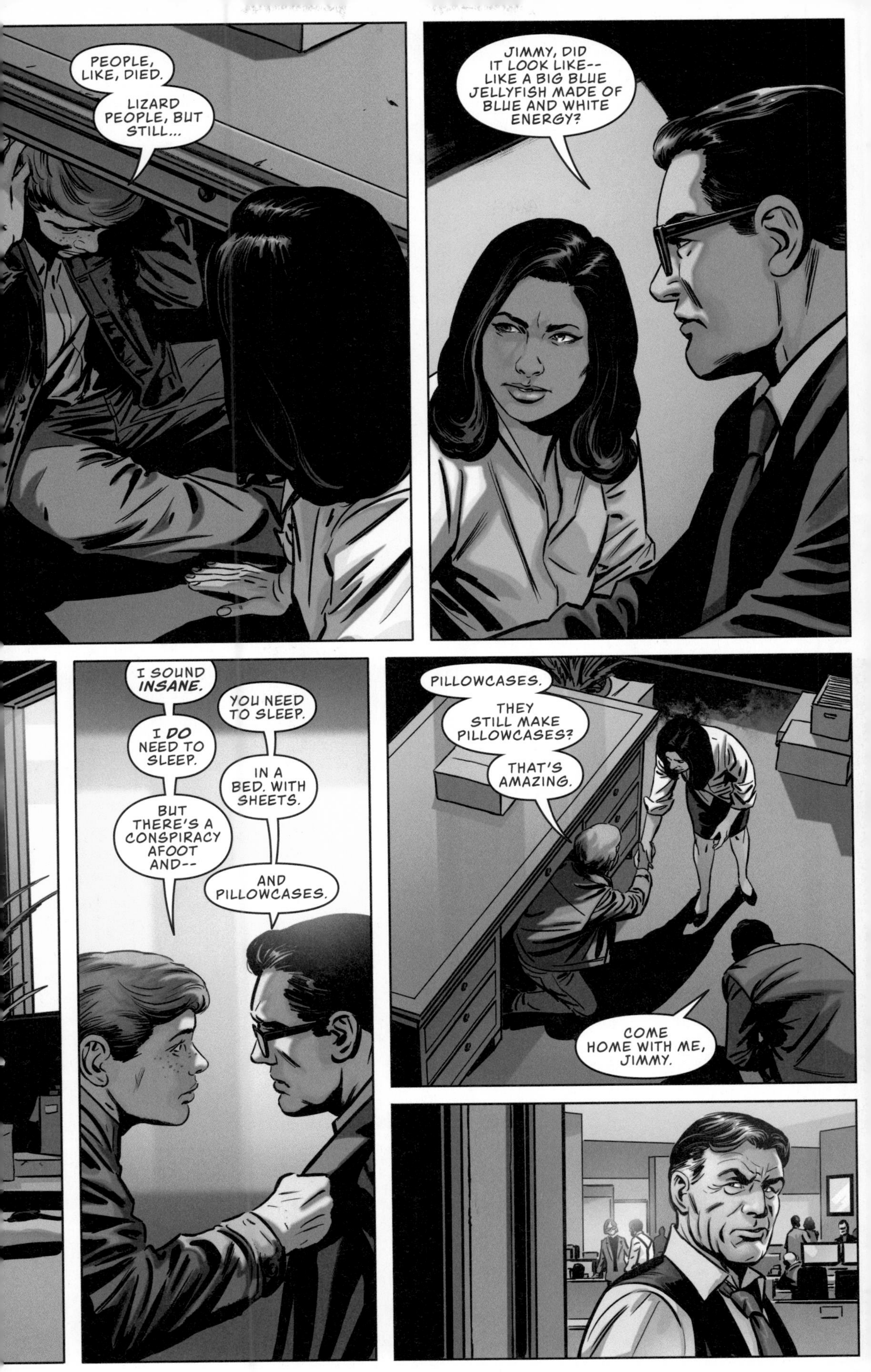
PEOPLE, LIKE, DIED.
LIZARD PEOPLE, BUT STILL...
JIMMY, DID IT LOOK LIKE-- LIKE A BIG BLUE JELLYFISH MADE OF BLUE AND WHITE ENERGY?
I SOUND INSANE.
YOU NEED TO SLEEP.
I DO NEED TO SLEEP.
IN A BED. WITH SHEETS.
BUT THERE'S A CONSPIRACY AFOOT AND--
AND PILLOWCASES.
PILLOWCASES.
THEY STILL MAKE PILLOWCASES?
THAT'S AMAZING.
COME HOME WITH ME, JIMMY.

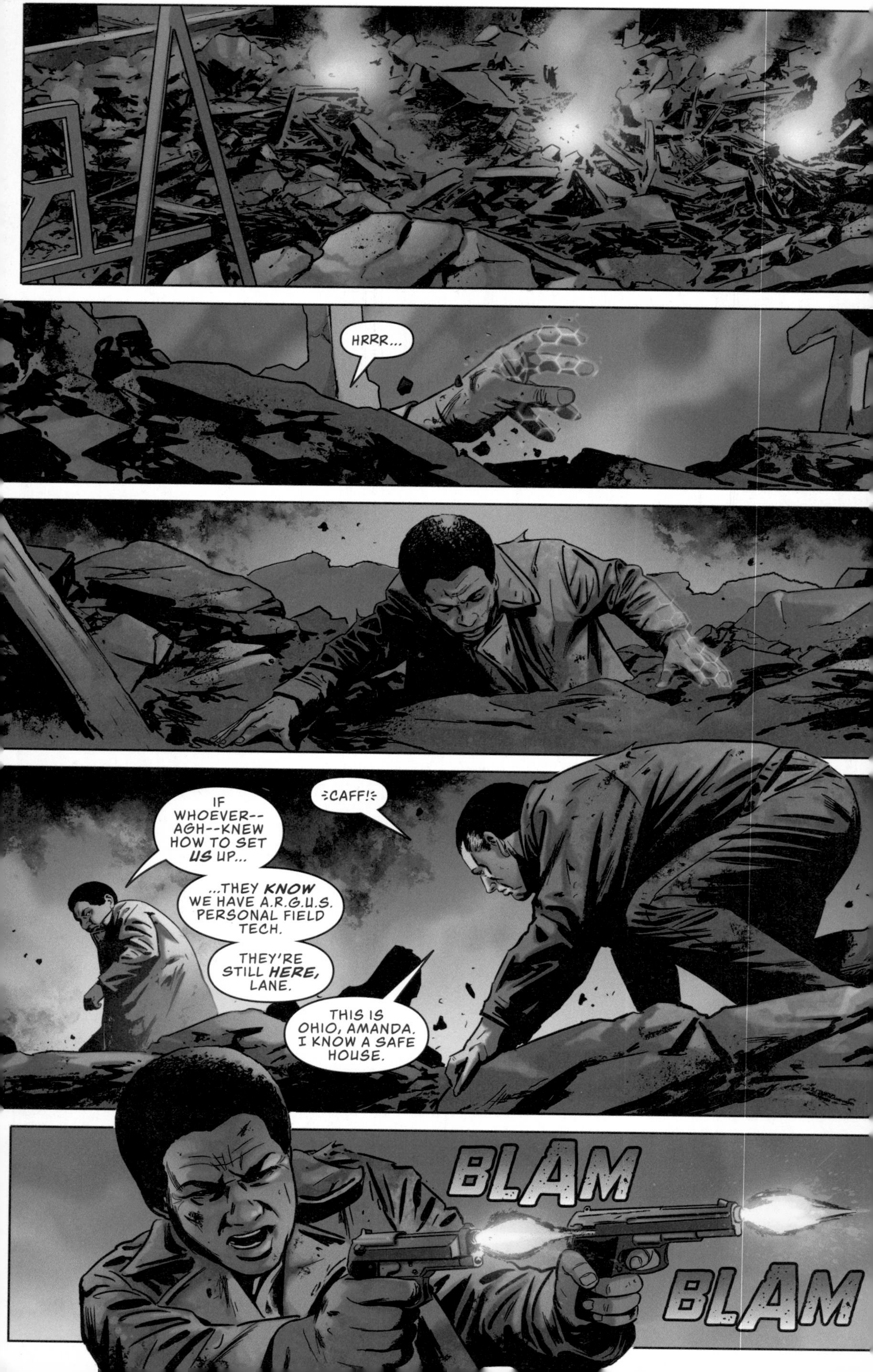
HRRR...
IF WHOEVER--AGH--KNEW HOW TO SET US UP...
...THEY KNOW WE HAVE A.R.G.U.S. PERSONAL FIELD TECH.
THEY'RE STILL HERE, LANE.
CAFF!
THIS IS OHIO, AMANDA. I KNOW A SAFE HOUSE.
BLAM
BLAM

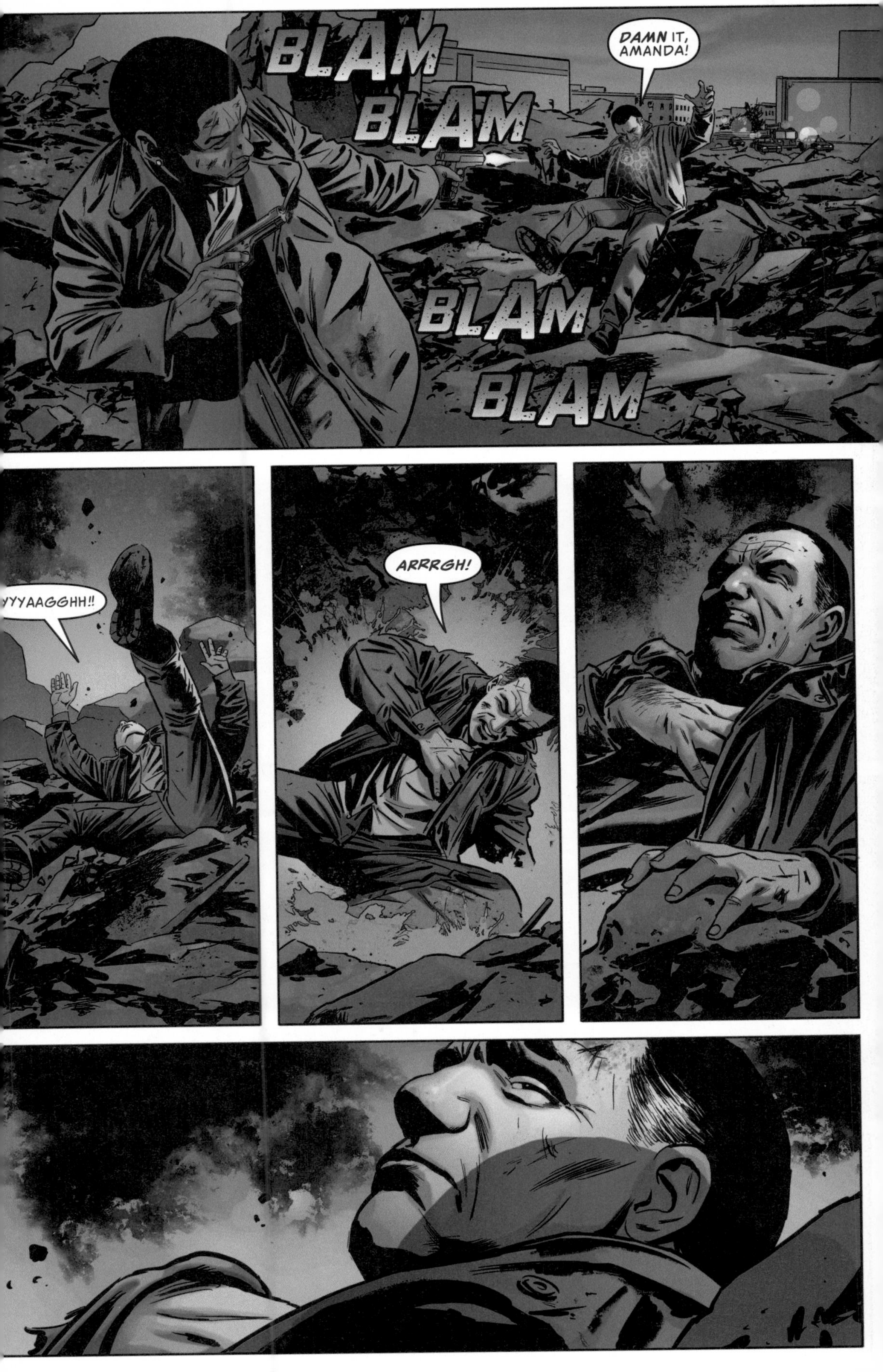
BLAM
BLAM
DAMN IT, AMANDA!
BLAM
BLAM
YYYAAGGHH!!
ARRRGH!

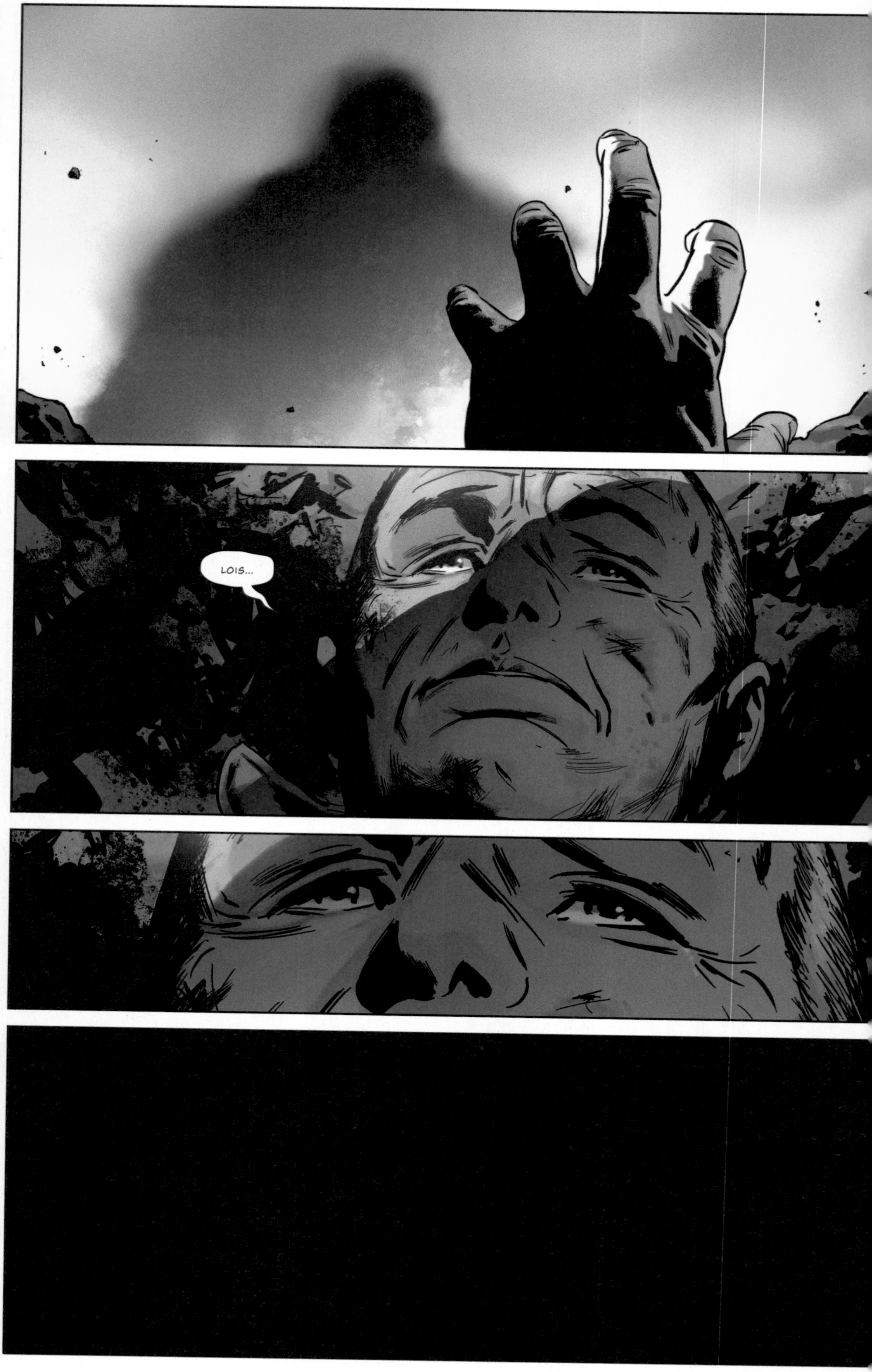
LOIS...

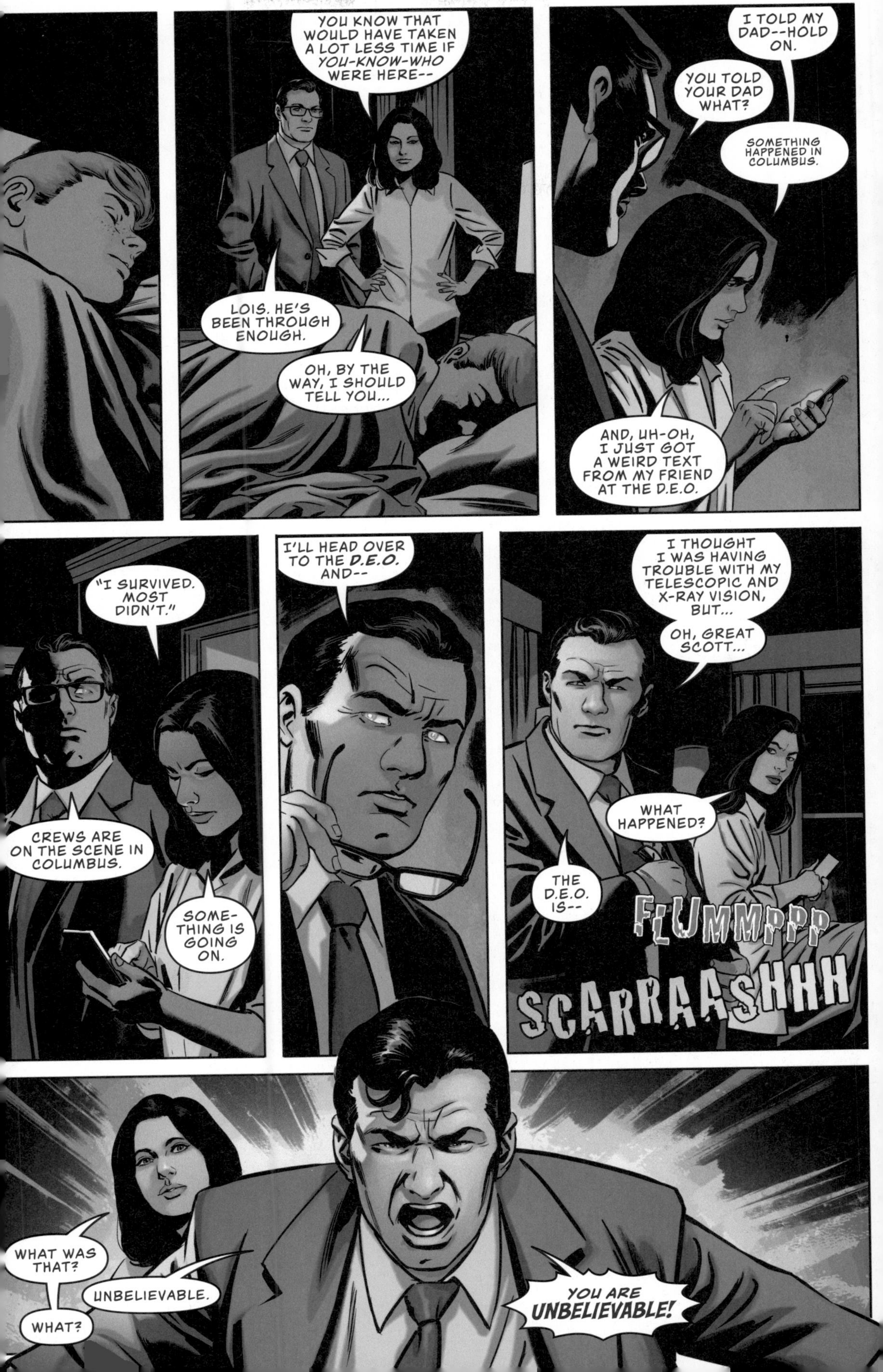
YOU KNOW THAT WOULD HAVE TAKEN A LOT LESS TIME IF YOU-KNOW-WHO WERE HERE--
LOIS. HE'S BEEN THROUGH ENOUGH.
OH, BY THE WAY, I SHOULD TELL YOU...
I TOLD MY DAD--HOLD ON.
YOU TOLD YOUR DAD WHAT?
SOMETHING HAPPENED IN COLUMBUS.
AND, UH-OH, I JUST GOT A WEIRD TEXT FROM MY FRIEND AT THE D.E.O.
"I SURVIVED. MOST DIDN'T."
CREWS ARE ON THE SCENE IN COLUMBUS.
SOME-THING IS GOING ON.
I'LL HEAD OVER TO THE D.E.O. AND--
I THOUGHT I WAS HAVING TROUBLE WITH MY TELESCOPIC AND X-RAY VISION, BUT...
OH, GREAT SCOTT...
WHAT HAPPENED?
THE D.E.O. IS--
FLUMMPPP
SCARRAASHHH
WHAT WAS THAT?
UNBELIEVABLE.
WHAT?
YOU ARE UNBELIEVABLE!

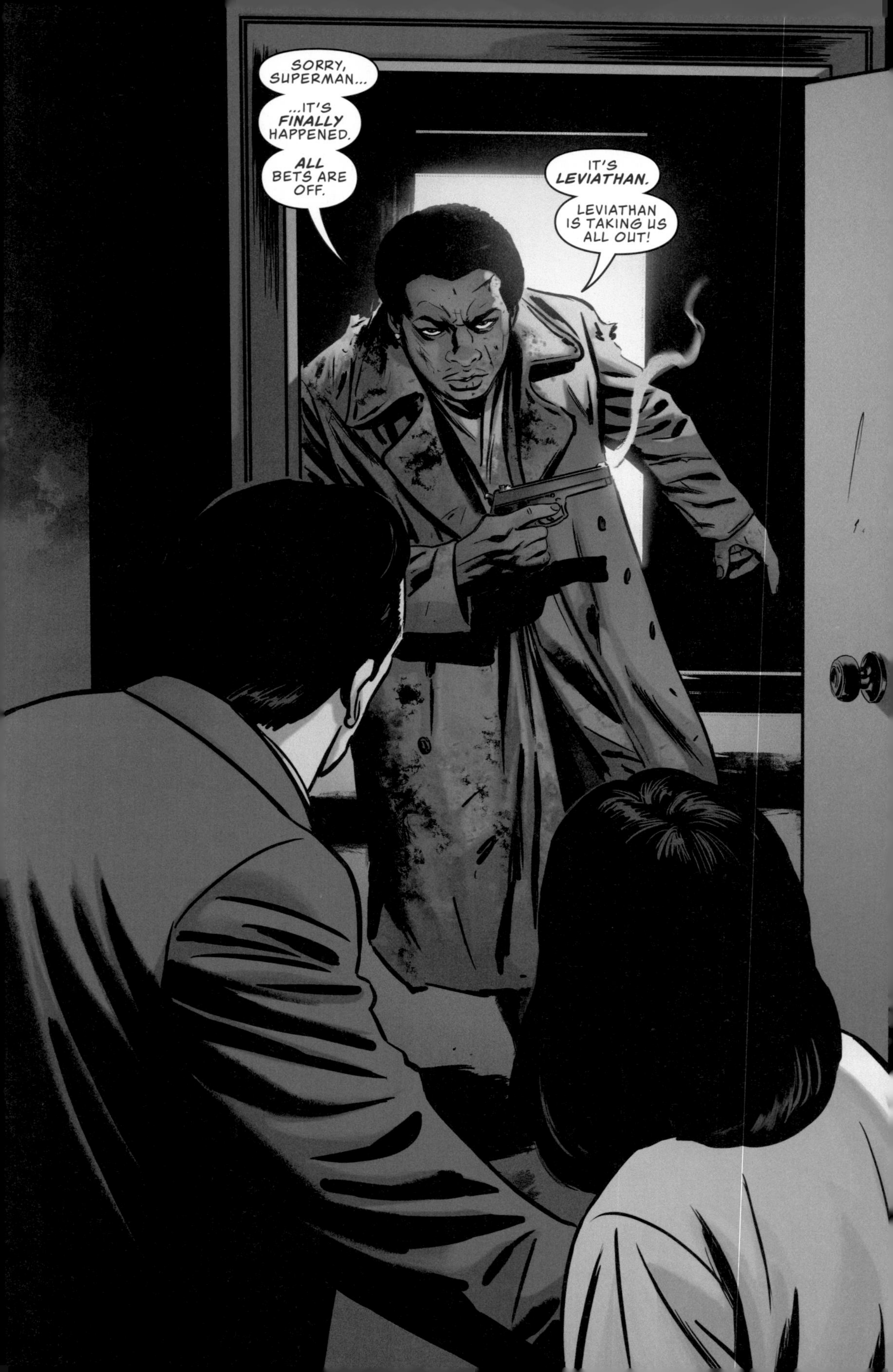
SORRY, SUPERMAN...
...IT'S FINALLY HAPPENED.
ALL BETS ARE OFF.
IT'S LEVIATHAN.
LEVIATHAN IS TAKING US ALL OUT!

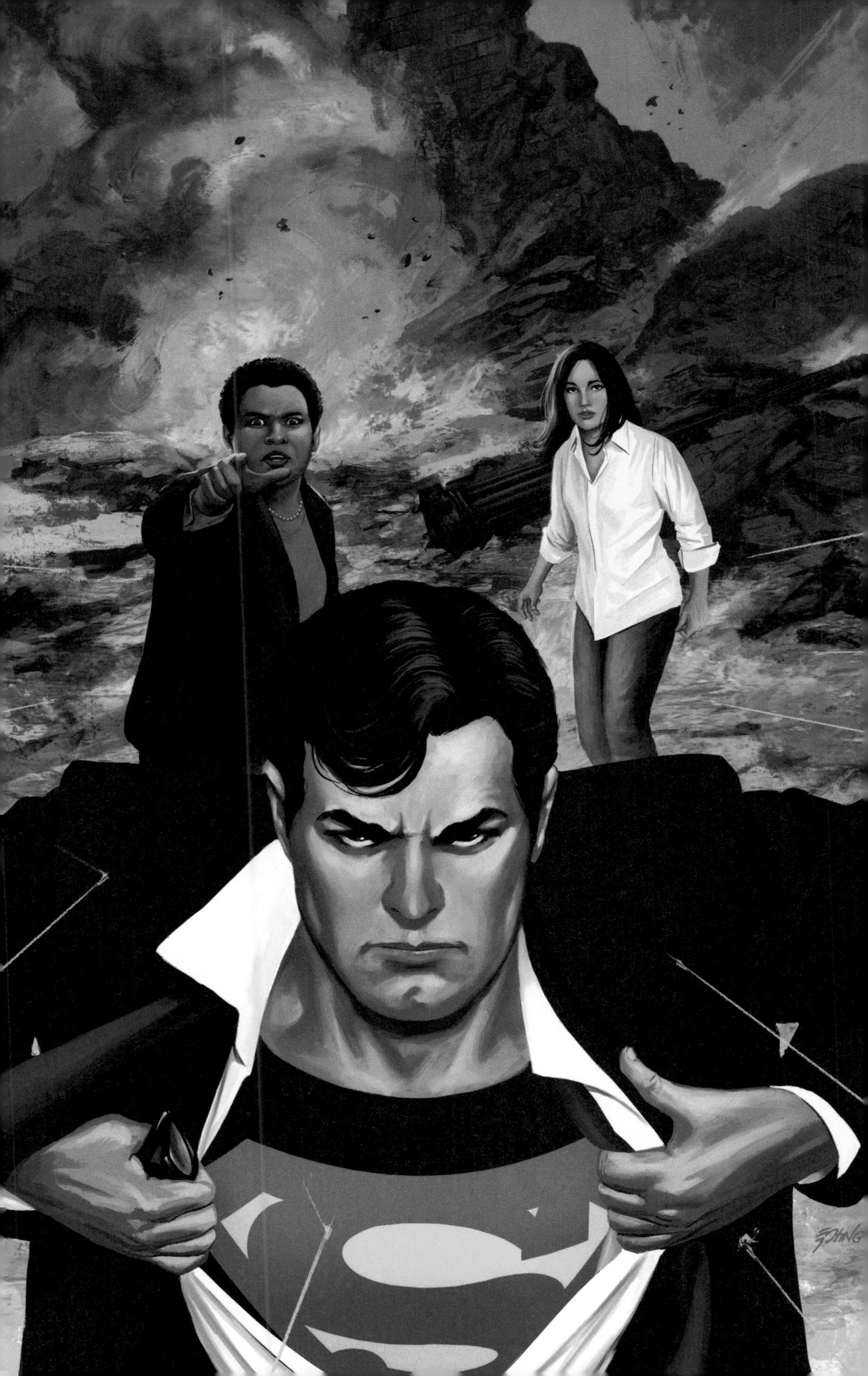

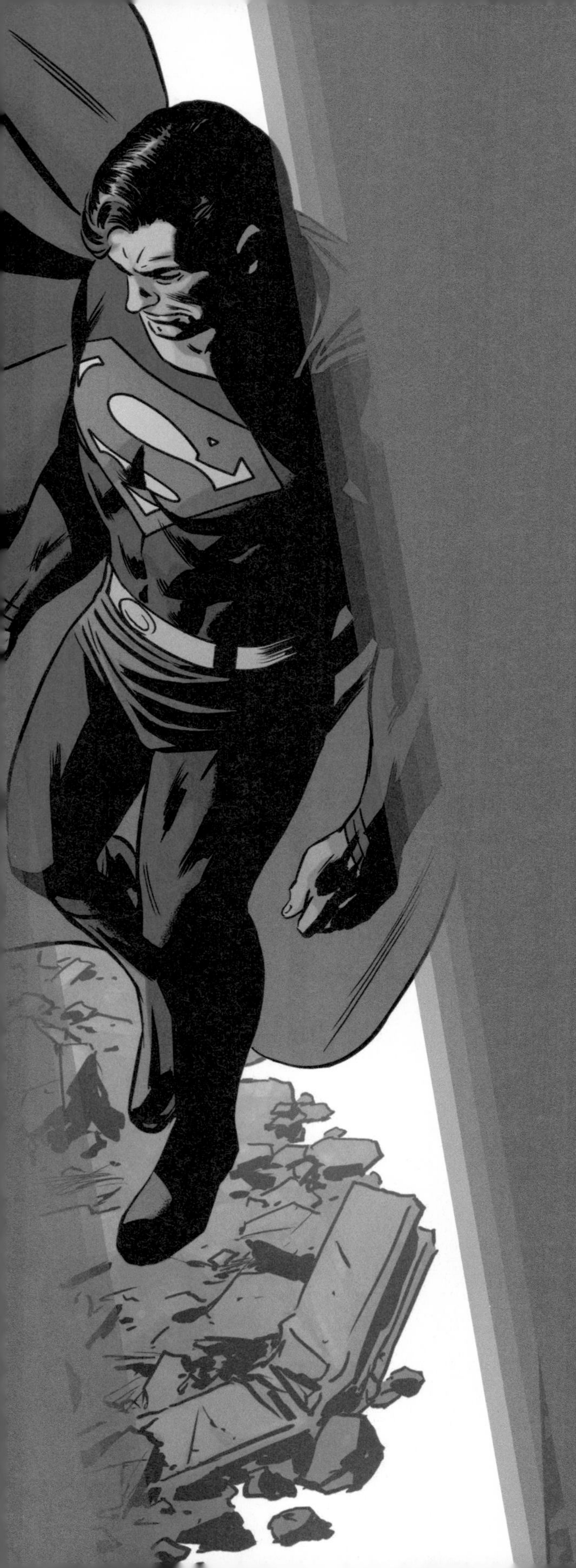

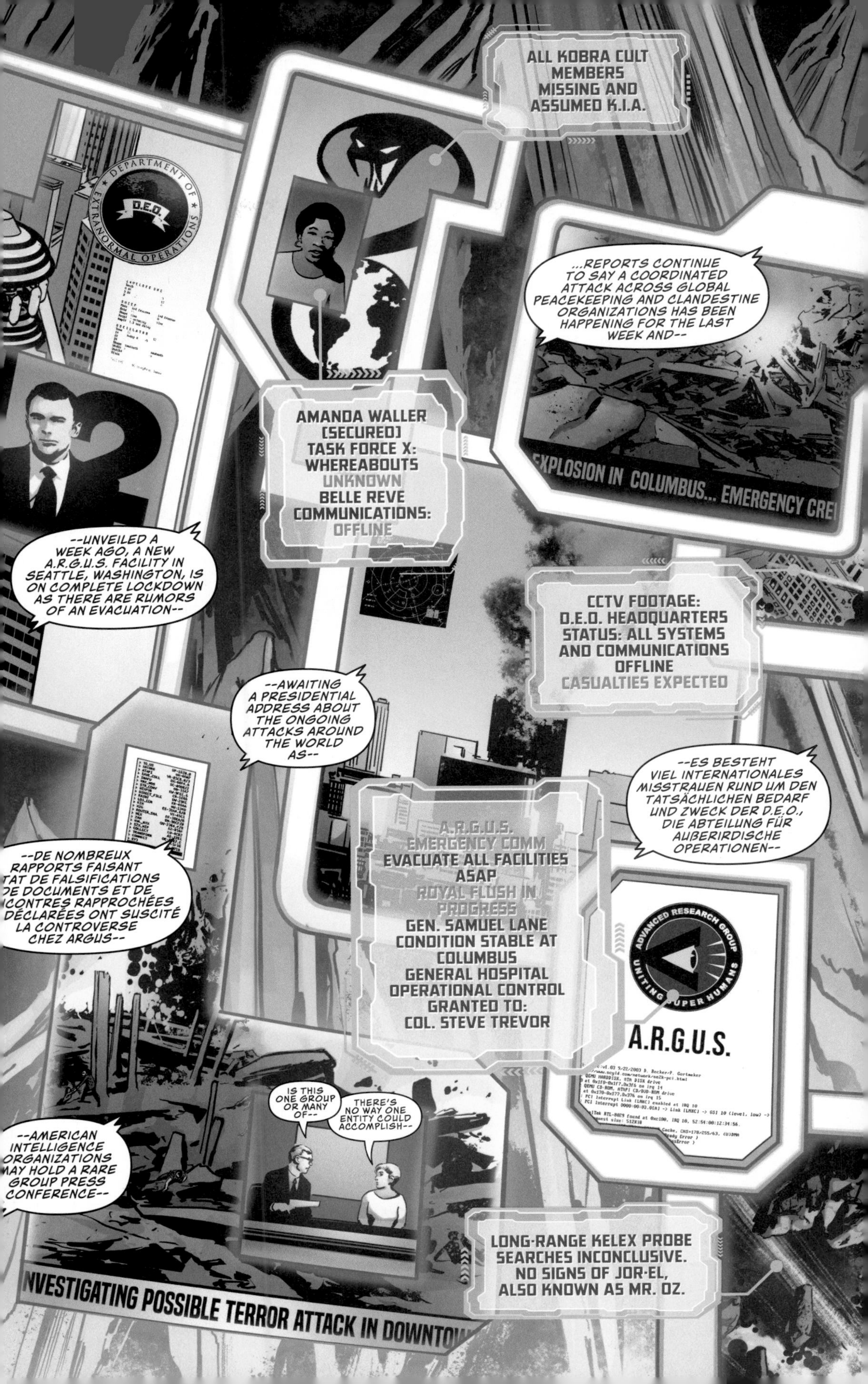
ALL KOBRA CULT MEMBERS MISSING AND ASSUMED K.I.A.
DEPARTMENT OF EXTRANORMAL OPERATIONS
D.E.O.
...REPORTS CONTINUE TO SAY A COORDINATED ATTACK ACROSS GLOBAL PEACEKEEPING AND CLANDESTINE ORGANIZATIONS HAS BEEN HAPPENING FOR THE LAST WEEK AND--
AMANDA WALLER [SECURED] TASK FORCE X: WHEREABOUTS UNKNOWN BELLE REVE COMMUNICATIONS: OFFLINE
EXPLOSION IN COLUMBUS... EMERGENCY CRE
--UNVEILED A WEEK AGO, A NEW A.R.G.U.S. FACILITY IN SEATTLE, WASHINGTON, IS ON COMPLETE LOCKDOWN AS THERE ARE RUMORS OF AN EVACUATION--
CCTV FOOTAGE: D.E.O. HEADQUARTERS STATUS: ALL SYSTEMS AND COMMUNICATIONS OFFLINE CASUALTIES EXPECTED
--AWAITING A PRESIDENTIAL ADDRESS ABOUT THE ONGOING ATTACKS AROUND THE WORLD AS--
--ES BESTEHT VIEL INTERNATIONALES MISSTRAUEN RUND UM DEN TATSÄCHLICHEN BEDARF UND ZWECK DER D.E.O., DIE ABTEILUNG FÜR AUßERIRDISCHE OPERATIONEN--
A.R.G.U.S. EMERGENCY COMM EVACUATE ALL FACILITIES ASAP ROYAL FLUSH IN PROGRESS GEN. SAMUEL LANE CONDITION STABLE AT COLUMBUS GENERAL HOSPITAL OPERATIONAL CONTROL GRANTED TO: COL. STEVE TREVOR
--DE NOMBREUX RAPPORTS FAISANT TAT DE FALSIFICATIONS DE DOCUMENTS ET DE CONTRES RAPPROCHÉES DÉCLARÉES ONT SUSCITÉ LA CONTROVERSE CHEZ ARGUS--
ADVANCED RESEARCH GROUP UNITING SUPER HUMANS
A.R.G.U.S.
IS THIS ONE GROUP OR MANY OF--
THERE'S NO WAY ONE ENTITY COULD ACCOMPLISH--
--AMERICAN INTELLIGENCE ORGANIZATIONS MAY HOLD A RARE GROUP PRESS CONFERENCE--
LONG-RANGE KELEX PROBE SEARCHES INCONCLUSIVE. NO SIGNS OF JOR-EL, ALSO KNOWN AS MR. OZ.
NVESTIGATING POSSIBLE TERROR ATTACK IN DOWNTOW

BRIAN MICHAEL BENDIS Script · STEVE EPTING Art & Cover
BRAD ANDERSON Colors · ROB LEIGH Letters
JESSICA CHEN Associate Editor · MIKE COTTON Editor · BRIAN CUNNINGHAM Group Editor

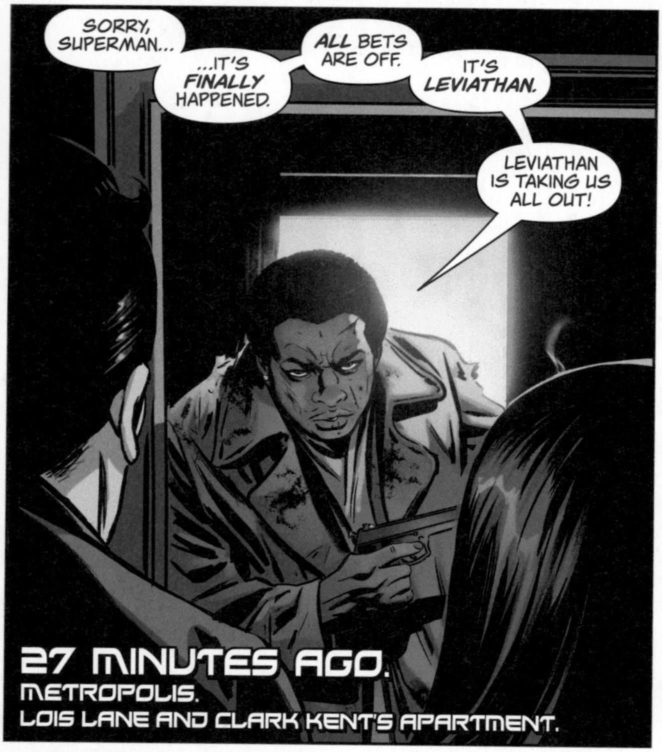
SORRY, SUPERMAN...
...IT'S *FINALLY* HAPPENED.
ALL BETS ARE OFF.
IT'S *LEVIATHAN.*
LEVIATHAN IS TAKING US ALL OUT!
27 MINUTES AGO.
METROPOLIS.
LOIS LANE AND CLARK KENT'S APARTMENT.

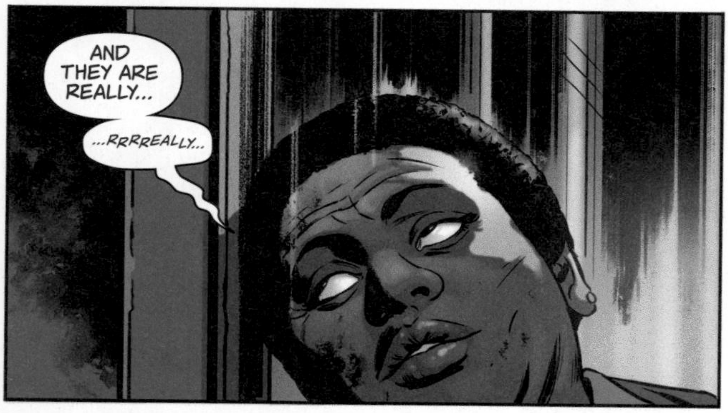
AND THEY ARE REALLY...
...RRRREALLY...

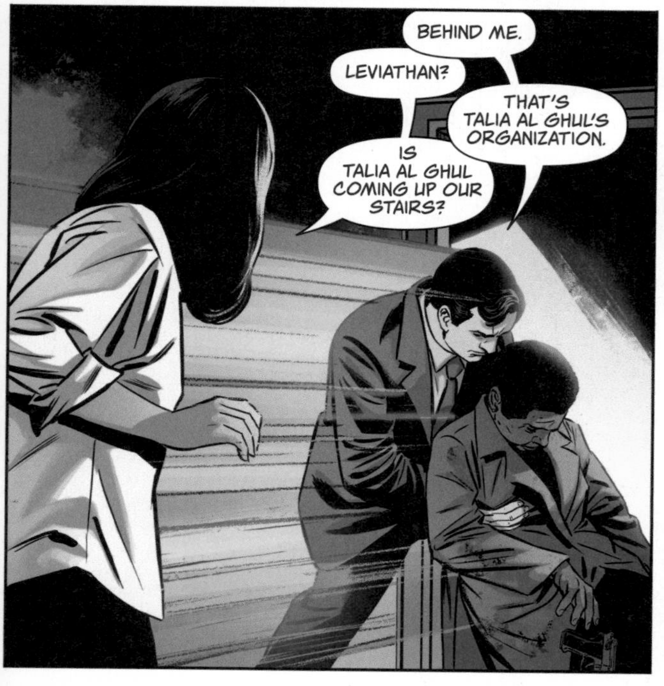
BEHIND ME.
LEVIATHAN?
THAT'S TALIA AL GHUL'S ORGANIZATION.
IS TALIA AL GHUL COMING UP OUR STAIRS?

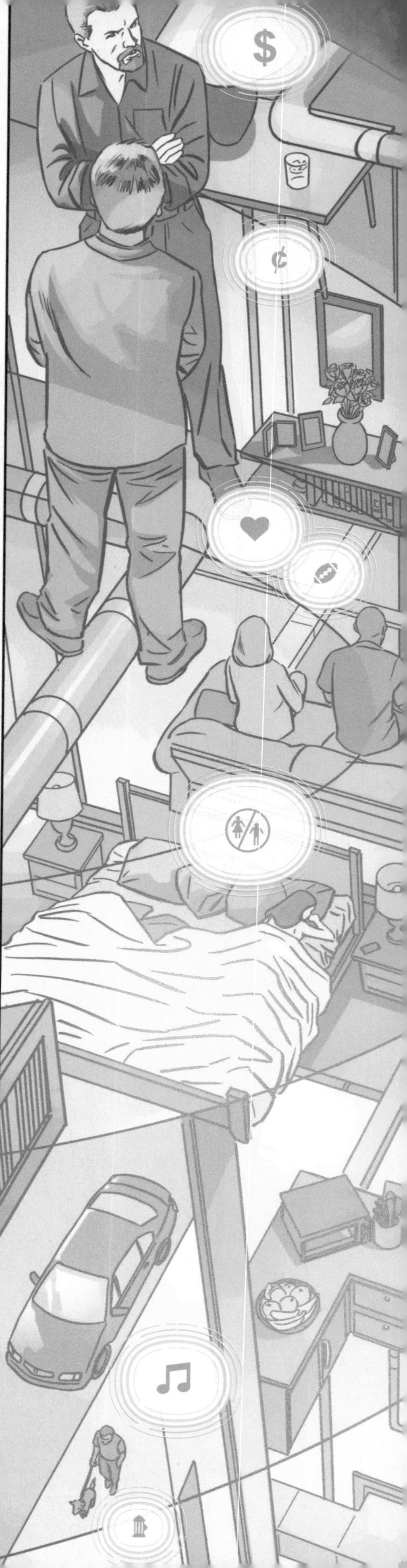

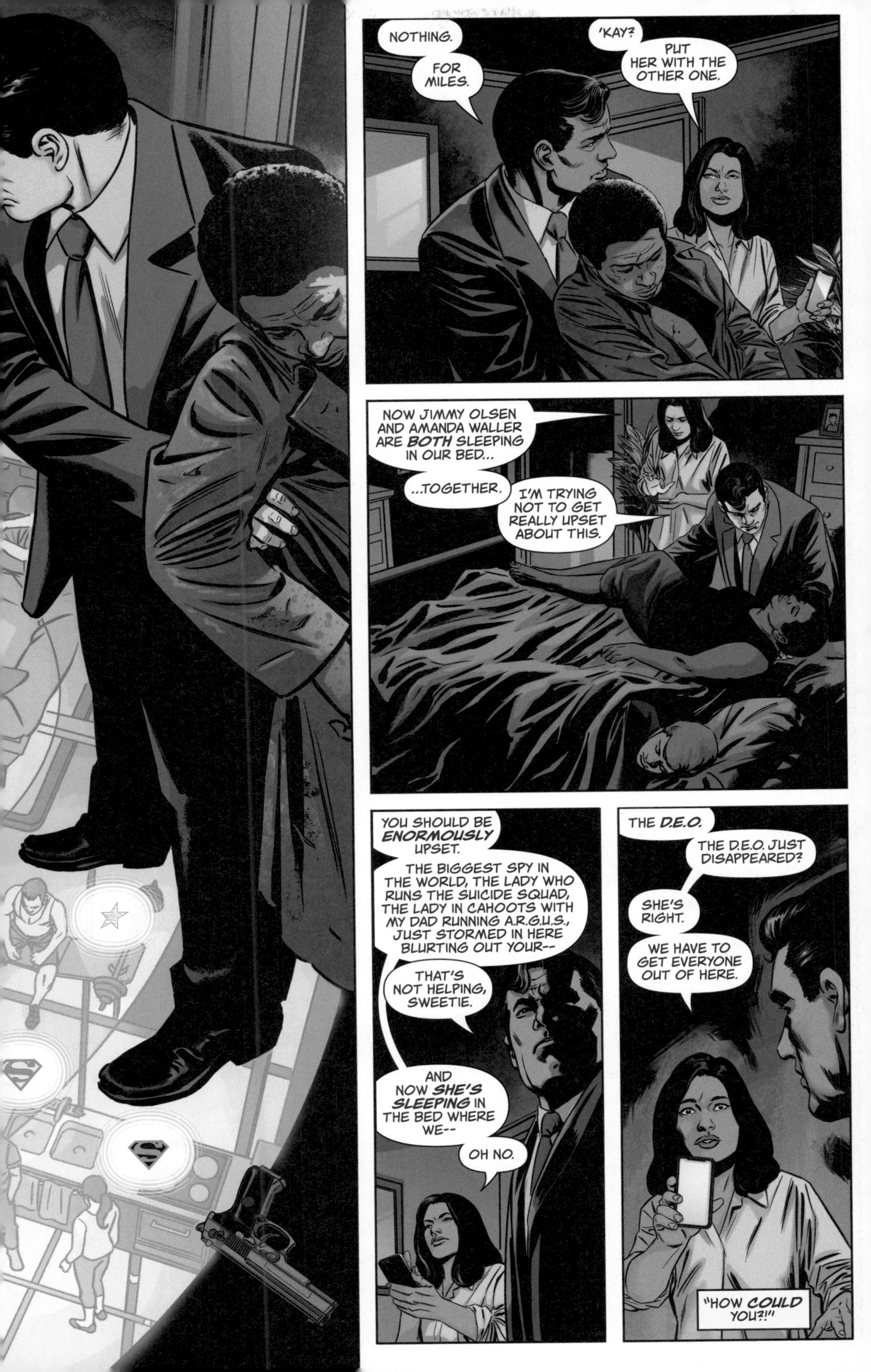
NOTHING.
FOR MILES.
'KAY?
PUT HER WITH THE OTHER ONE.
NOW JIMMY OLSEN AND AMANDA WALLER ARE BOTH SLEEPING IN OUR BED...
...TOGETHER.
I'M TRYING NOT TO GET REALLY UPSET ABOUT THIS.
YOU SHOULD BE ENORMOUSLY UPSET.
THE BIGGEST SPY IN THE WORLD, THE LADY WHO RUNS THE SUICIDE SQUAD, THE LADY IN CAHOOTS WITH MY DAD RUNNING A.R.G.U.S., JUST STORMED IN HERE BLURTING OUT YOUR--
THAT'S NOT HELPING, SWEETIE.
AND NOW SHE'S SLEEPING IN THE BED WHERE WE--
OH NO.
THE D.E.O.
THE D.E.O. JUST DISAPPEARED?
SHE'S RIGHT.
WE HAVE TO GET EVERYONE OUT OF HERE.
"HOW COULD YOU?!"

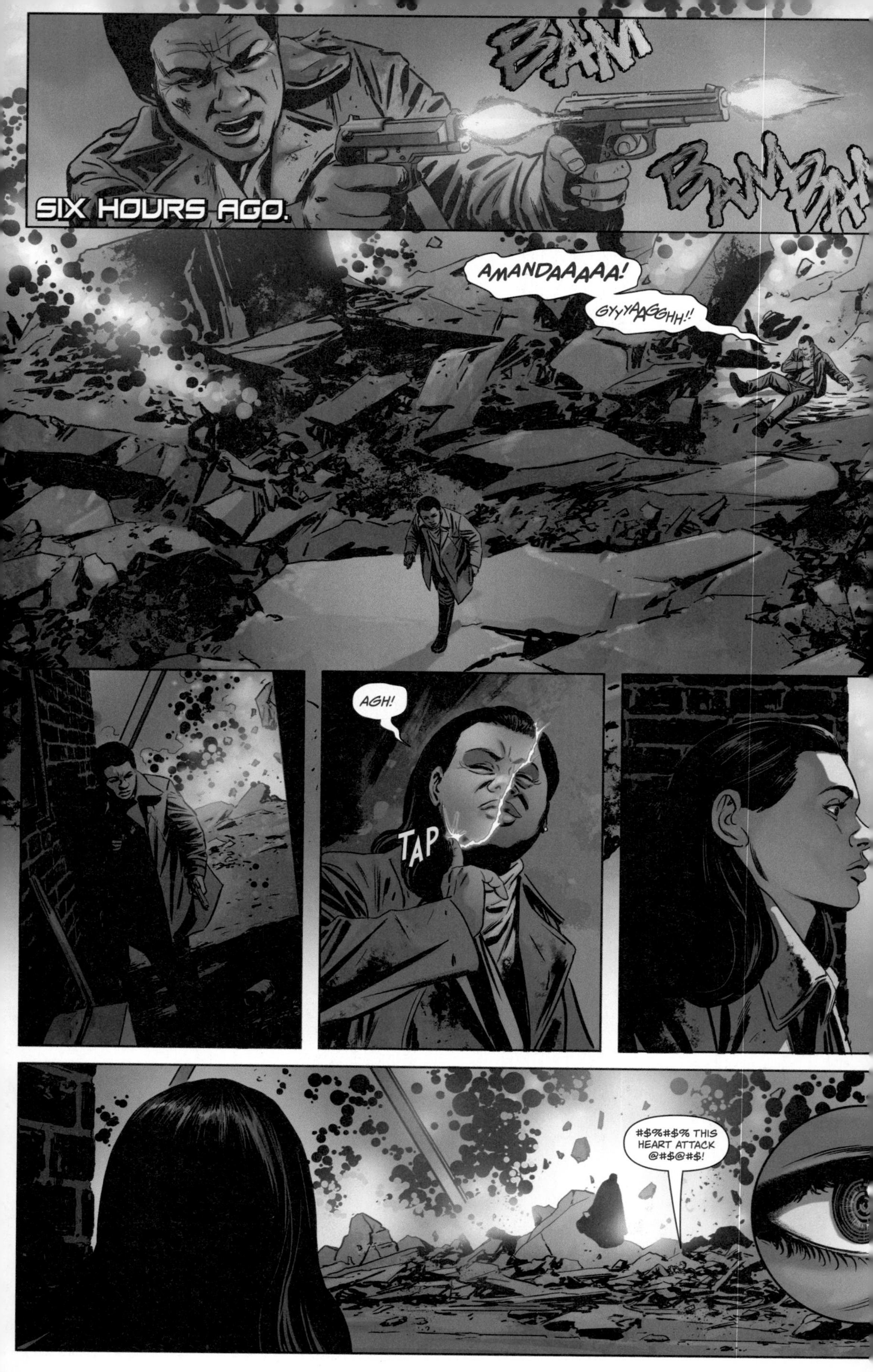

SIX HOURS AGO.
BAM
BAM BAM
AMANDAAAAA!
GYYYAAGGHH!!
AGH!
TAP
#$%#$% THIS
HEART ATTACK
@#$@#$!

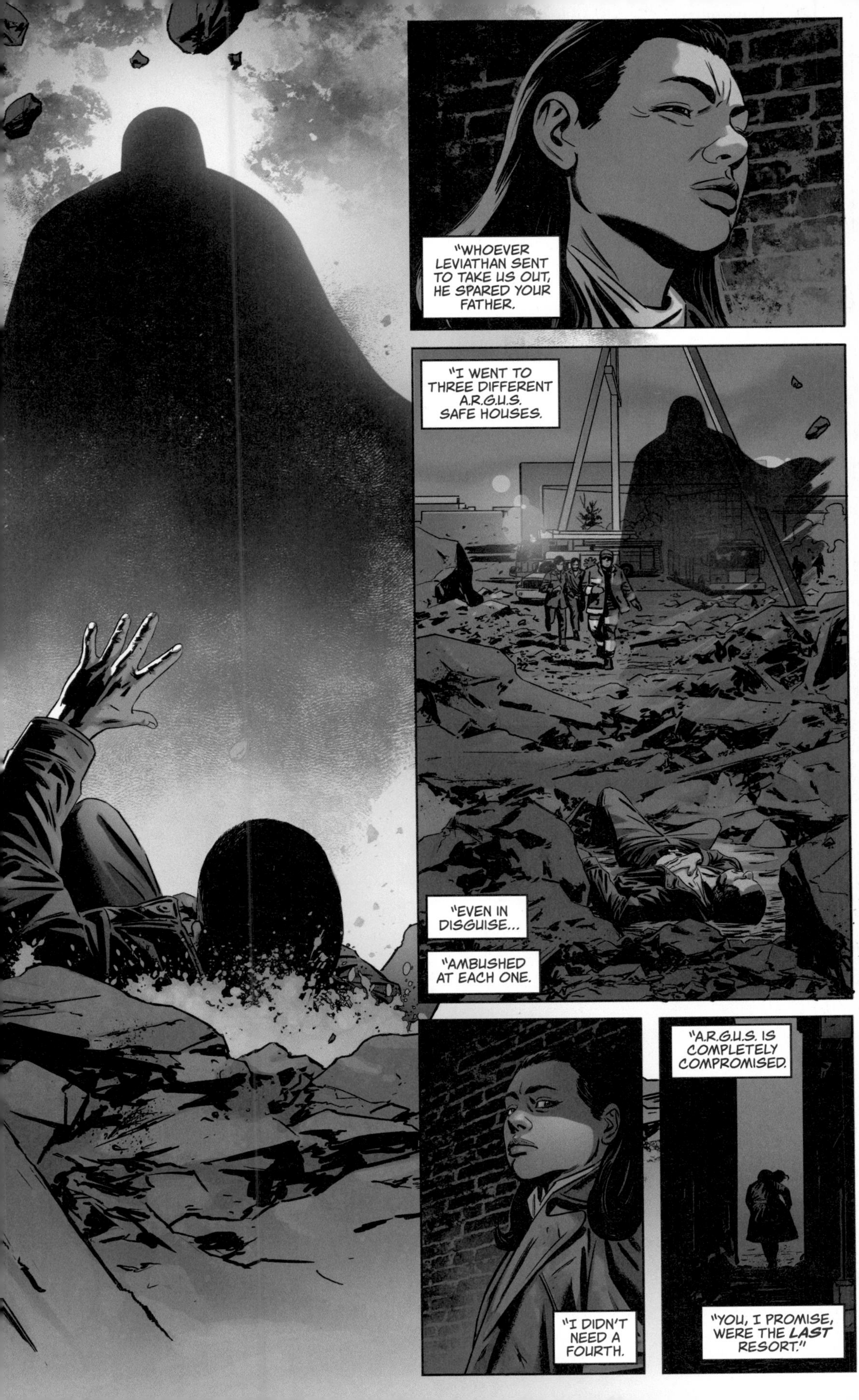
"WHOEVER LEVIATHAN SENT TO TAKE US OUT, HE SPARED YOUR FATHER.
"I WENT TO THREE DIFFERENT A.R.G.U.S. SAFE HOUSES.
"EVEN IN DISGUISE...
"AMBUSHED AT EACH ONE.
"I DIDN'T NEED A FOURTH.
"A.R.G.U.S. IS COMPLETELY COMPROMISED.
"YOU, I PROMISE, WERE THE *LAST* RESORT."

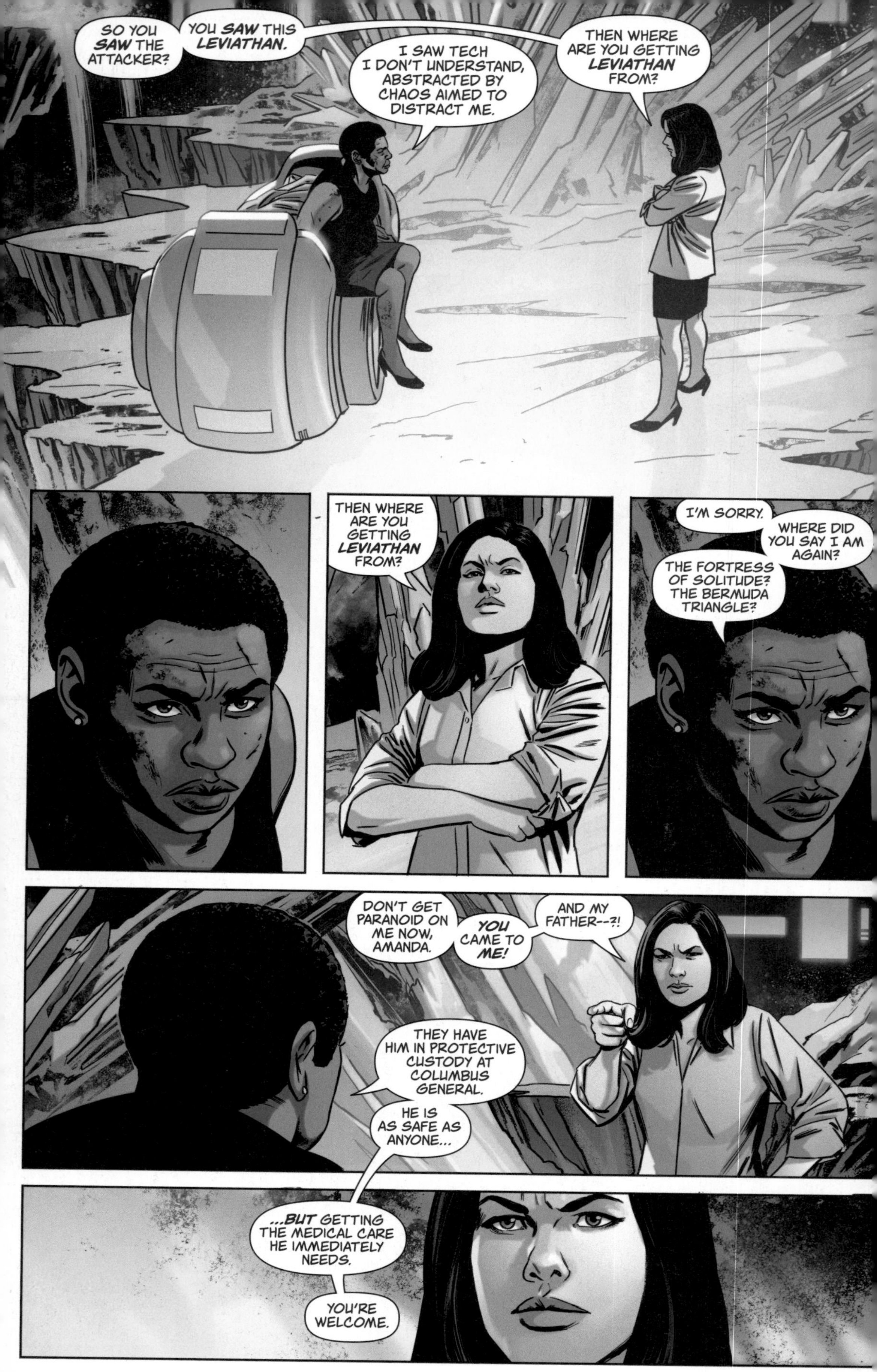
SO YOU SAW THE ATTACKER?
YOU SAW THIS LEVIATHAN.
I SAW TECH I DON'T UNDERSTAND, ABSTRACTED BY CHAOS AIMED TO DISTRACT ME.
THEN WHERE ARE YOU GETTING LEVIATHAN FROM?
THEN WHERE ARE YOU GETTING LEVIATHAN FROM?
I'M SORRY.
WHERE DID YOU SAY I AM AGAIN?
THE FORTRESS OF SOLITUDE? THE BERMUDA TRIANGLE?
DON'T GET PARANOID ON ME NOW, AMANDA.
YOU CAME TO ME!
AND MY FATHER--?!
THEY HAVE HIM IN PROTECTIVE CUSTODY AT COLUMBUS GENERAL.
HE IS AS SAFE AS ANYONE...
...BUT GETTING THE MEDICAL CARE HE IMMEDIATELY NEEDS.
YOU'RE WELCOME.

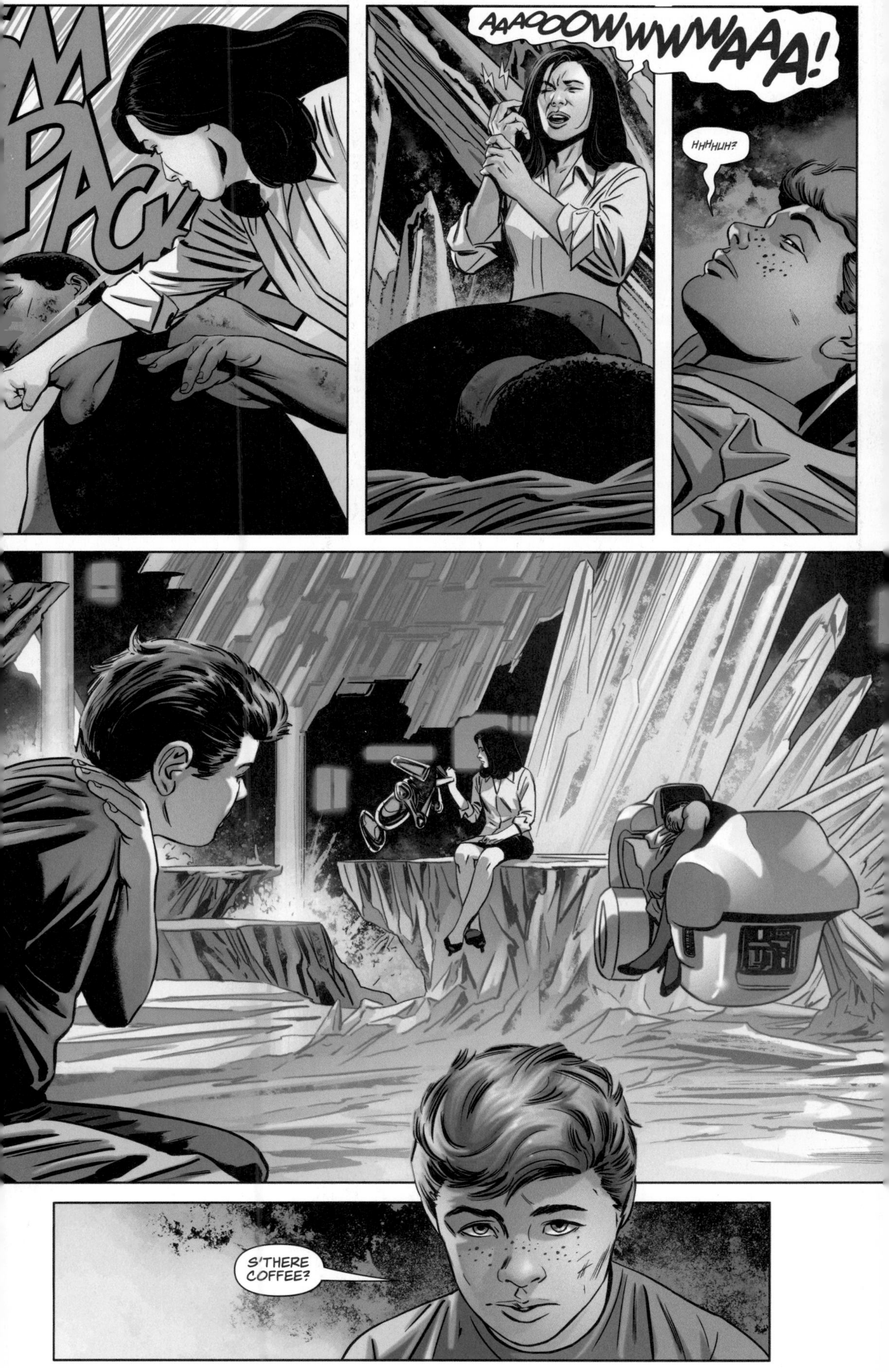
AAAOOOWWWWAAA!
HHHHUH?
S'THERE COFFEE?

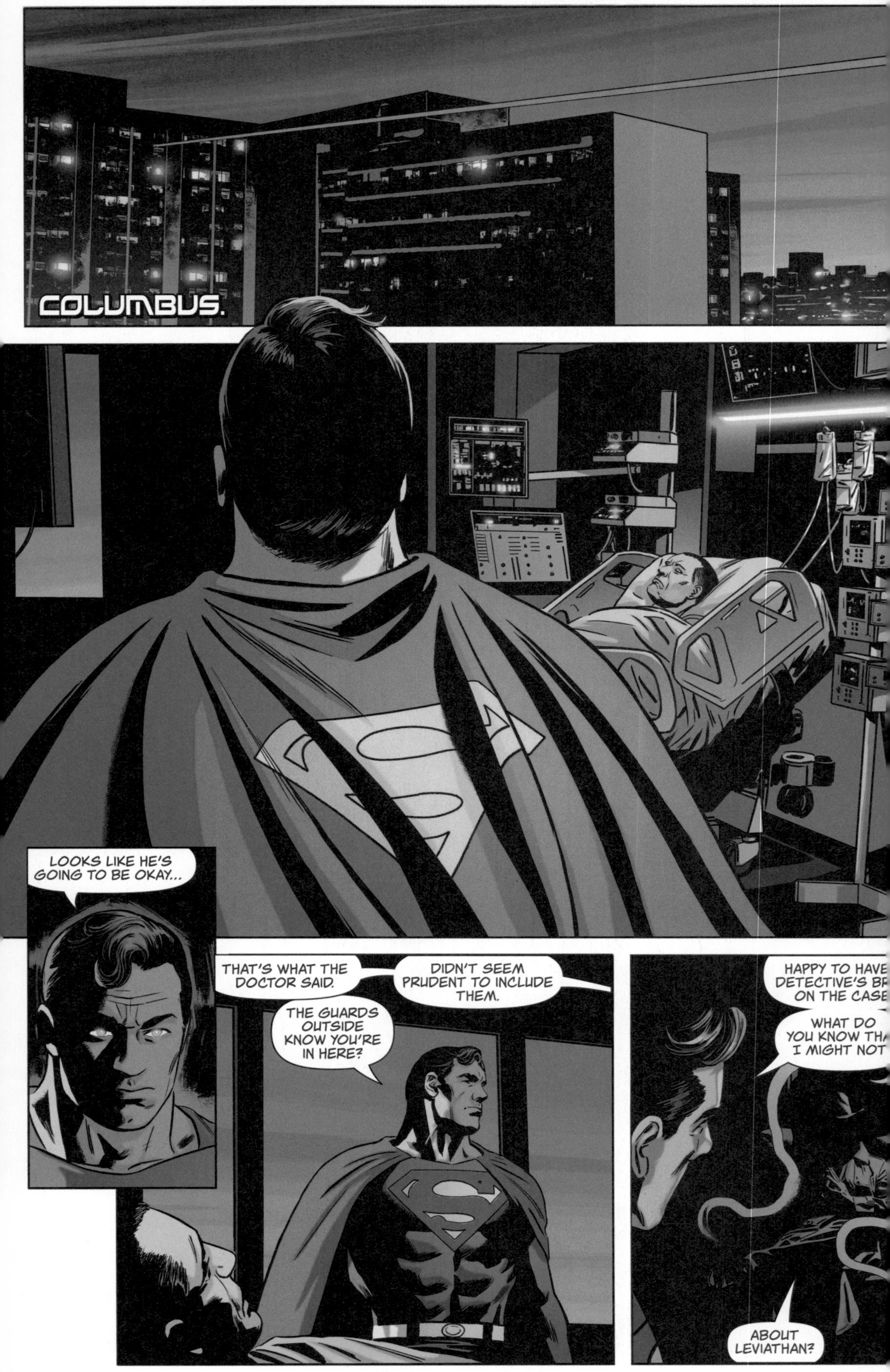
COLUMBUS.
LOOKS LIKE HE'S GOING TO BE OKAY...
THAT'S WHAT THE DOCTOR SAID.
DIDN'T SEEM PRUDENT TO INCLUDE THEM.
THE GUARDS OUTSIDE KNOW YOU'RE IN HERE?
HAPPY TO HAVE DETECTIVE'S BR ON THE CASE
WHAT DO YOU KNOW THA I MIGHT NOT
ABOUT LEVIATHAN?

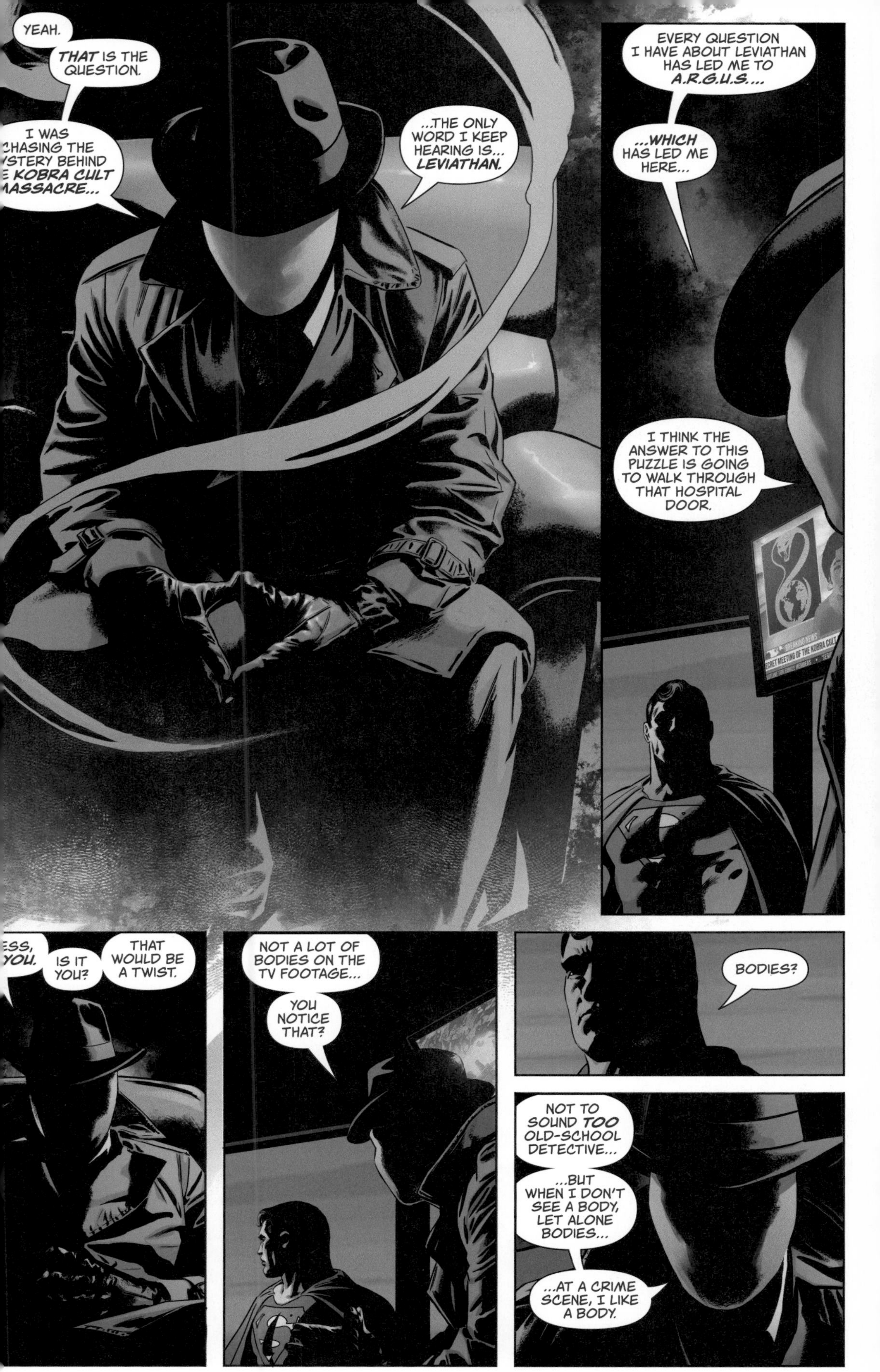
YEAH.
THAT IS THE QUESTION.
I WAS CHASING THE YSTERY BEHIND E KOBRA CULT MASSACRE...
...THE ONLY WORD I KEEP HEARING IS... LEVIATHAN.
EVERY QUESTION I HAVE ABOUT LEVIATHAN HAS LED ME TO A.R.G.U.S....
...WHICH HAS LED ME HERE...
I THINK THE ANSWER TO THIS PUZZLE IS GOING TO WALK THROUGH THAT HOSPITAL DOOR.
BREAKING NEWS
SECRET MEETING OF THE KOBRA CULT
ESS, YOU.
IS IT YOU?
THAT WOULD BE A TWIST.
NOT A LOT OF BODIES ON THE TV FOOTAGE...
YOU NOTICE THAT?
BODIES?
NOT TO SOUND TOO OLD-SCHOOL DETECTIVE...
...BUT WHEN I DON'T SEE A BODY, LET ALONE BODIES...
...AT A CRIME SCENE, I LIKE A BODY.

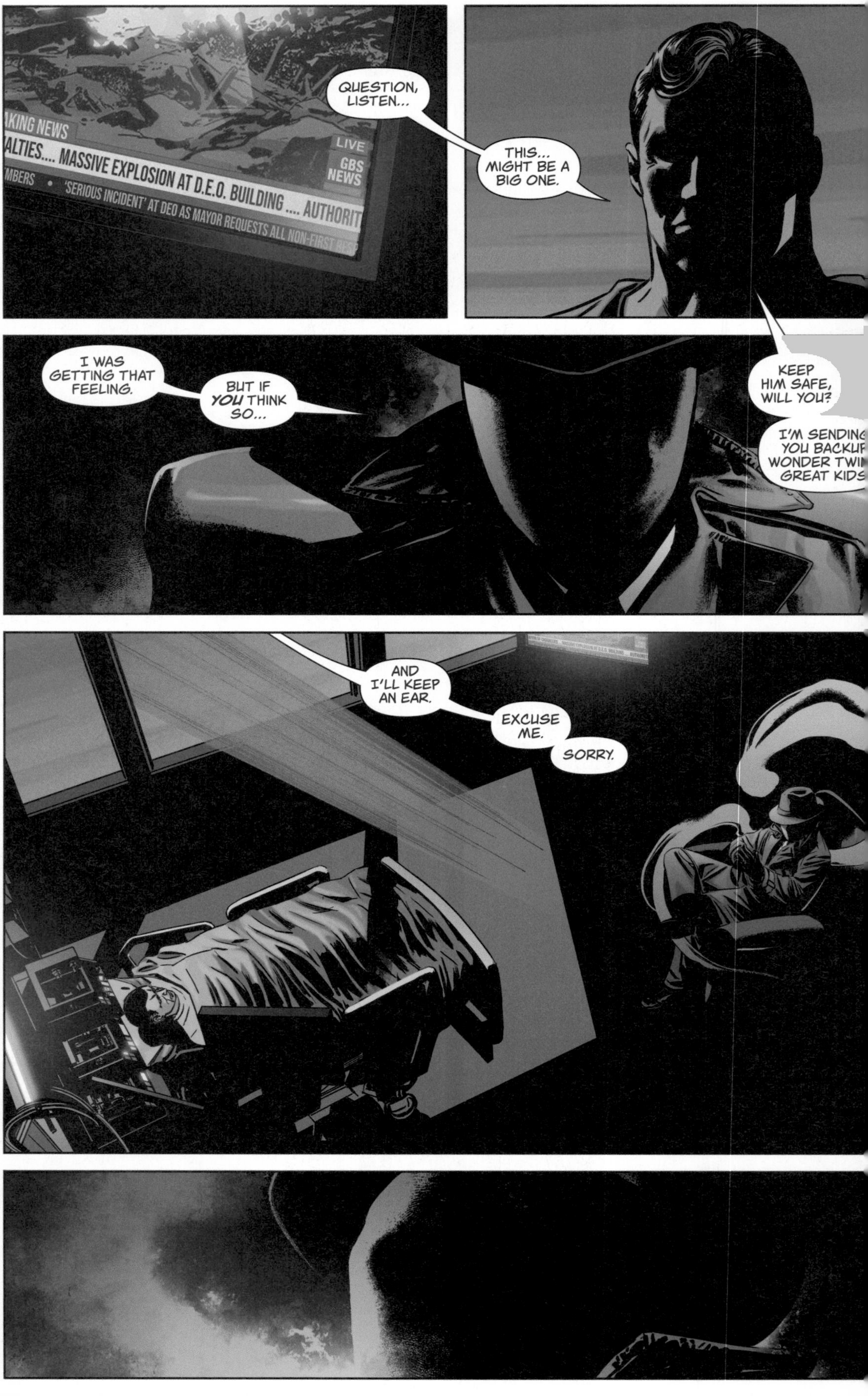

AKING NEWS
LTIES.... MASSIVE EXPLOSION AT D.E.O. BUILDING .... AUTHORIT
LIVE
GBS NEWS
'SERIOUS INCIDENT' AT DEO AS MAYOR REQUESTS ALL NON-FIRST RES
QUESTION, LISTEN...
THIS... MIGHT BE A BIG ONE.
I WAS GETTING THAT FEELING.
BUT IF YOU THINK SO...
KEEP HIM SAFE, WILL YOU?
I'M SENDING YOU BACKUP WONDER TWIN GREAT KIDS
AND I'LL KEEP AN EAR.
EXCUSE ME.
SORRY.

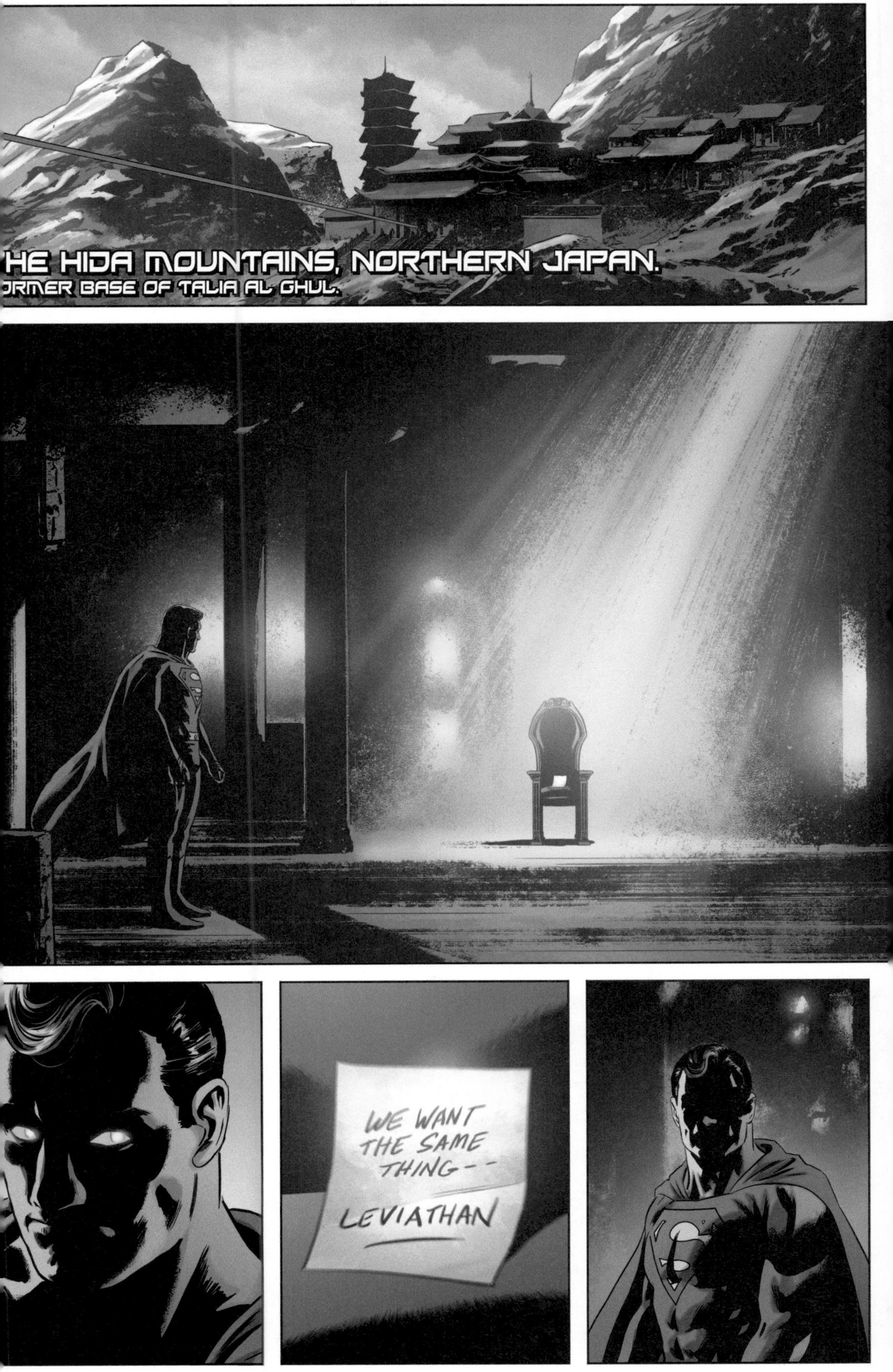
HE HIDA MOUNTAINS, NORTHERN JAPAN.
ORMER BASE OF TALIA AL GHUL.
WE WANT THE SAME THING--
LEVIATHAN

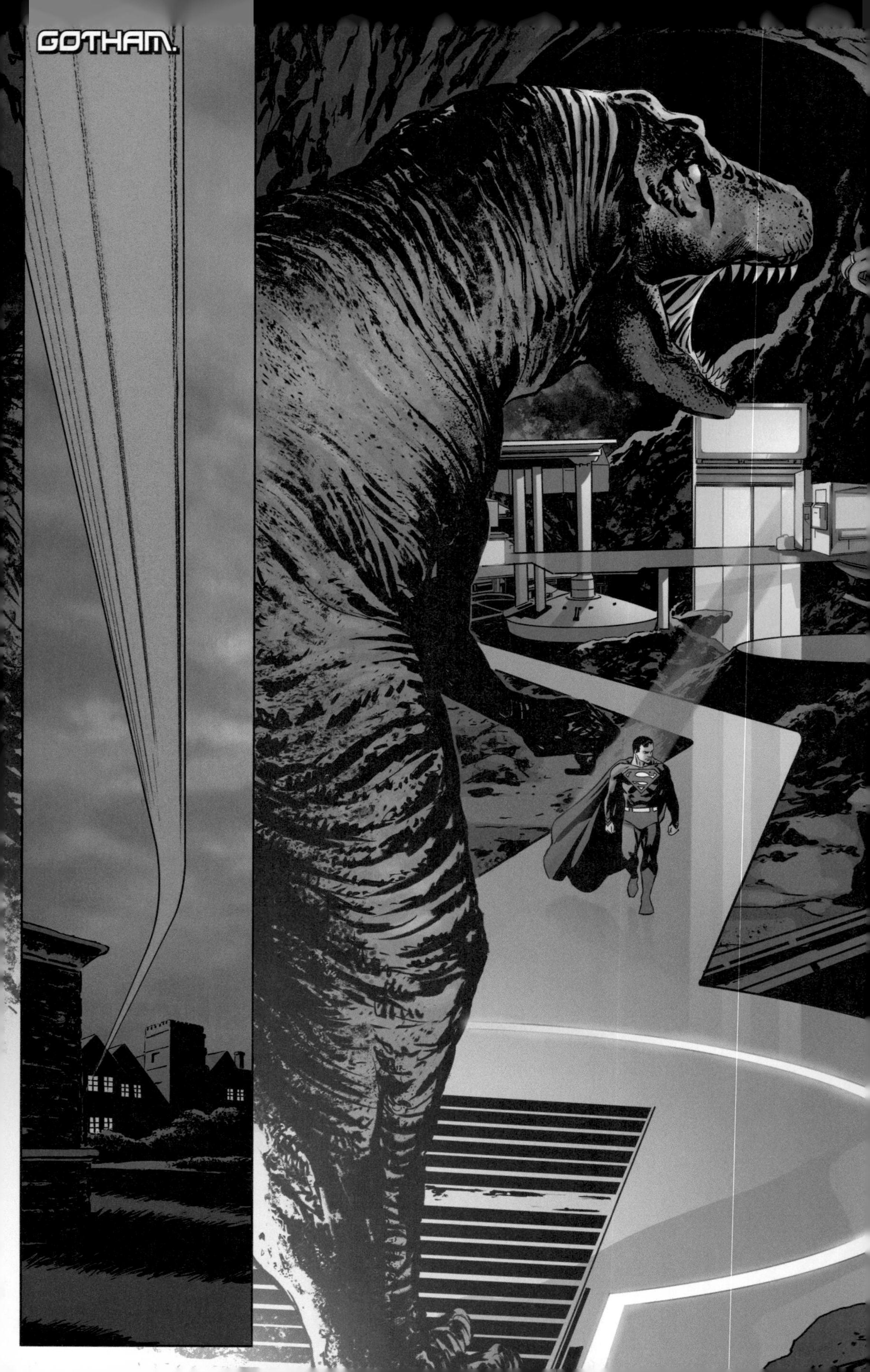
GOTHAM.

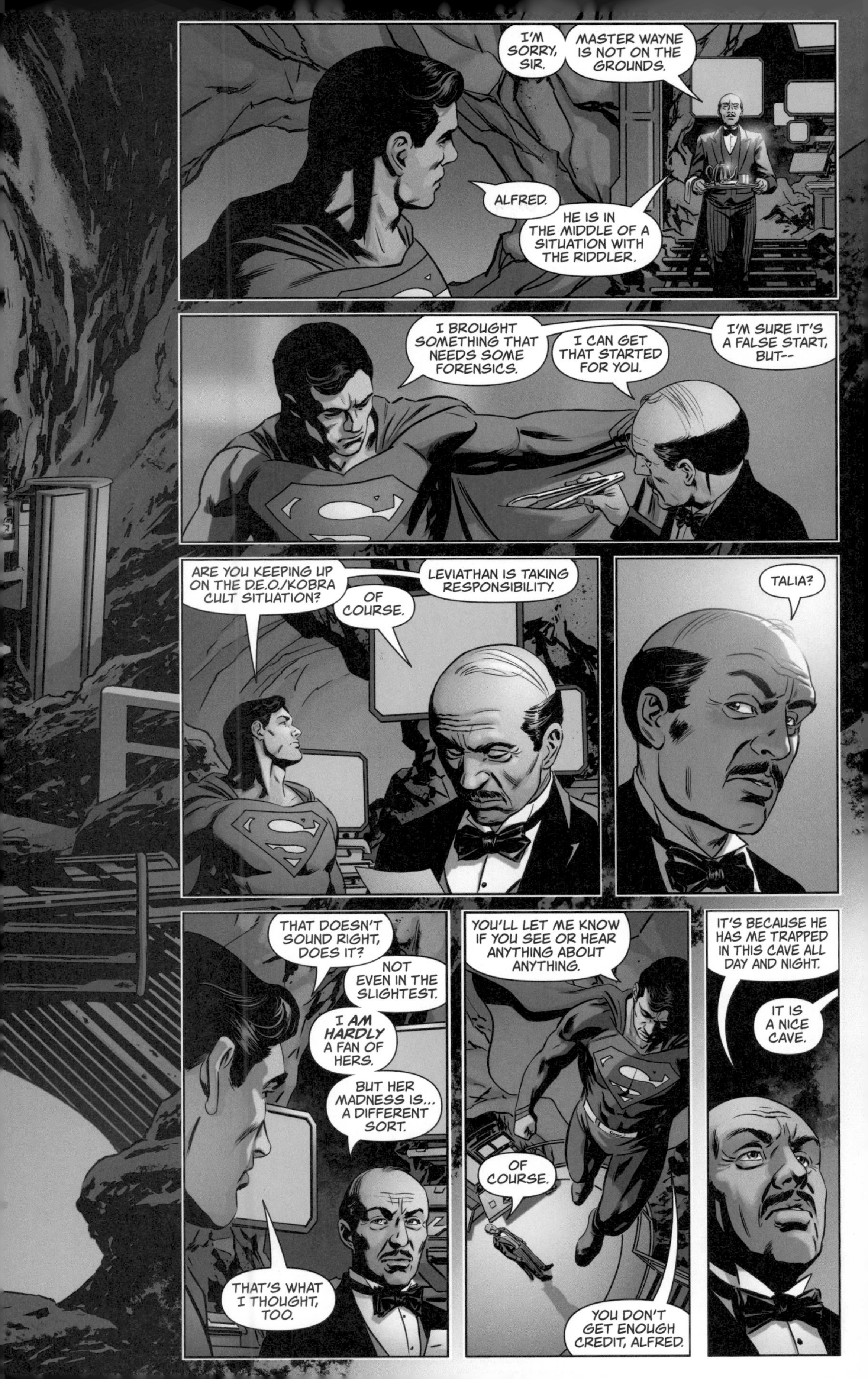
I'M SORRY, SIR.
MASTER WAYNE IS NOT ON THE GROUNDS.
ALFRED.
HE IS IN THE MIDDLE OF A SITUATION WITH THE RIDDLER.
I BROUGHT SOMETHING THAT NEEDS SOME FORENSICS.
I CAN GET THAT STARTED FOR YOU.
I'M SURE IT'S A FALSE START, BUT--
ARE YOU KEEPING UP ON THE D.E.O./KOBRA CULT SITUATION?
OF COURSE.
LEVIATHAN IS TAKING RESPONSIBILITY.
TALIA?
THAT DOESN'T SOUND RIGHT, DOES IT?
NOT EVEN IN THE SLIGHTEST.
I *AM HARDLY* A FAN OF HERS.
BUT HER MADNESS IS... A DIFFERENT SORT.
THAT'S WHAT I THOUGHT, TOO.
YOU'LL LET ME KNOW IF YOU SEE OR HEAR ANYTHING ABOUT ANYTHING.
OF COURSE.
YOU DON'T GET ENOUGH CREDIT, ALFRED.
IT'S BECAUSE HE HAS ME TRAPPED IN THIS CAVE ALL DAY AND NIGHT.
IT IS A NICE CAVE.

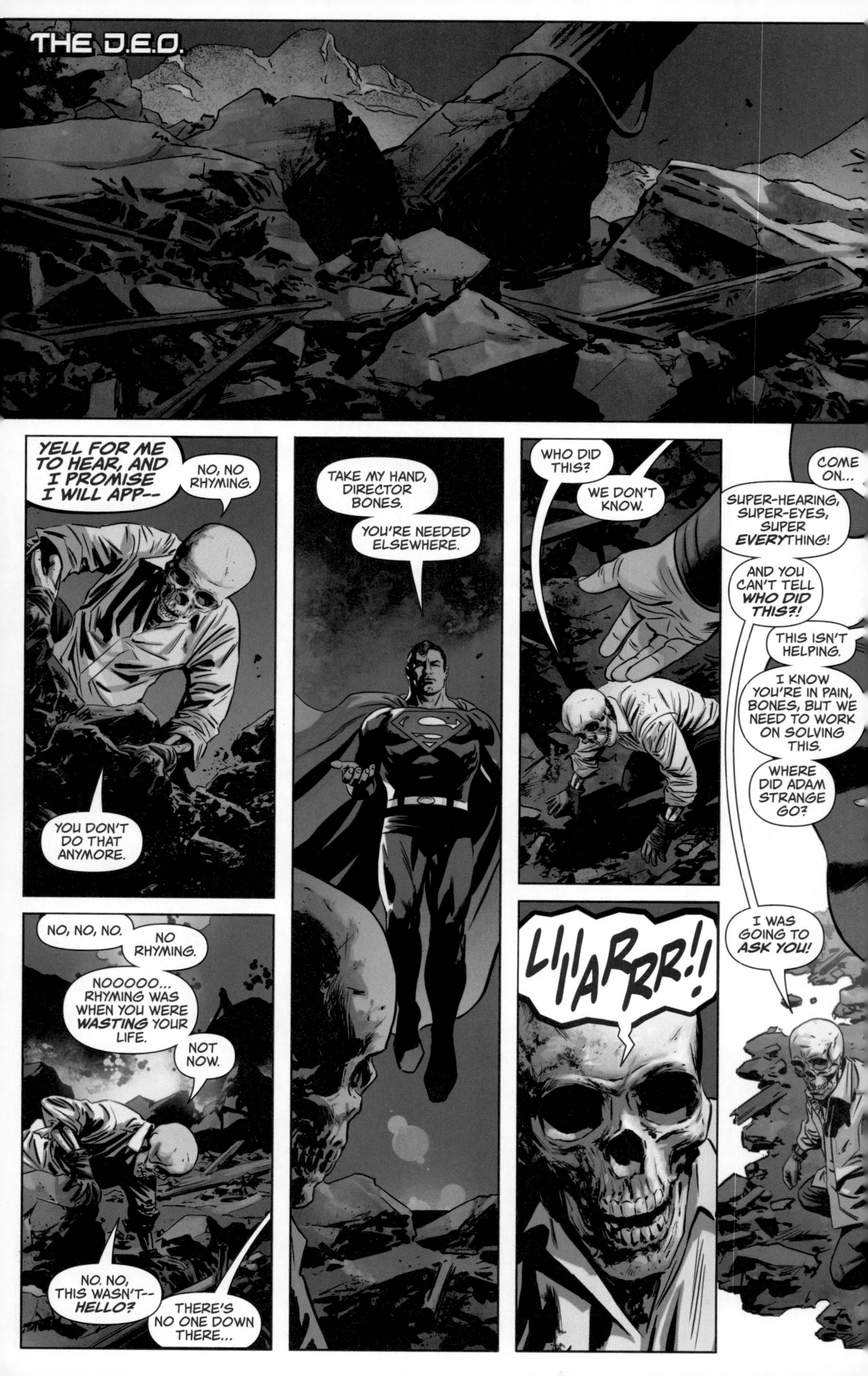
THE D.E.O.
YELL FOR ME TO HEAR, AND I PROMISE I WILL APP--
NO, NO RHYMING.
YOU DON'T DO THAT ANYMORE.
NO, NO, NO.
NO RHYMING.
NOOOOO... RHYMING WAS WHEN YOU WERE WASTING YOUR LIFE.
NOT NOW.
NO. NO, THIS WASN'T-- HELLO?
THERE'S NO ONE DOWN THERE...
TAKE MY HAND, DIRECTOR BONES.
YOU'RE NEEDED ELSEWHERE.
WHO DID THIS?
WE DON'T KNOW.
LIIIARRR!!
COME ON...
SUPER-HEARING, SUPER-EYES, SUPER EVERYTHING!
AND YOU CAN'T TELL WHO DID THIS?!
THIS ISN'T HELPING.
I KNOW YOU'RE IN PAIN, BONES, BUT WE NEED TO WORK ON SOLVING THIS.
WHERE DID ADAM STRANGE GO?
I WAS GOING TO ASK YOU!

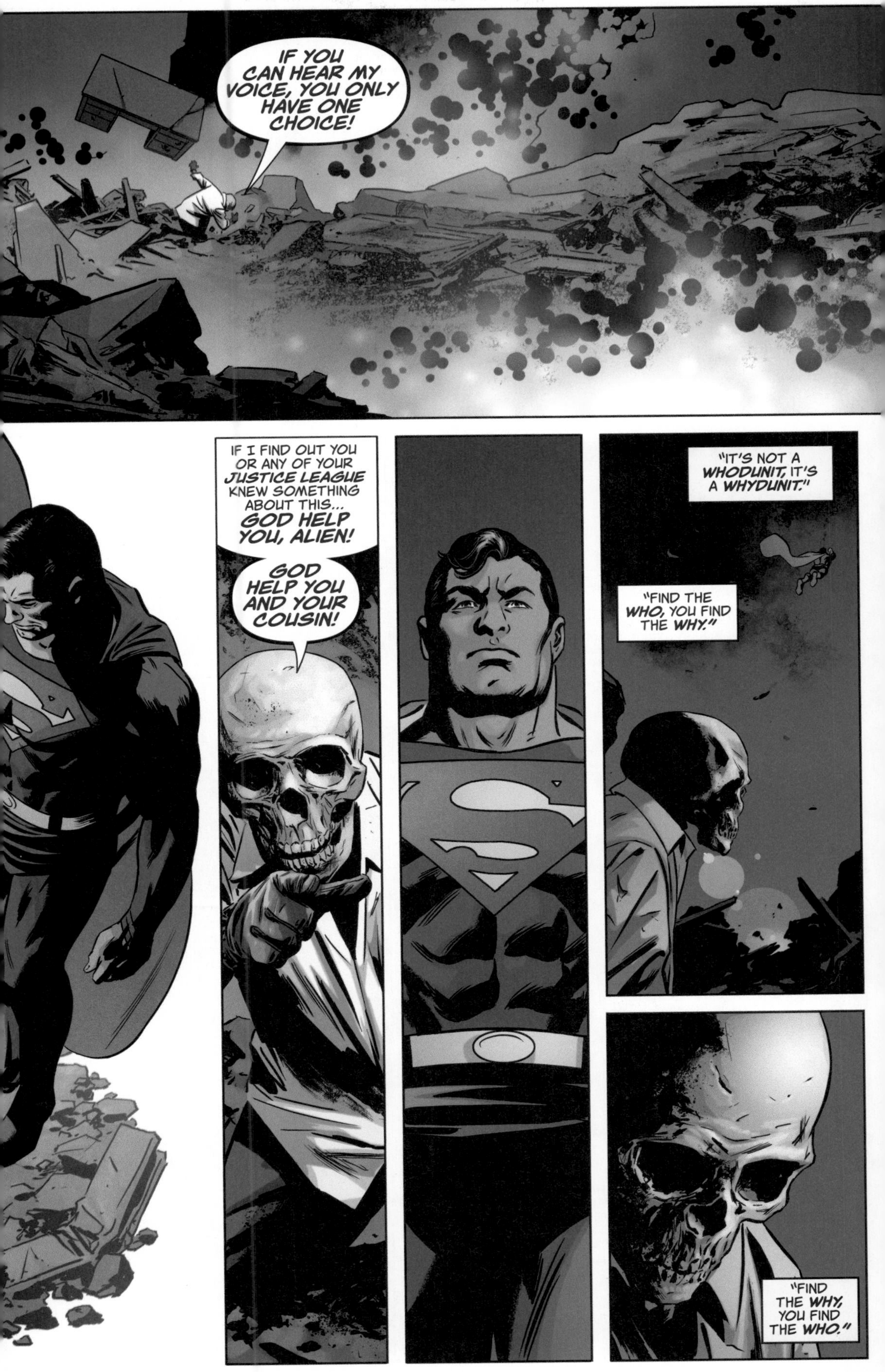
IF YOU CAN HEAR MY VOICE, YOU ONLY HAVE ONE CHOICE!
IF I FIND OUT YOU OR ANY OF YOUR JUSTICE LEAGUE KNEW SOMETHING ABOUT THIS... GOD HELP YOU, ALIEN!
GOD HELP YOU AND YOUR COUSIN!
"IT'S NOT A WHODUNIT, IT'S A WHYDUNIT."
"FIND THE WHO, YOU FIND THE WHY."
"FIND THE WHY, YOU FIND THE WHO."

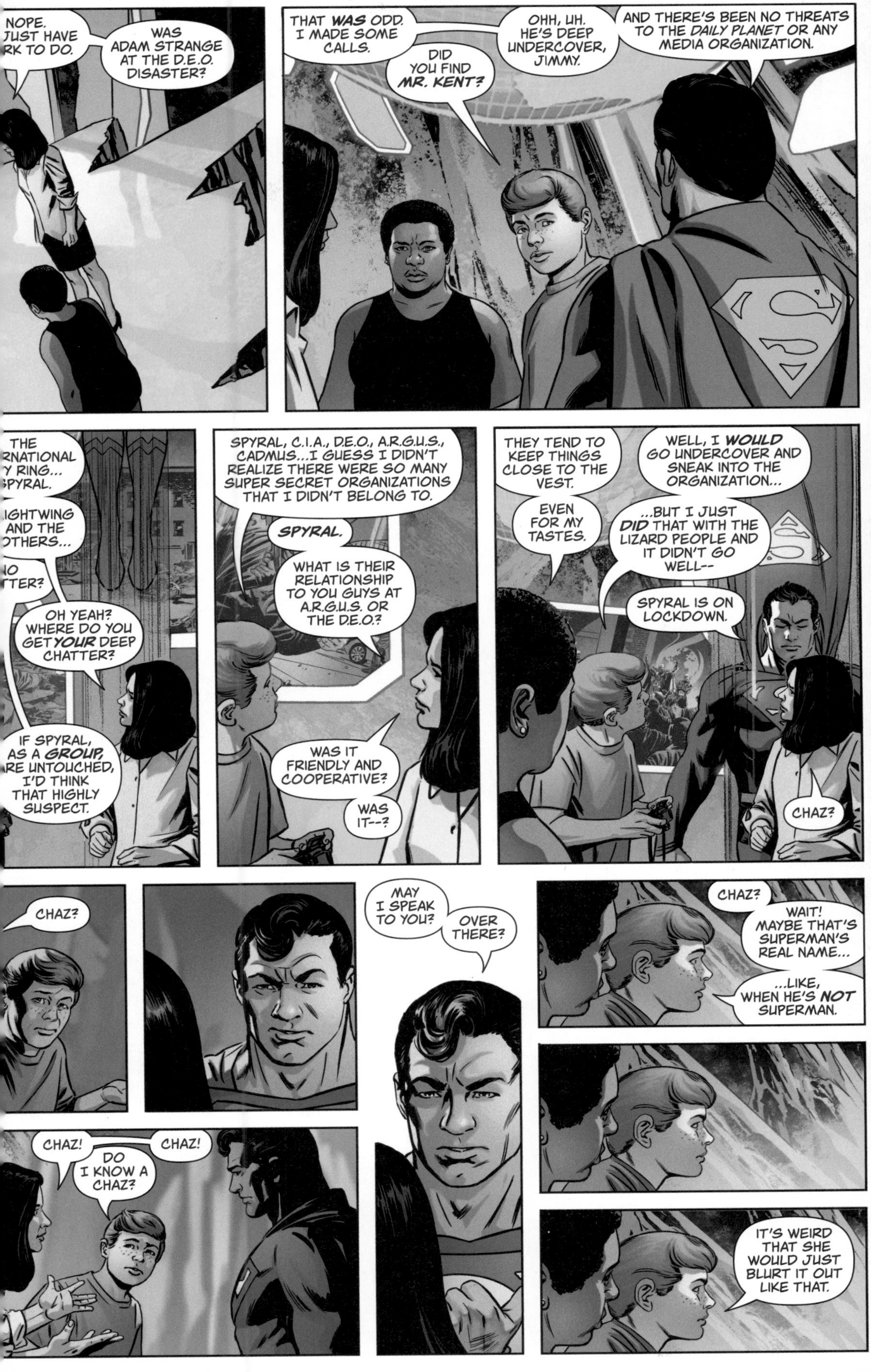

NOPE. JUST HAVE RK TO DO.
WAS ADAM STRANGE AT THE D.E.O. DISASTER?
THAT WAS ODD. I MADE SOME CALLS.
DID YOU FIND MR. KENT?
OHH, UH. HE'S DEEP UNDERCOVER, JIMMY.
AND THERE'S BEEN NO THREATS TO THE DAILY PLANET OR ANY MEDIA ORGANIZATION.
THE RNATIONAL Y RING... PYRAL.
IGHTWING AND THE OTHERS...
O TTER?
OH YEAH? WHERE DO YOU GET YOUR DEEP CHATTER?
IF SPYRAL, AS A GROUP, RE UNTOUCHED, I'D THINK THAT HIGHLY SUSPECT.
SPYRAL, C.I.A., D.E.O., A.R.G.U.S., CADMUS...I GUESS I DIDN'T REALIZE THERE WERE SO MANY SUPER SECRET ORGANIZATIONS THAT I DIDN'T BELONG TO.
SPYRAL.
WHAT IS THEIR RELATIONSHIP TO YOU GUYS AT A.R.G.U.S. OR THE D.E.O.?
WAS IT FRIENDLY AND COOPERATIVE?
WAS IT--?
THEY TEND TO KEEP THINGS CLOSE TO THE VEST.
EVEN FOR MY TASTES.
WELL, I WOULD GO UNDERCOVER AND SNEAK INTO THE ORGANIZATION...
...BUT I JUST DID THAT WITH THE LIZARD PEOPLE AND IT DIDN'T GO WELL--
SPYRAL IS ON LOCKDOWN.
CHAZ?
CHAZ?
MAY I SPEAK TO YOU?
OVER THERE?
CHAZ?
WAIT! MAYBE THAT'S SUPERMAN'S REAL NAME...
...LIKE, WHEN HE'S NOT SUPERMAN.
CHAZ!
CHAZ!
DO I KNOW A CHAZ?
IT'S WEIRD THAT SHE WOULD JUST BLURT IT OUT LIKE THAT.

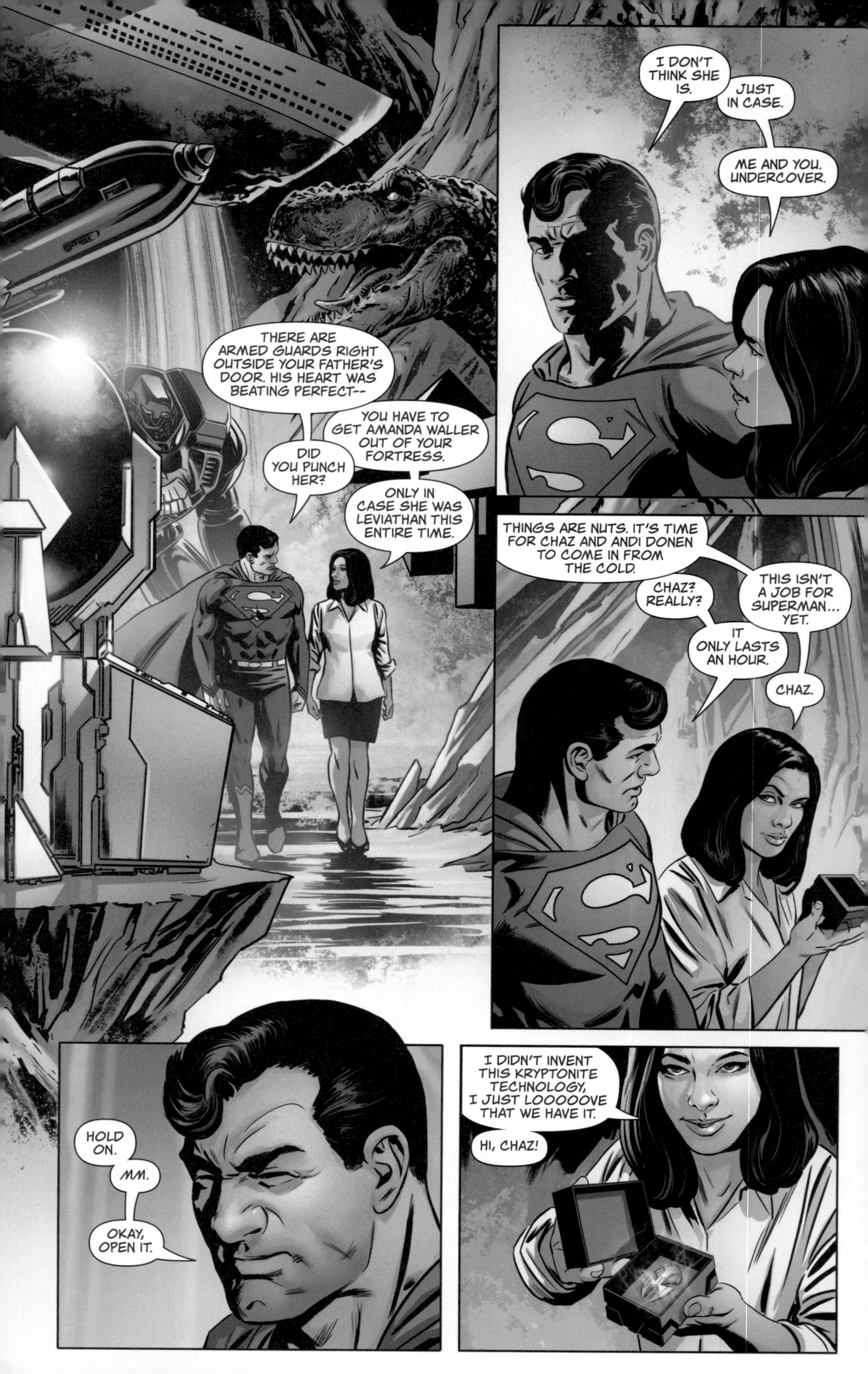
THERE ARE ARMED GUARDS RIGHT OUTSIDE YOUR FATHER'S DOOR. HIS HEART WAS BEATING PERFECT--
YOU HAVE TO GET AMANDA WALLER OUT OF YOUR FORTRESS.
DID YOU PUNCH HER?
ONLY IN CASE SHE WAS LEVIATHAN THIS ENTIRE TIME.
I DON'T THINK SHE IS.
JUST IN CASE.
ME AND YOU. UNDERCOVER.
THINGS ARE NUTS. IT'S TIME FOR CHAZ AND ANDI DONEN TO COME IN FROM THE COLD.
THIS ISN'T A JOB FOR SUPERMAN... YET.
CHAZ? REALLY?
IT ONLY LASTS AN HOUR.
CHAZ.
HOLD ON.
MM.
OKAY, OPEN IT.
I DIDN'T INVENT THIS KRYPTONITE TECHNOLOGY, I JUST LOOOOOVE THAT WE HAVE IT.
HI, CHAZ!

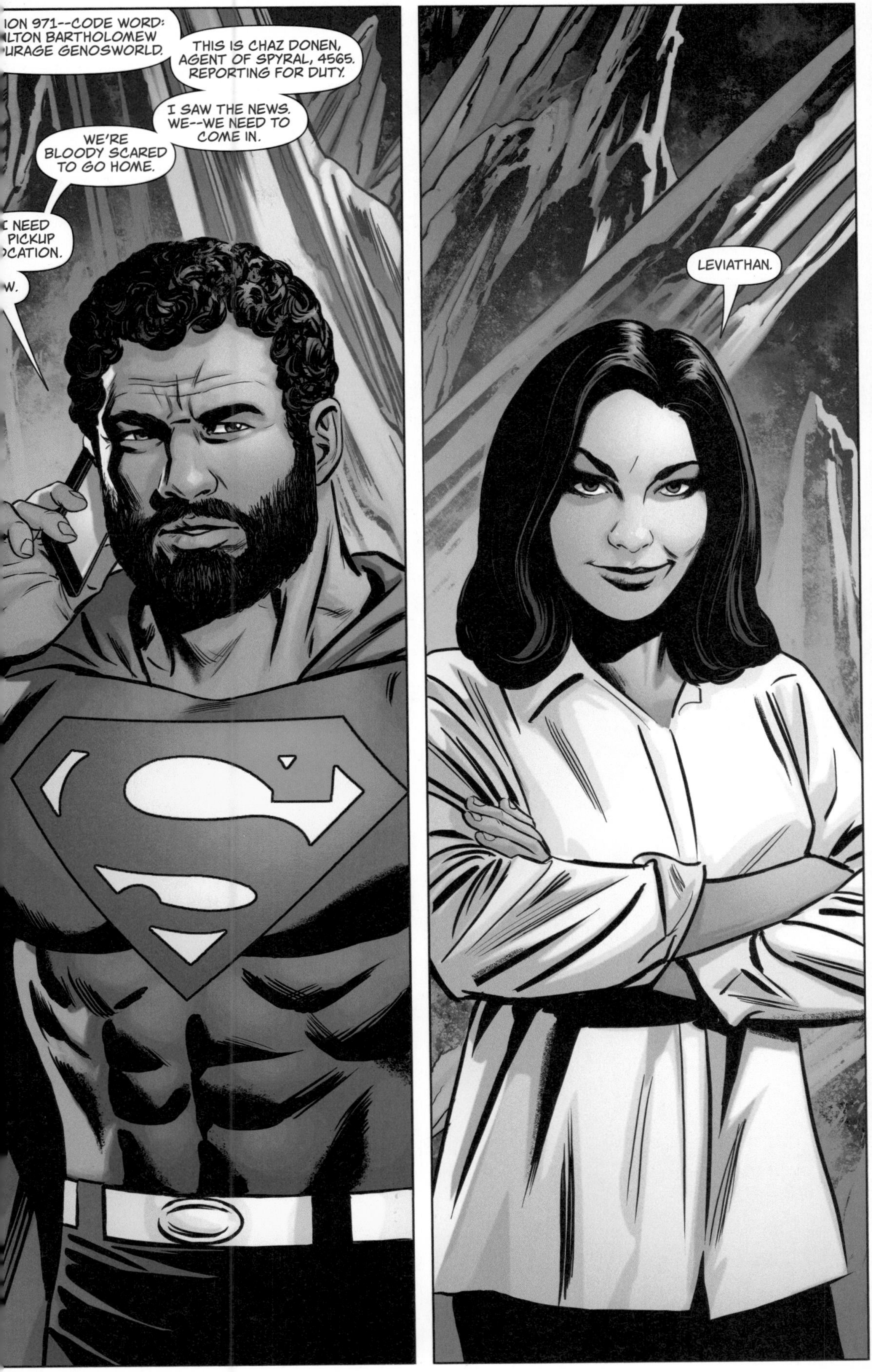

ION 971--CODE WORD:
LTON BARTHOLOMEW
URAGE GENOSWORLD.
THIS IS CHAZ DONEN, AGENT OF SPYRAL, 4565. REPORTING FOR DUTY.
I SAW THE NEWS. WE--WE NEED TO COME IN.
WE'RE BLOODY SCARED TO GO HOME.
NEED
PICKUP
CATION.
W.
LEVIATHAN.

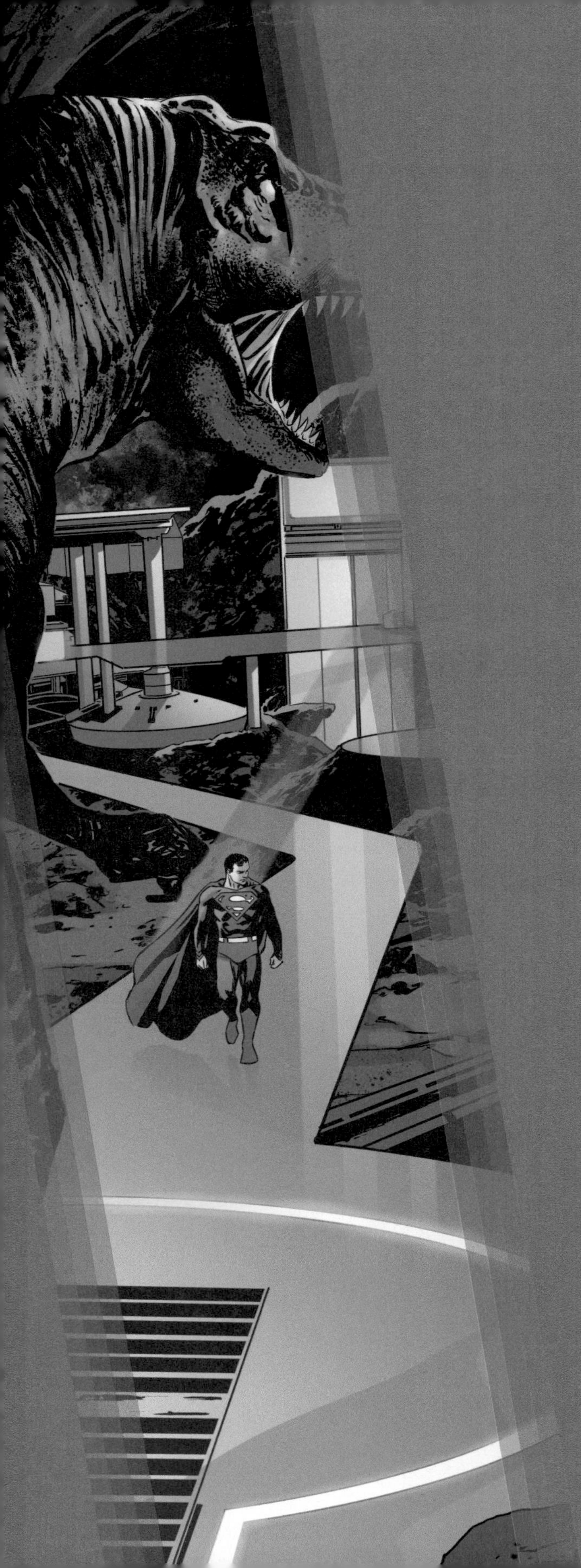

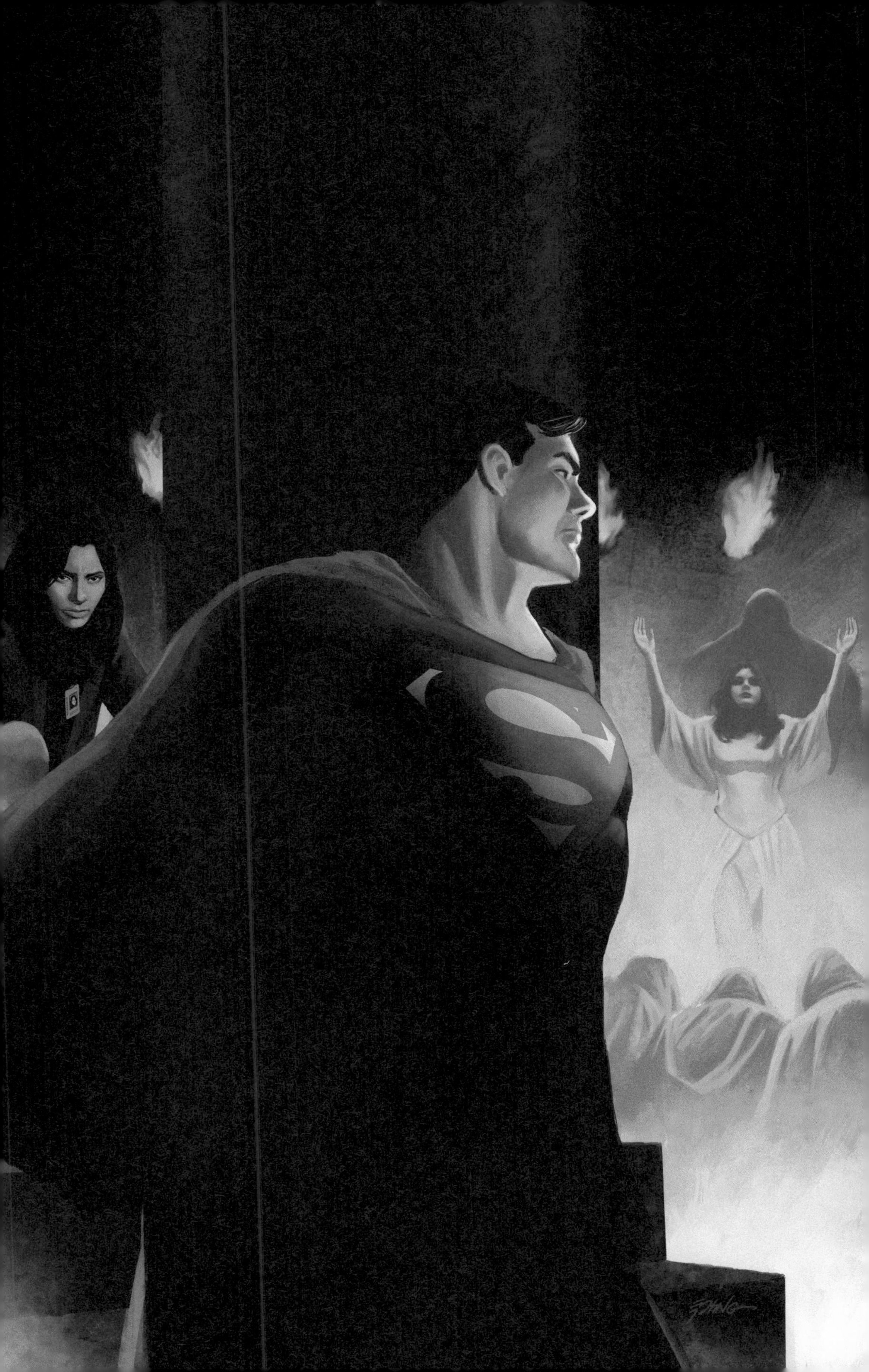

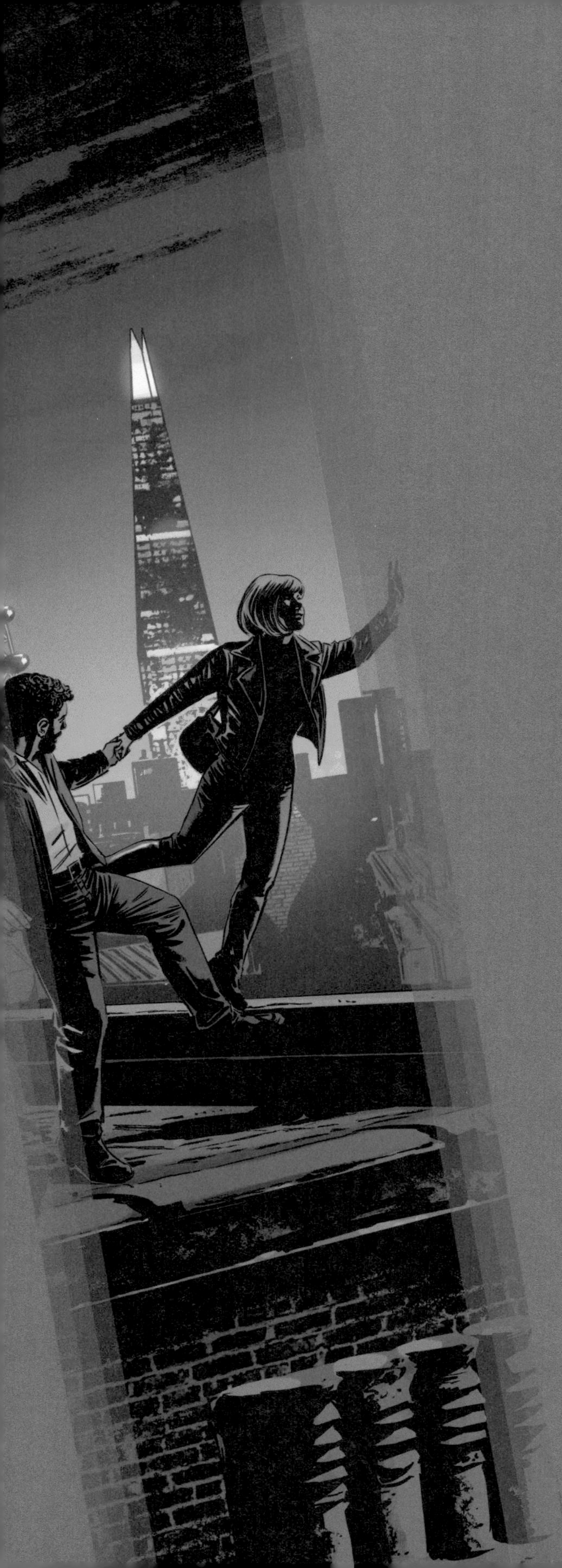

SUPERMAN
BATMAN
FLASH
CYBORG
S.P.Y.R.A.L. — Agent Zero?
TIGER
AMANDA WALLER
STEVE TREVOR
RICK FLAGG
KOBI
TASK FORCE X
ARGUS
THANAGARIANS
STARRO
XUDARIAN
TAMARA
DHOR
DEO
ADAM STRANGE
CHECKM

D.E.O. DIRECTOR BONES, I AM KATE SPENCER.

I AM *SO* SORRY FOR WHAT YOU HAVE BEEN THROUGH.

I CAN'T EVEN IMAGINE.

CAN YOU TELL ME *EXACTLY* WHAT HAPPENED?

KATE SPENCER. I KNOW YOU.

WHAT ARE *YOU* DOING HERE?

YOU NEED A LAWYER.

A FRIEND OF A FRIEND OF A *FRIEND* CALLED ME.

FOR A SECOND THERE...

...I THOUGHT YOU WERE *THEM.*

COME TO FINISH THE JOB.

WE'VE MET.

I REMEMBER.

I NEED YOU TO TELL ME EXACTLY WHAT HAPPENED TO THE D.E.O. BECAUSE A NARRATIVE IS BEING FORMED IN THE PRESS...

...AND IT IS *NOT* KIND TO YOU.

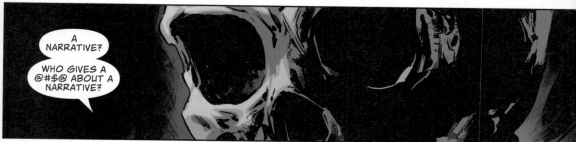

A NARRATIVE?

WHO GIVES A @#$@ ABOUT A NARRATIVE?

THE *TRUTH*.

THE TRUTH CARES.

THEY TOLD ME OUTSIDE--YOU WERE RESCUED BY *ADAM STRANGE?*

THE ADAM STRANGE? FROM OUTER SPACE?

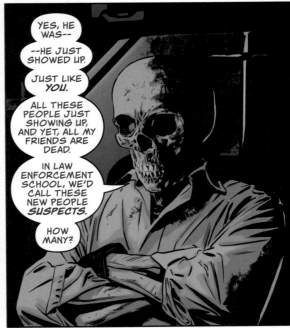

YES, HE WAS--

--HE JUST SHOWED UP.

JUST LIKE *YOU.*

ALL THESE PEOPLE JUST SHOWING UP, AND YET, ALL MY FRIENDS ARE DEAD.

IN LAW ENFORCEMENT SCHOOL, WE'D CALL THESE NEW PEOPLE *SUSPECTS.*

HOW MANY?

HOW MANY PEOPLE ARE *SUSPECTS?*

HOW MANY PEOPLE AT THE D.E.O. DIED HORRIFICALLY UNDER MY PROTECTION TODAY?

I DON'T KNOW.

THEY'RE STILL SIFTING THROUGH IT.

DO YOU--DO YOU HAVE *ANY* IDEA *WHO* DID IT?

WAS IT--*WAS* IT ADAM STRANGE?

I KNOW *EXACTLY* WHO IT WAS.

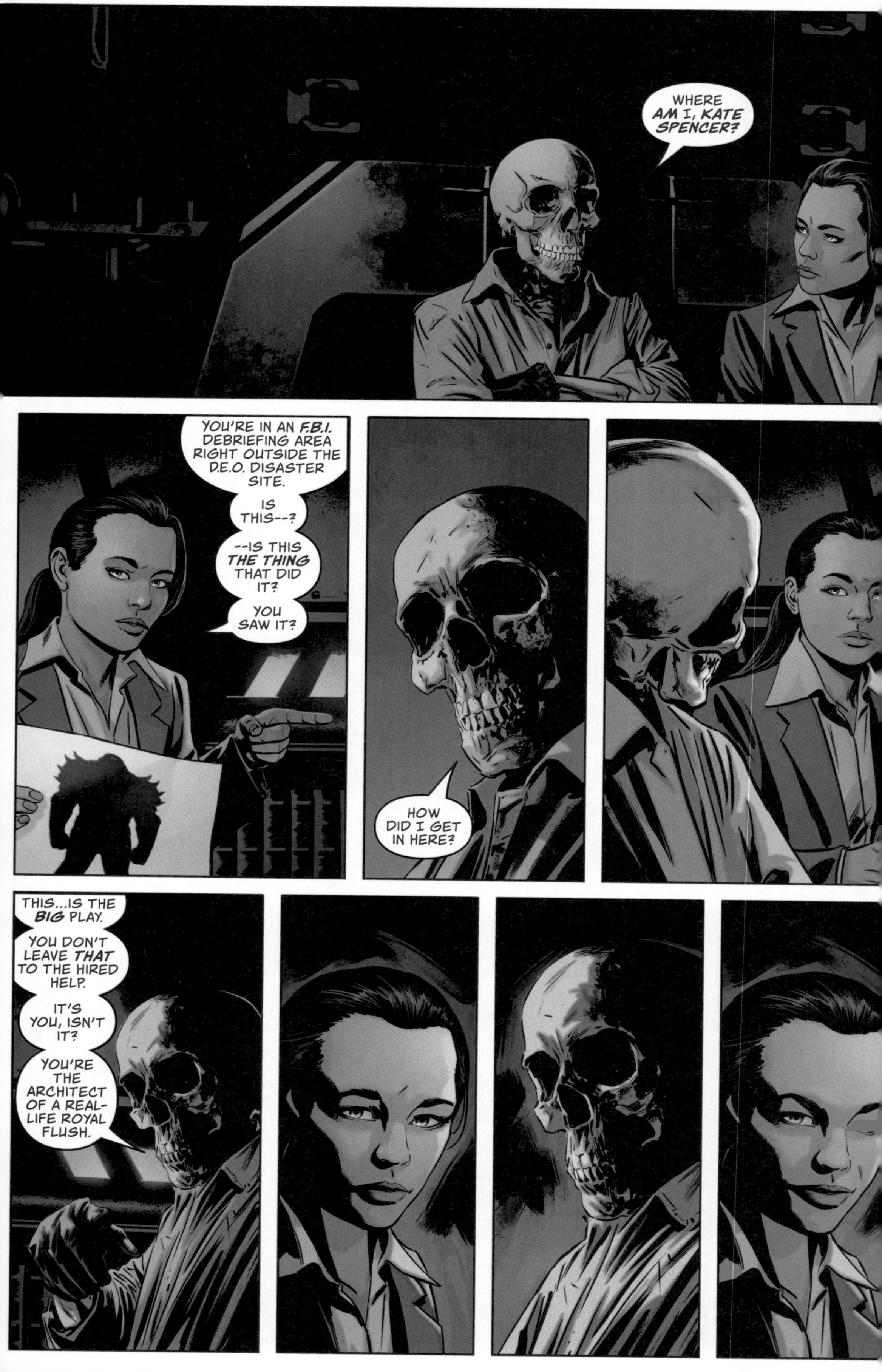
WHERE AM I, KATE SPENCER?
YOU'RE IN AN F.B.I. DEBRIEFING AREA RIGHT OUTSIDE THE D.E.O. DISASTER SITE.
IS THIS--?
--IS THIS THE THING THAT DID IT?
YOU SAW IT?
HOW DID I GET IN HERE?
THIS...IS THE BIG PLAY.
YOU DON'T LEAVE THAT TO THE HIRED HELP.
IT'S YOU, ISN'T IT?
YOU'RE THE ARCHITECT OF A REAL-LIFE ROYAL FLUSH.

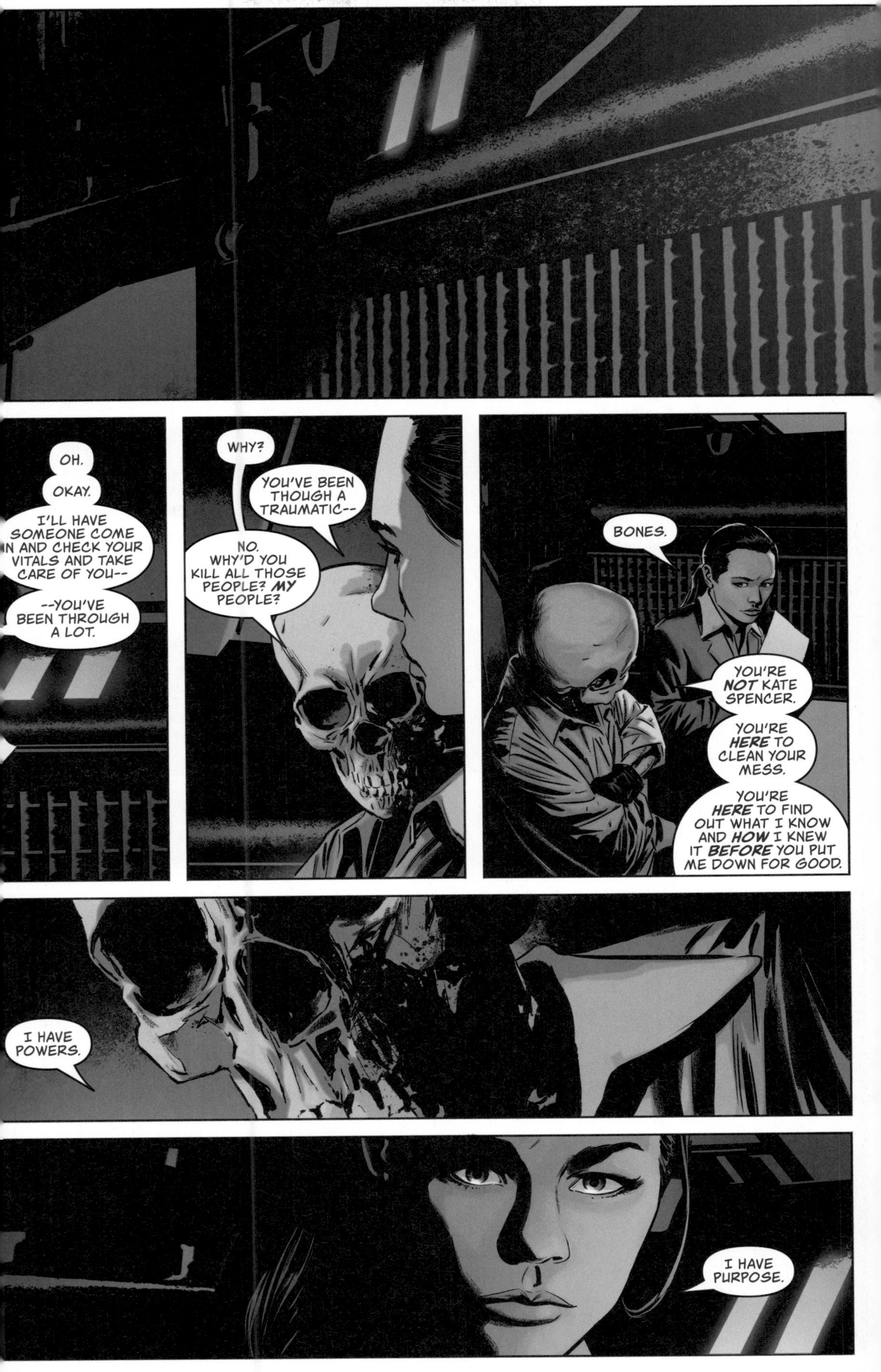
OH.
OKAY.
I'LL HAVE SOMEONE COME IN AND CHECK YOUR VITALS AND TAKE CARE OF YOU--
--YOU'VE BEEN THROUGH A LOT.
WHY?
YOU'VE BEEN THOUGH A TRAUMATIC--
NO. WHY'D YOU KILL ALL THOSE PEOPLE? MY PEOPLE?
BONES.
YOU'RE NOT KATE SPENCER.
YOU'RE HERE TO CLEAN YOUR MESS.
YOU'RE HERE TO FIND OUT WHAT I KNOW AND HOW I KNEW IT BEFORE YOU PUT ME DOWN FOR GOOD.
I HAVE POWERS.
I HAVE PURPOSE.

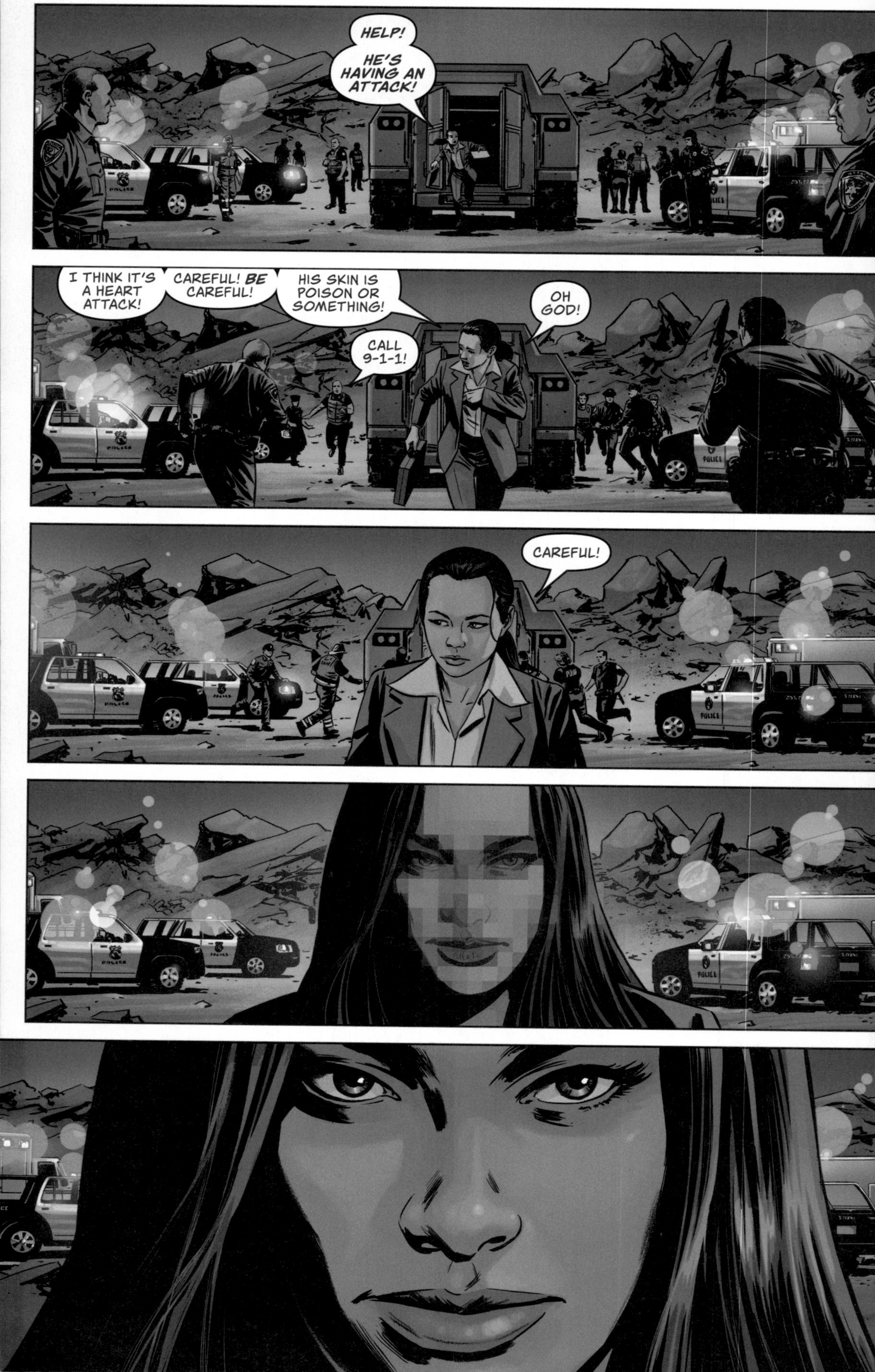
HELP!
HE'S HAVING AN ATTACK!
I THINK IT'S A HEART ATTACK!
CAREFUL! BE CAREFUL!
HIS SKIN IS POISON OR SOMETHING!
CALL 9-1-1!
OH GOD!
CAREFUL!

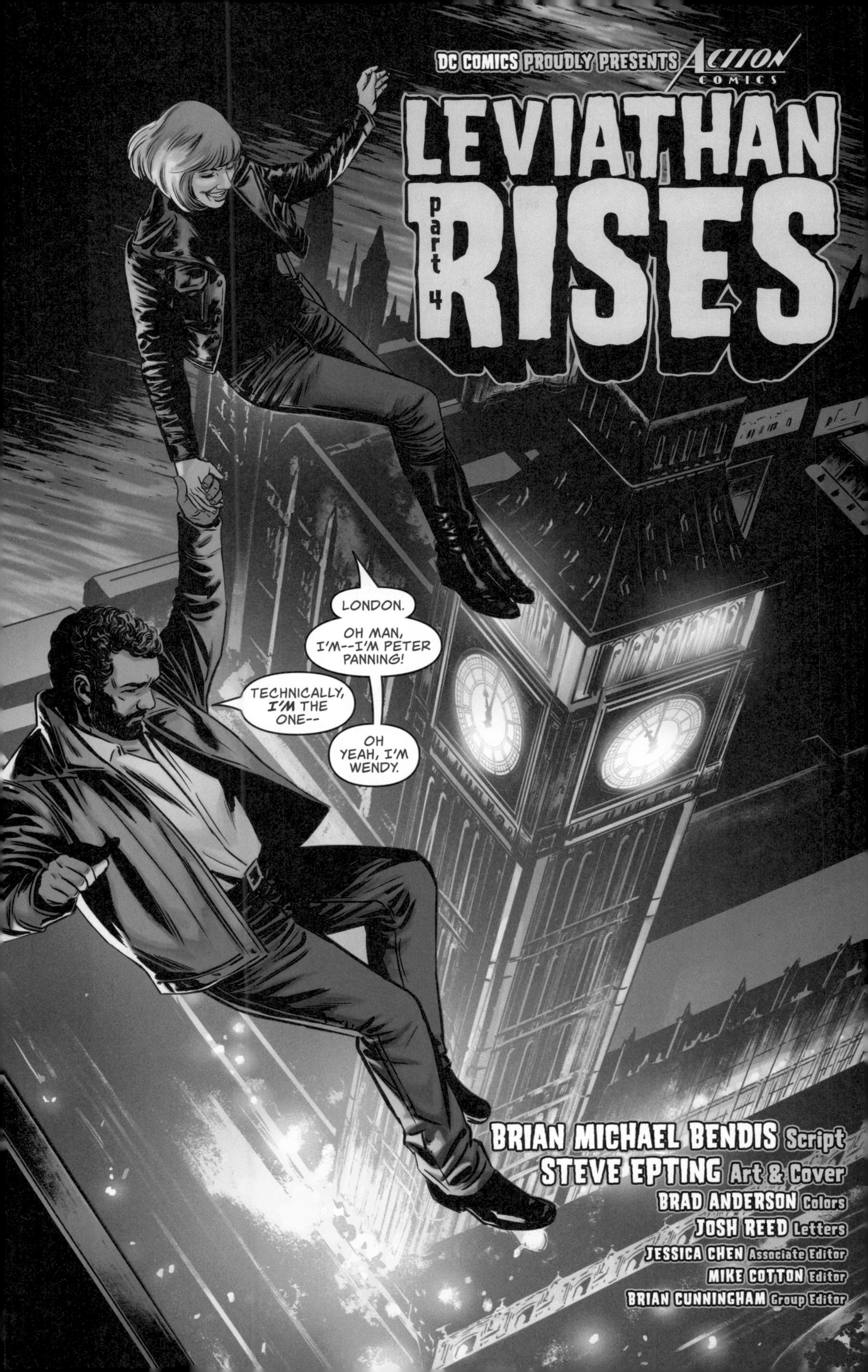

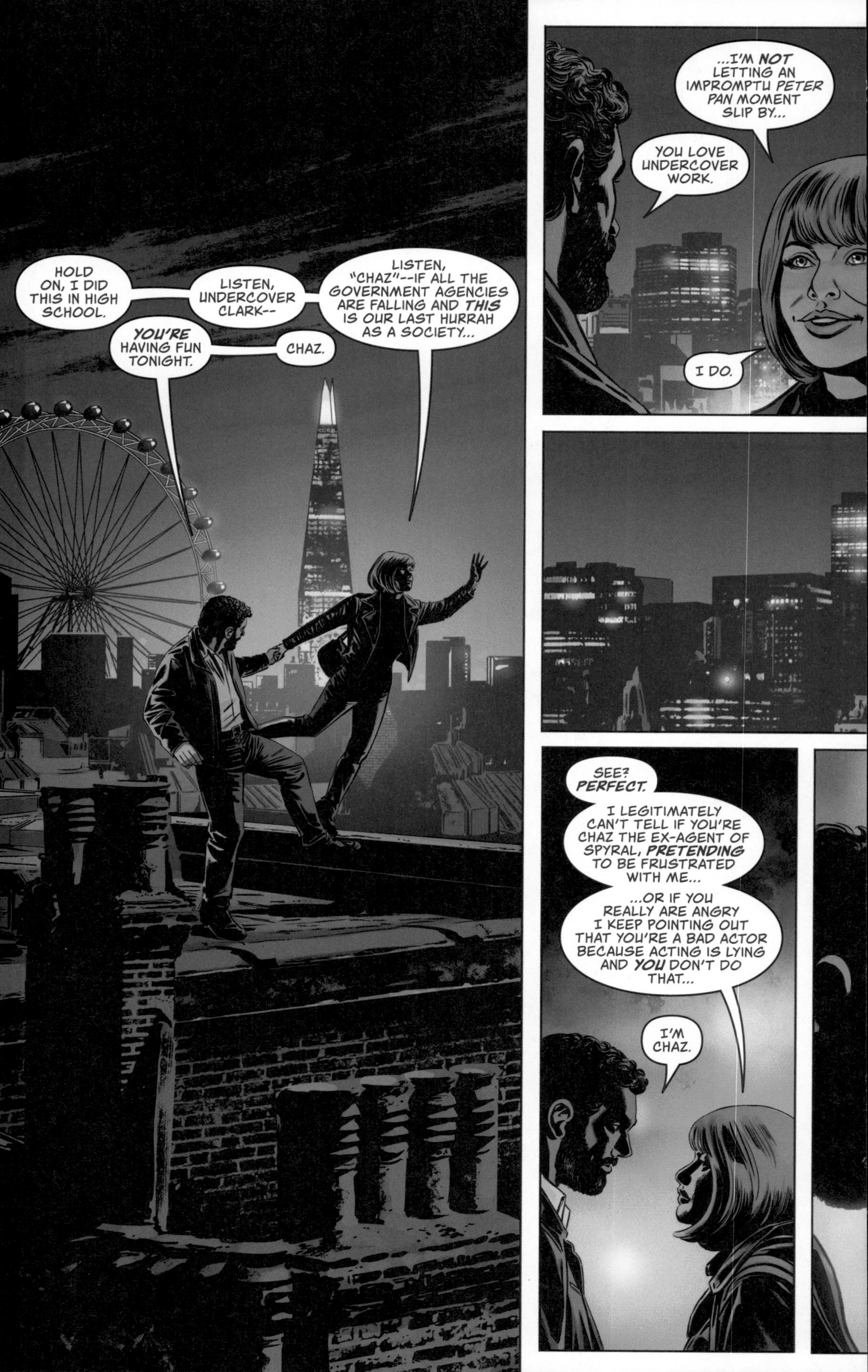
HOLD ON, I DID THIS IN HIGH SCHOOL.
LISTEN, UNDERCOVER CLARK--
LISTEN, "CHAZ"--IF ALL THE GOVERNMENT AGENCIES ARE FALLING AND *THIS* IS OUR LAST HURRAH AS A SOCIETY...
YOU'RE HAVING FUN TONIGHT.
CHAZ.
...I'M *NOT* LETTING AN IMPROMPTU PETER PAN MOMENT SLIP BY...
YOU LOVE UNDERCOVER WORK.
I DO.
SEE? *PERFECT.*
I LEGITIMATELY CAN'T TELL IF YOU'RE CHAZ THE EX-AGENT OF SPYRAL, *PRETENDING* TO BE FRUSTRATED WITH ME...
...OR IF YOU REALLY ARE ANGRY I KEEP POINTING OUT THAT YOU'RE A BAD ACTOR BECAUSE ACTING IS LYING AND *YOU* DON'T DO THAT...
I'M CHAZ.

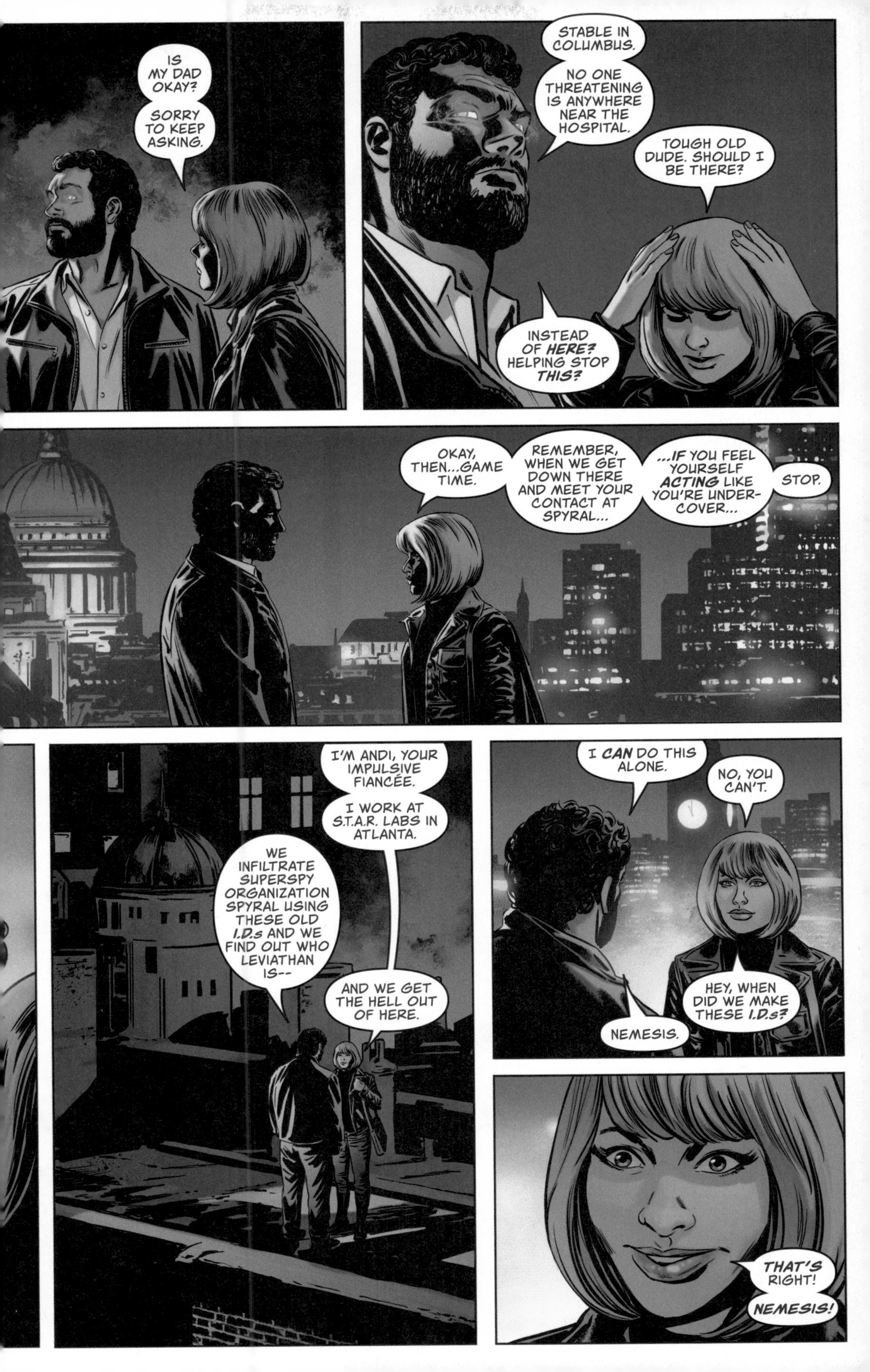
IS MY DAD OKAY?
SORRY TO KEEP ASKING.
STABLE IN COLUMBUS.
NO ONE THREATENING IS ANYWHERE NEAR THE HOSPITAL.
TOUGH OLD DUDE. SHOULD I BE THERE?
INSTEAD OF *HERE?* HELPING STOP *THIS?*
OKAY, THEN...GAME TIME.
REMEMBER, WHEN WE GET DOWN THERE AND MEET YOUR CONTACT AT SPYRAL...
...*IF* YOU FEEL YOURSELF *ACTING* LIKE YOU'RE UNDER-COVER...
STOP.
I'M ANDI, YOUR IMPULSIVE FIANCÉE.
I WORK AT S.T.A.R. LABS IN ATLANTA.
WE INFILTRATE SUPERSPY ORGANIZATION SPYRAL USING THESE OLD *I.D.s* AND WE FIND OUT WHO LEVIATHAN IS--
AND WE GET THE HELL OUT OF HERE.
I *CAN* DO THIS ALONE.
NO, YOU CAN'T.
HEY, WHEN DID WE MAKE THESE *I.D.s?*
NEMESIS.
THAT'S RIGHT!
NEMESIS!

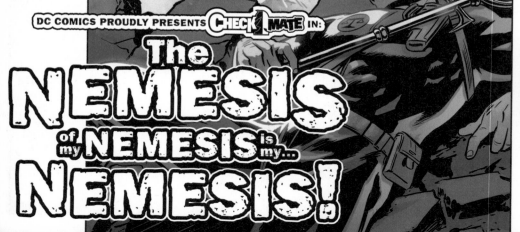

WELL, NOW WE KNOW WHO WAS BEHIND THE COUNCIL!

YOU'RE SHARING THE BYLINE!

I THINK *THIS* MIGHT HAVE TURNED INTO A JOB FOR *SUPERMAN*, "CHAZ"!

SUPERMAN CALLED A FRIEND IN, ANDI!

SUPERGIRL!

WHEYP!

DC COMICS PROUDLY PRESENTS CHECKMATE IN:

The NEMESIS of my NEMESIS is my... NEMESIS!

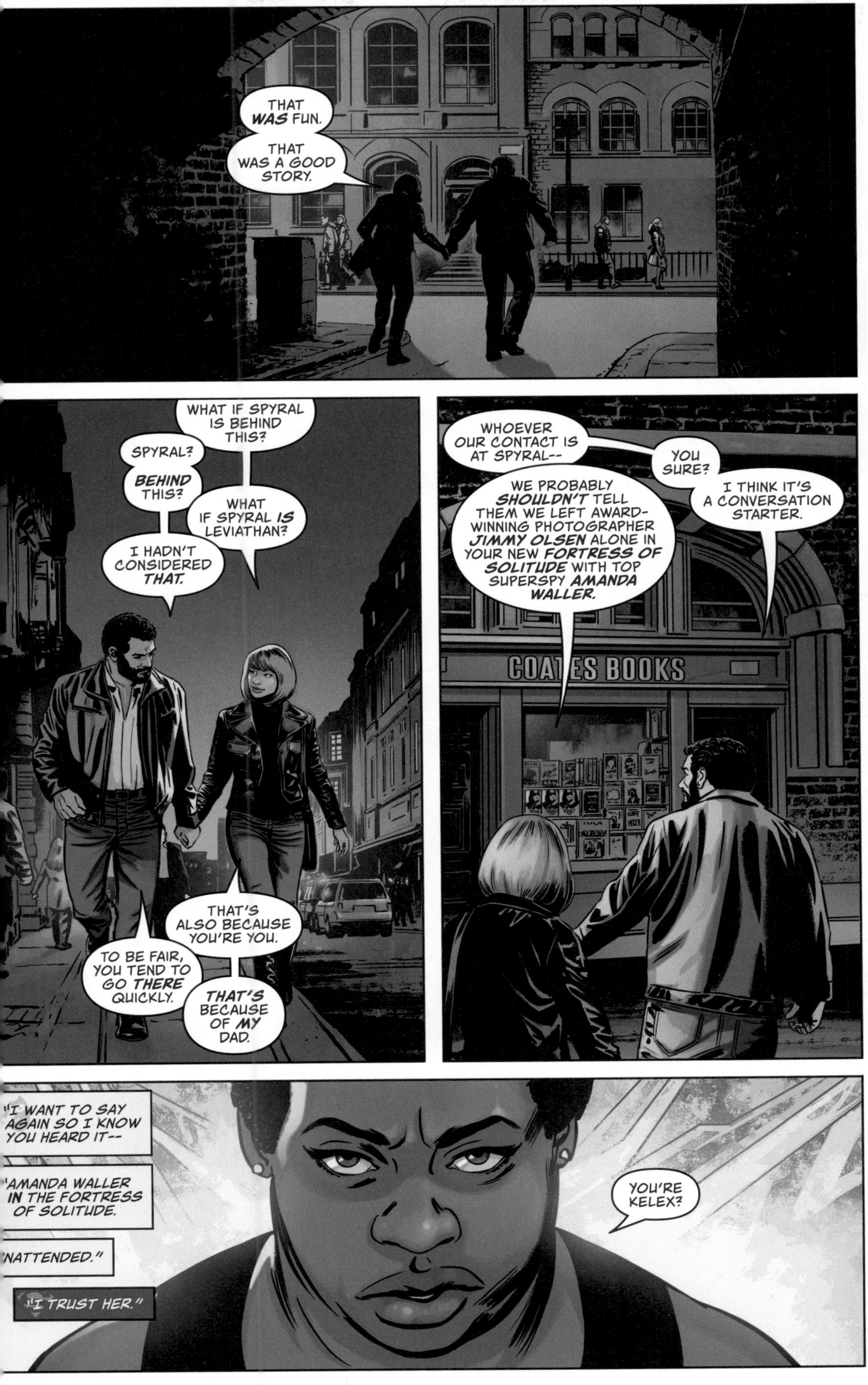
THAT WAS FUN.
THAT WAS A GOOD STORY.
WHAT IF SPYRAL IS BEHIND THIS?
SPYRAL?
BEHIND THIS?
WHAT IF SPYRAL IS LEVIATHAN?
I HADN'T CONSIDERED THAT.
TO BE FAIR, YOU TEND TO GO THERE QUICKLY.
THAT'S ALSO BECAUSE YOU'RE YOU.
THAT'S BECAUSE OF MY DAD.
WHOEVER OUR CONTACT IS AT SPYRAL--
YOU SURE?
WE PROBABLY SHOULDN'T TELL THEM WE LEFT AWARD-WINNING PHOTOGRAPHER JIMMY OLSEN ALONE IN YOUR NEW FORTRESS OF SOLITUDE WITH TOP SUPERSPY AMANDA WALLER.
I THINK IT'S A CONVERSATION STARTER.
COATES BOOKS
"I WANT TO SAY AGAIN SO I KNOW YOU HEARD IT--
"AMANDA WALLER IN THE FORTRESS OF SOLITUDE.
"NATTENDED."
"I TRUST HER."
YOU'RE KELEX?

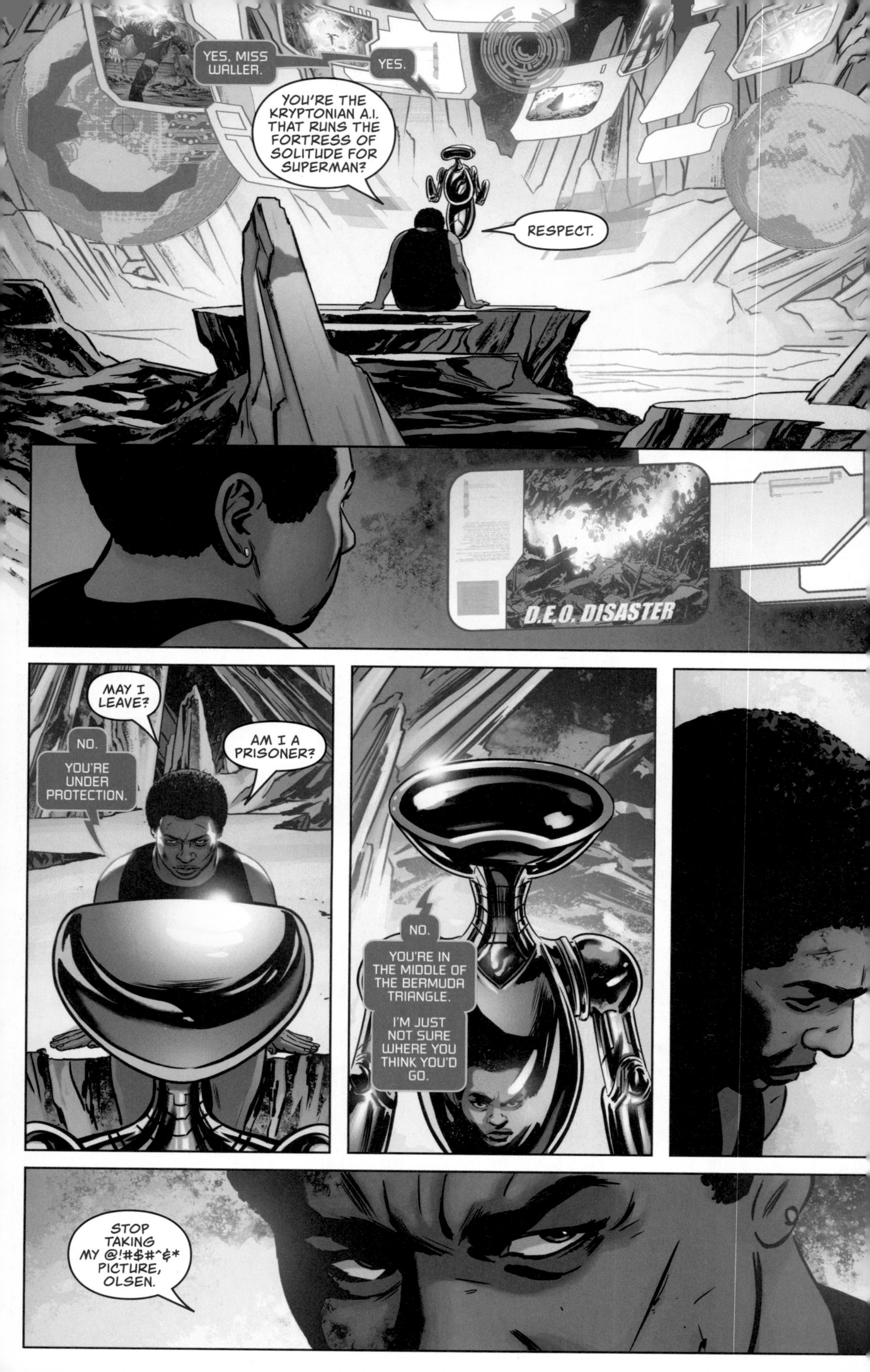

YES, MISS WALLER.
YES.
YOU'RE THE KRYPTONIAN A.I. THAT RUNS THE FORTRESS OF SOLITUDE FOR SUPERMAN?
RESPECT.
D.E.O. DISASTER
MAY I LEAVE?
NO.
YOU'RE UNDER PROTECTION.
AM I A PRISONER?
NO.
YOU'RE IN THE MIDDLE OF THE BERMUDA TRIANGLE.
I'M JUST NOT SURE WHERE YOU THINK YOU'D GO.
STOP TAKING MY @!#$#^&* PICTURE, OLSEN.

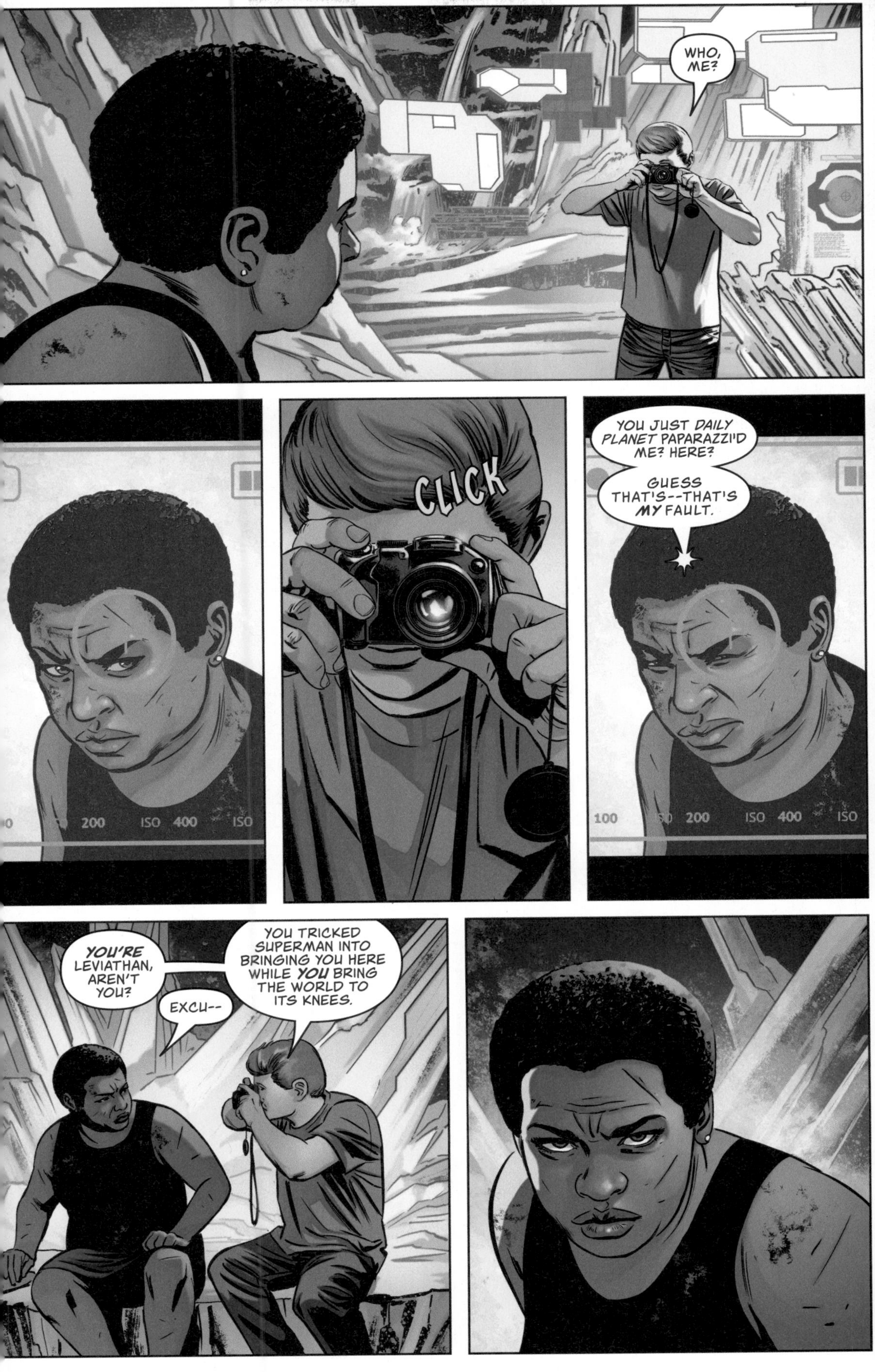
WHO, ME?
YOU JUST *DAILY PLANET* PAPARAZZI'D ME? HERE?
GUESS THAT'S--THAT'S *MY* FAULT.
CLICK
200 ISO 400 ISO
100 ISO 200 ISO 400 ISO
YOU'RE LEVIATHAN, AREN'T YOU?
EXCU--
YOU TRICKED SUPERMAN INTO BRINGING YOU HERE WHILE ***YOU*** BRING THE WORLD TO ITS KNEES.

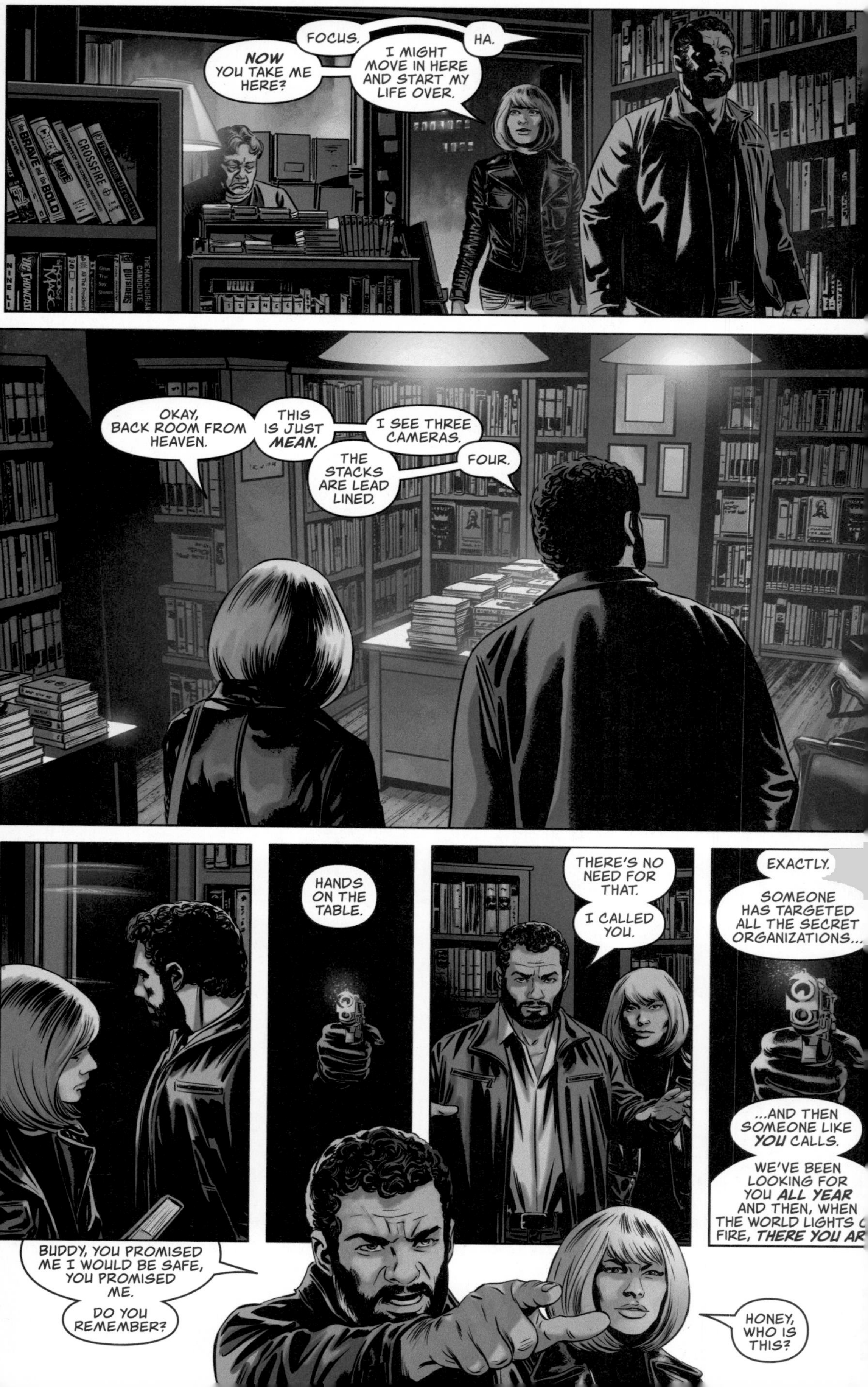
NOW YOU TAKE ME HERE?
FOCUS.
I MIGHT MOVE IN HERE AND START MY LIFE OVER.
HA.
OKAY, BACK ROOM FROM HEAVEN.
THIS IS JUST MEAN.
I SEE THREE CAMERAS.
THE STACKS ARE LEAD LINED.
FOUR.
HANDS ON THE TABLE.
THERE'S NO NEED FOR THAT.
I CALLED YOU.
EXACTLY.
SOMEONE HAS TARGETED ALL THE SECRET ORGANIZATIONS...
...AND THEN SOMEONE LIKE YOU CALLS.
WE'VE BEEN LOOKING FOR YOU ALL YEAR AND THEN, WHEN THE WORLD LIGHTS O FIRE, THERE YOU AR
BUDDY, YOU PROMISED ME I WOULD BE SAFE, YOU PROMISED ME.
DO YOU REMEMBER?
HONEY, WHO IS THIS?

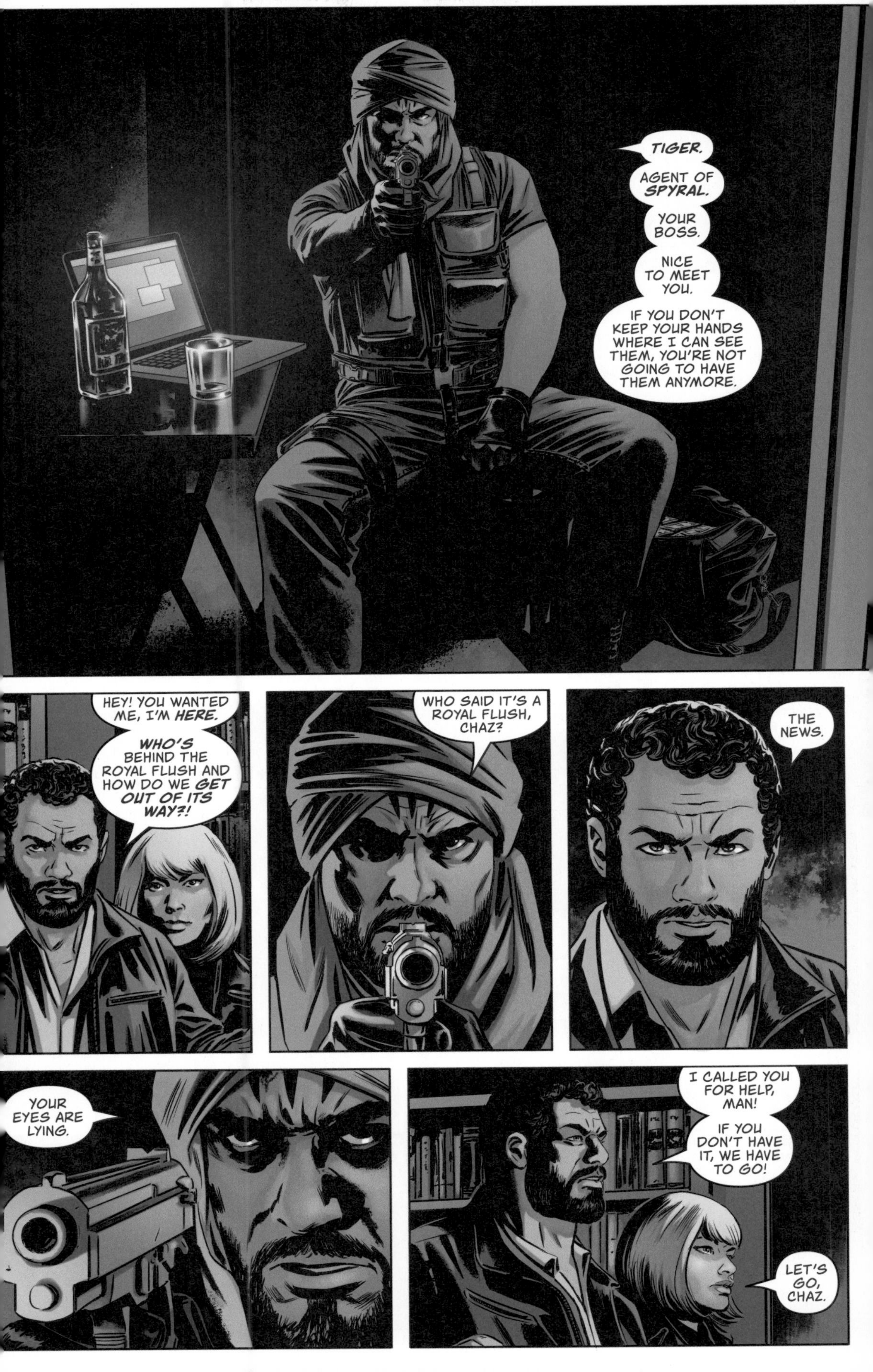
TIGER.
AGENT OF SPYRAL.
YOUR BOSS.
NICE TO MEET YOU.
IF YOU DON'T KEEP YOUR HANDS WHERE I CAN SEE THEM, YOU'RE NOT GOING TO HAVE THEM ANYMORE.
HEY! YOU WANTED ME, I'M HERE.
WHO'S BEHIND THE ROYAL FLUSH AND HOW DO WE GET OUT OF ITS WAY?!
WHO SAID IT'S A ROYAL FLUSH, CHAZ?
THE NEWS.
YOUR EYES ARE LYING.
I CALLED YOU FOR HELP, MAN!
IF YOU DON'T HAVE IT, WE HAVE TO GO!
LET'S GO, CHAZ.

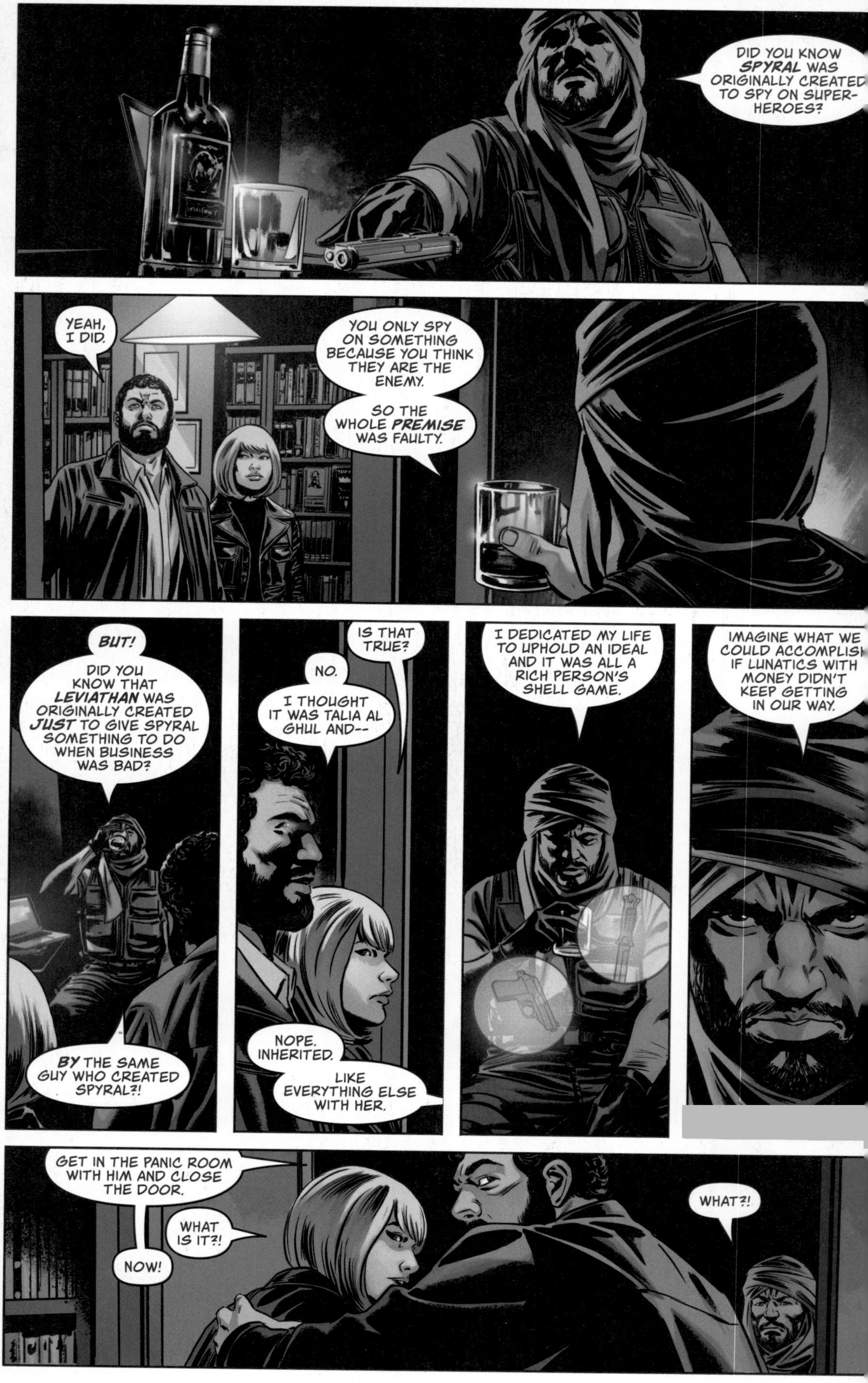
DID YOU KNOW SPYRAL WAS ORIGINALLY CREATED TO SPY ON SUPER-HEROES?
YEAH, I DID.
YOU ONLY SPY ON SOMETHING BECAUSE YOU THINK THEY ARE THE ENEMY.
SO THE WHOLE PREMISE WAS FAULTY.
BUT!
DID YOU KNOW THAT LEVIATHAN WAS ORIGINALLY CREATED JUST TO GIVE SPYRAL SOMETHING TO DO WHEN BUSINESS WAS BAD?
BY THE SAME GUY WHO CREATED SPYRAL?!
IS THAT TRUE?
NO.
I THOUGHT IT WAS TALIA AL GHUL AND--
NOPE. INHERITED.
LIKE EVERYTHING ELSE WITH HER.
I DEDICATED MY LIFE TO UPHOLD AN IDEAL AND IT WAS ALL A RICH PERSON'S SHELL GAME.
IMAGINE WHAT WE COULD ACCOMPLIS IF LUNATICS WITH MONEY DIDN'T KEEP GETTING IN OUR WAY.
GET IN THE PANIC ROOM WITH HIM AND CLOSE THE DOOR.
WHAT IS IT?!
NOW!
WHAT?!

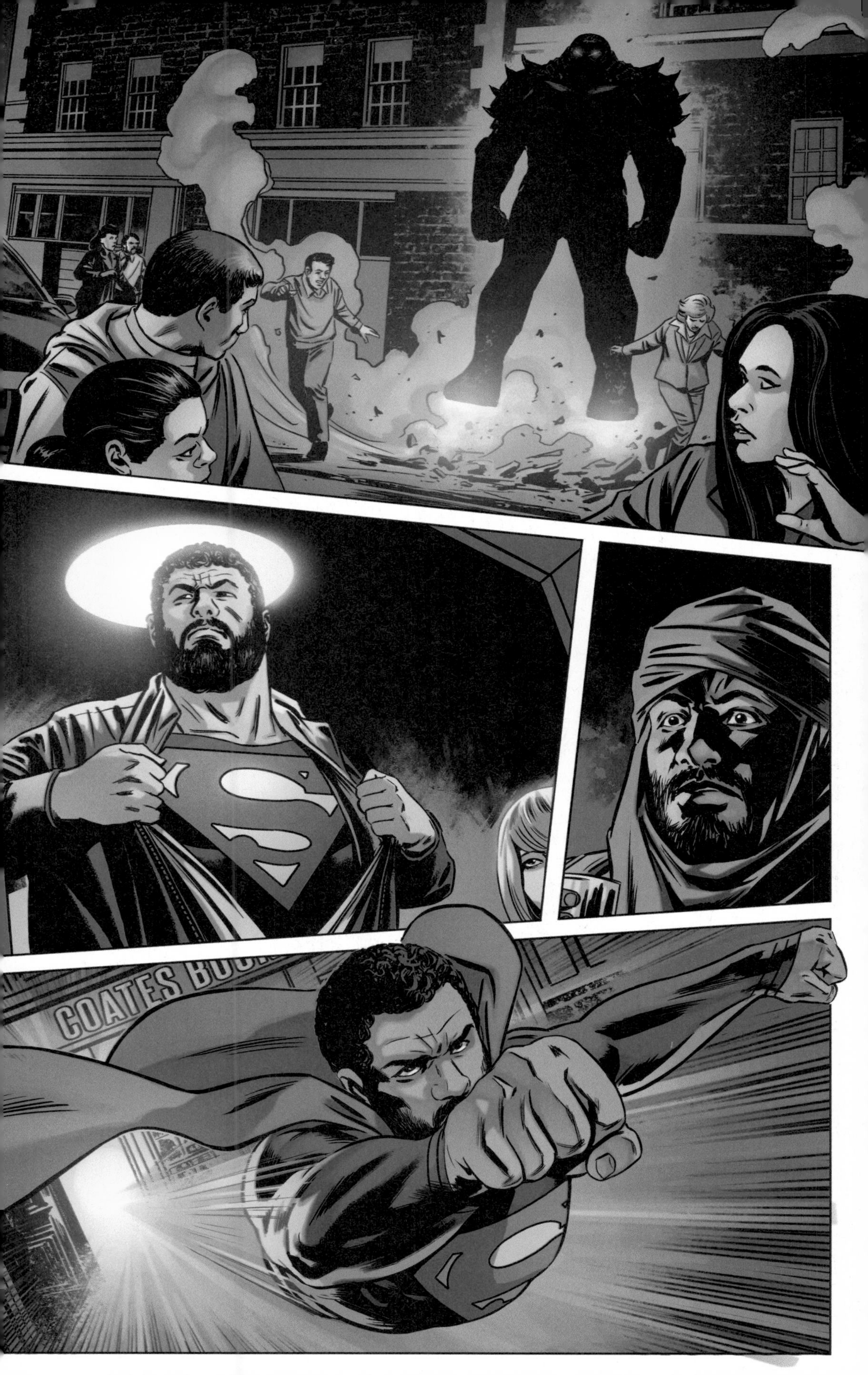
COATES

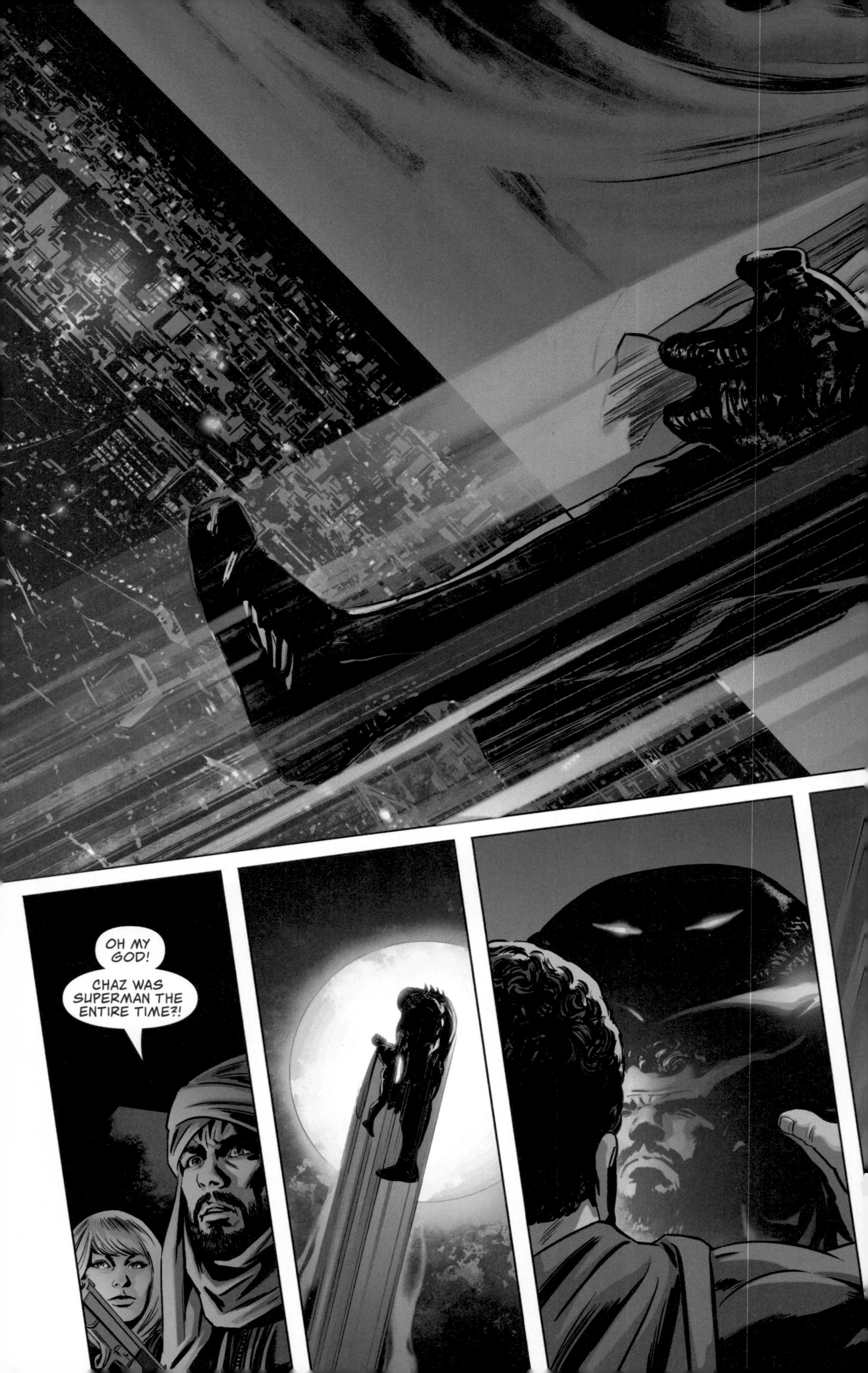
OH MY GOD!
CHAZ WAS SUPERMAN THE ENTIRE TIME?!

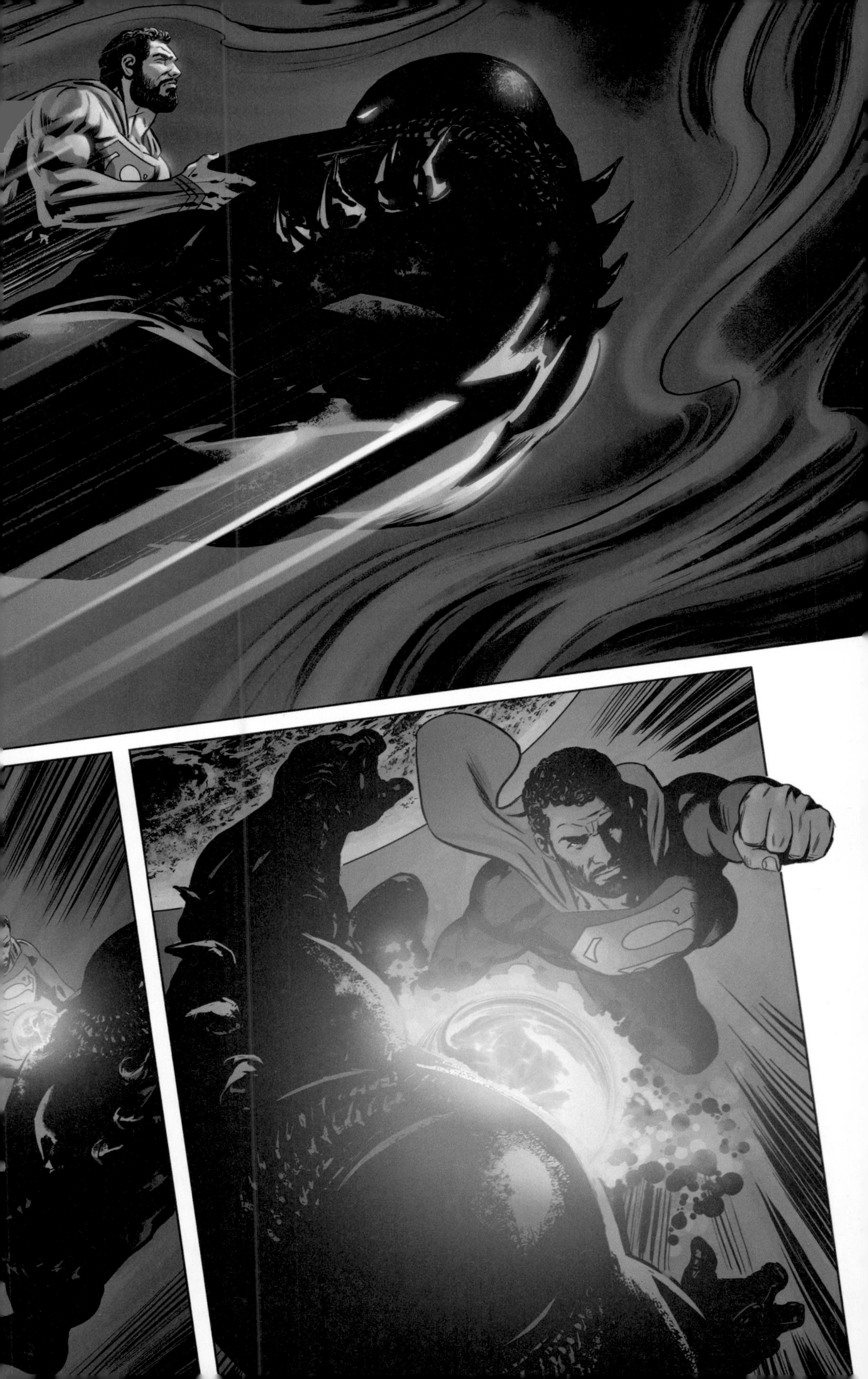

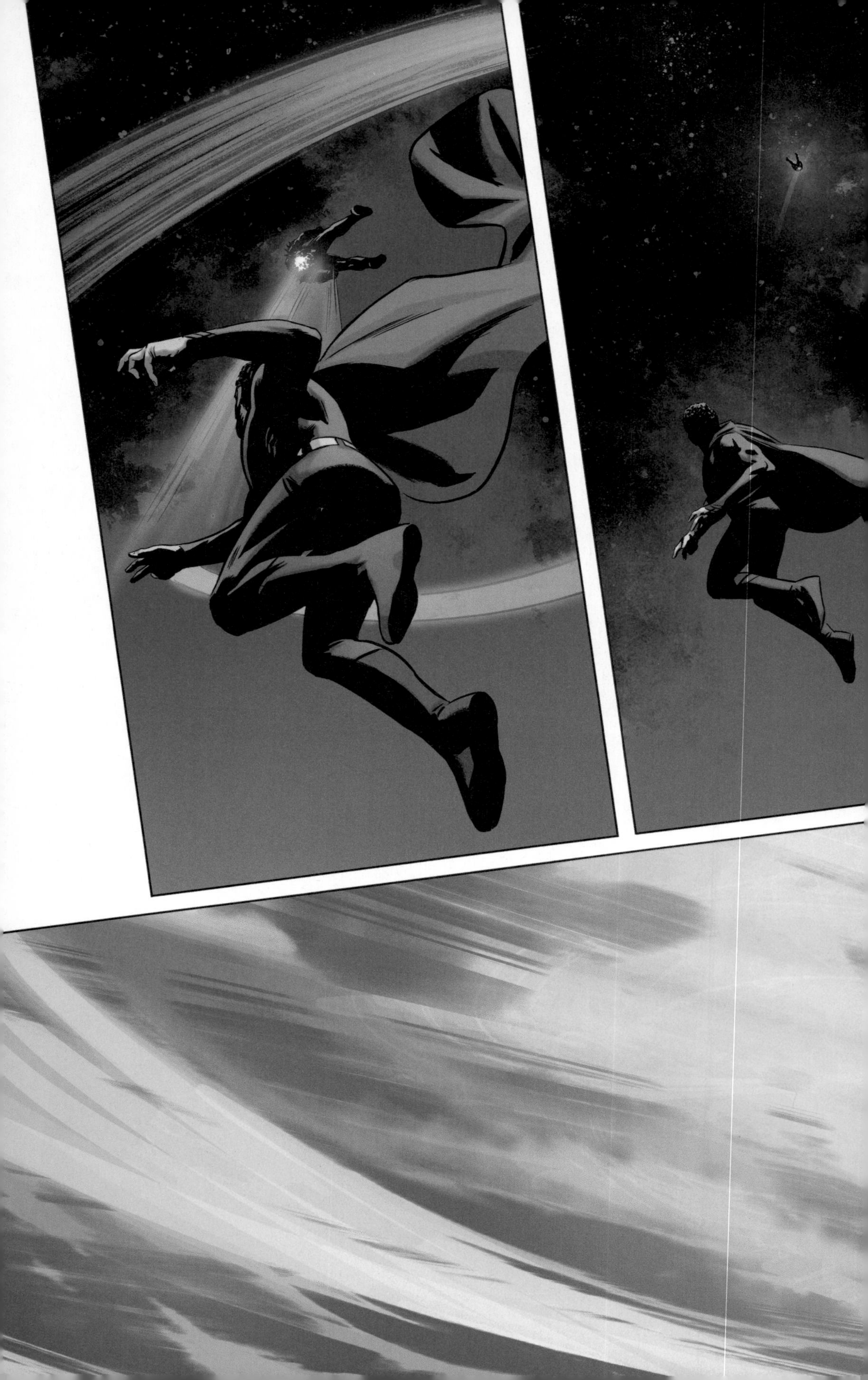

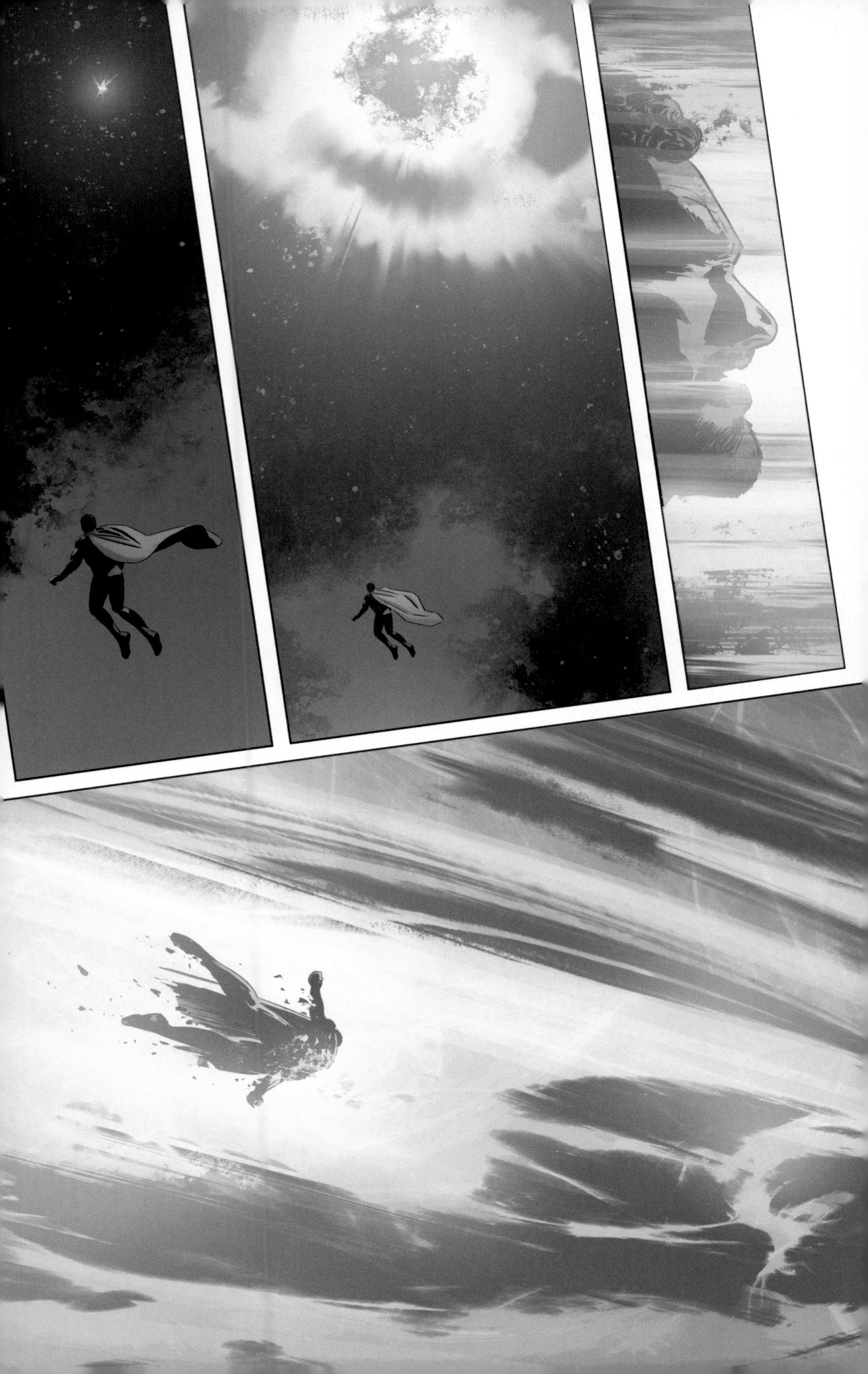

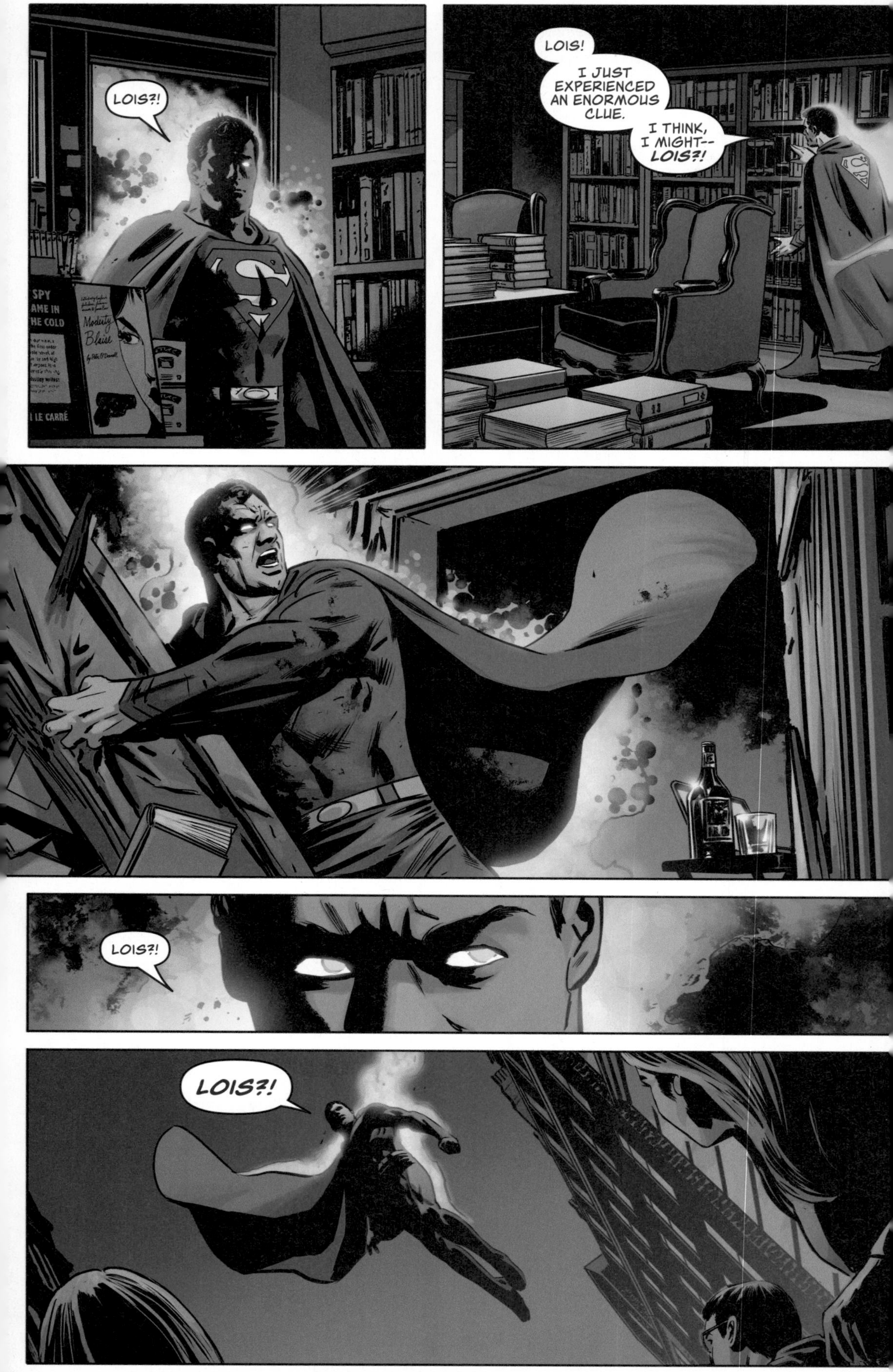
LOIS?!
Modesty Blaise
LOIS!
I JUST EXPERIENCED AN ENORMOUS CLUE.
I THINK, I MIGHT-- LOIS?!
LOIS?!
LOIS?!

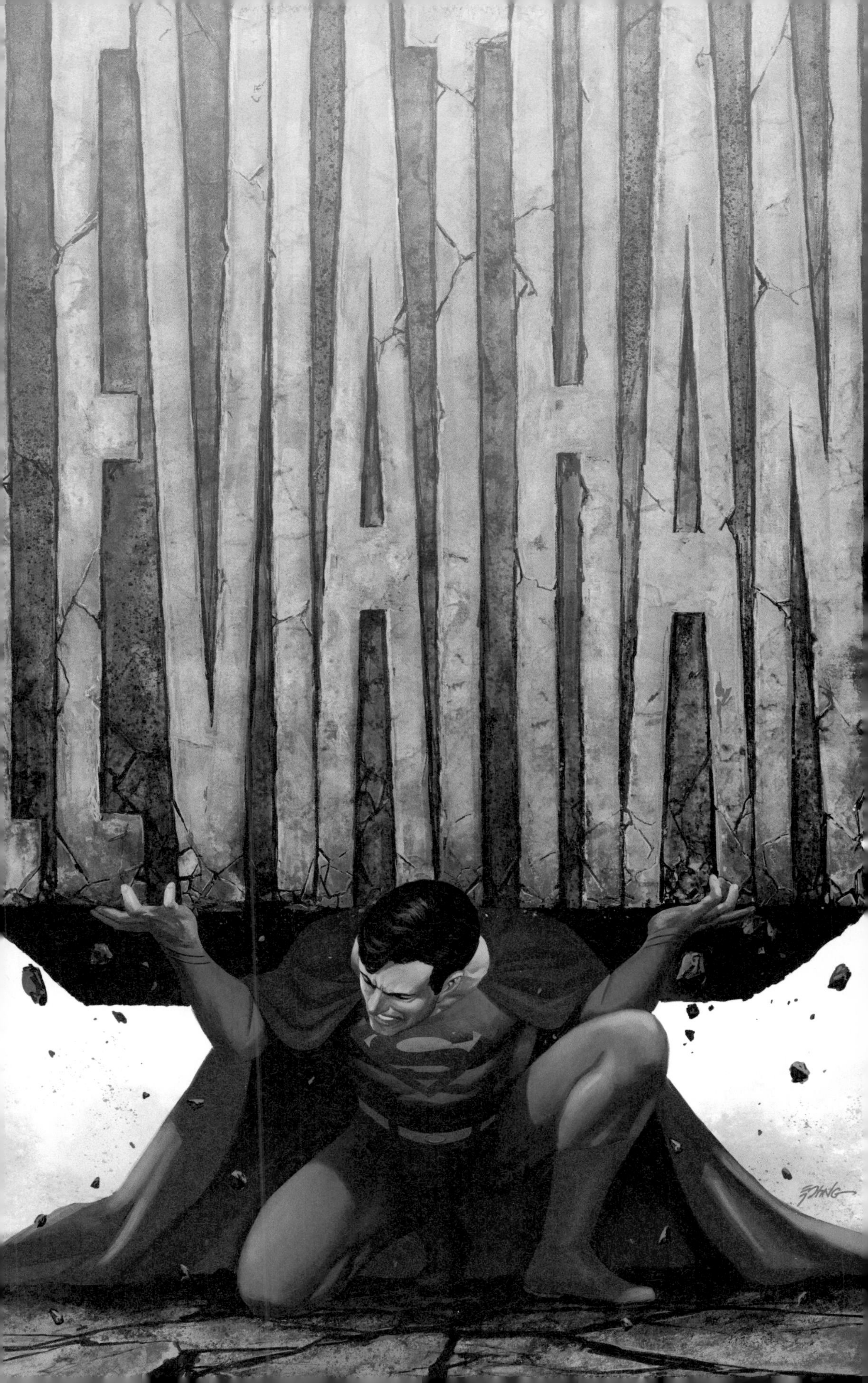

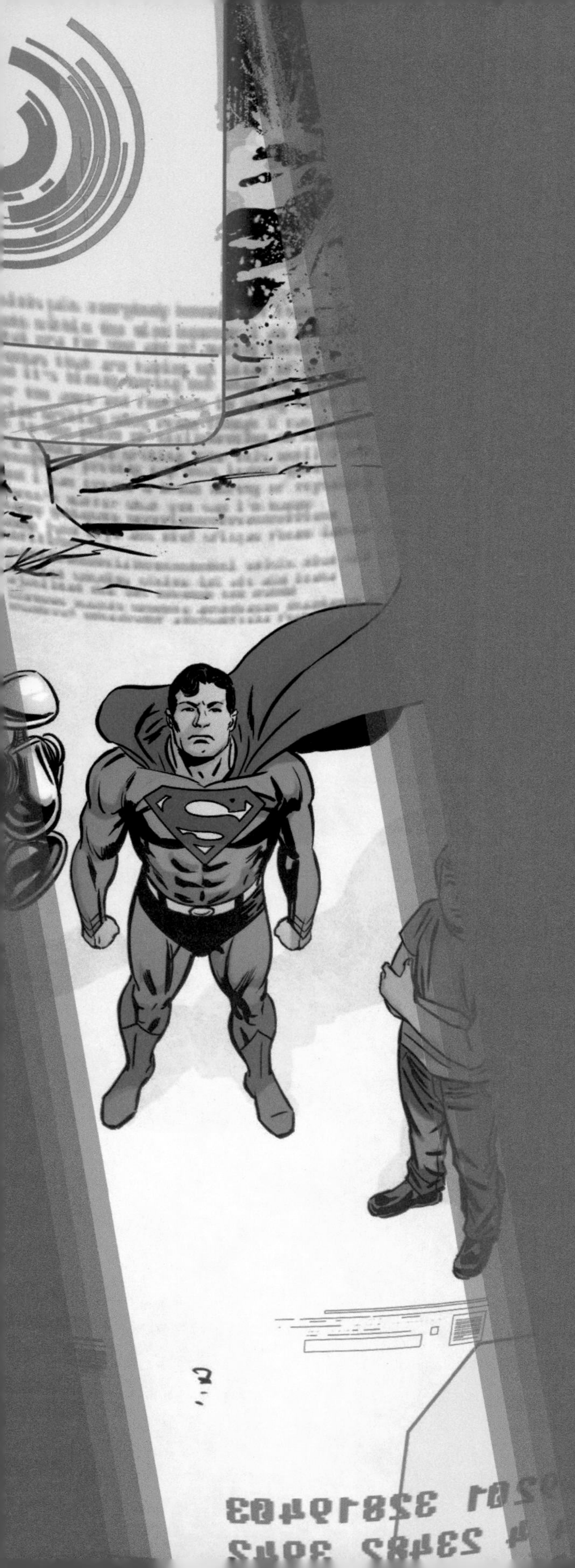

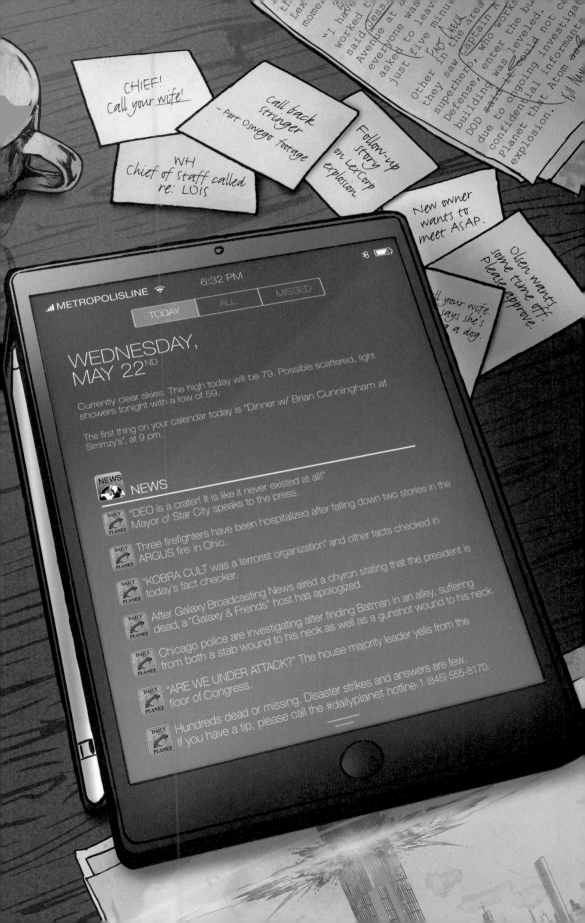

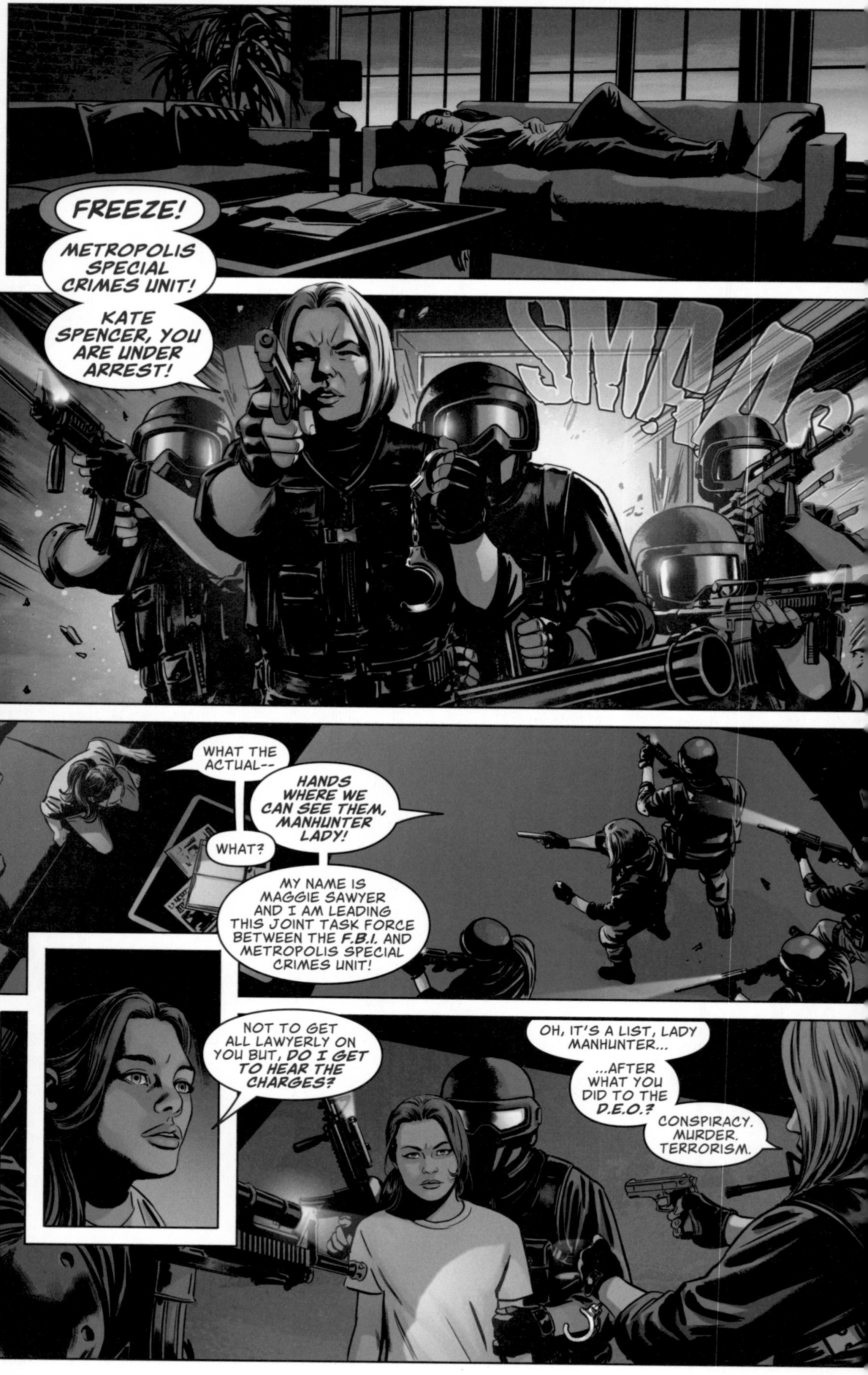
FREEZE!
METROPOLIS SPECIAL CRIMES UNIT!
KATE SPENCER, YOU ARE UNDER ARREST!
SMAAASH
WHAT THE ACTUAL--
WHAT?
HANDS WHERE WE CAN SEE THEM, MANHUNTER LADY!
MY NAME IS MAGGIE SAWYER AND I AM LEADING THIS JOINT TASK FORCE BETWEEN THE F.B.I. AND METROPOLIS SPECIAL CRIMES UNIT!
NOT TO GET ALL LAWYERLY ON YOU BUT, DO I GET TO HEAR THE CHARGES?
OH, IT'S A LIST, LADY MANHUNTER...
...AFTER WHAT YOU DID TO THE D.E.O.?
CONSPIRACY. MURDER. TERRORISM.

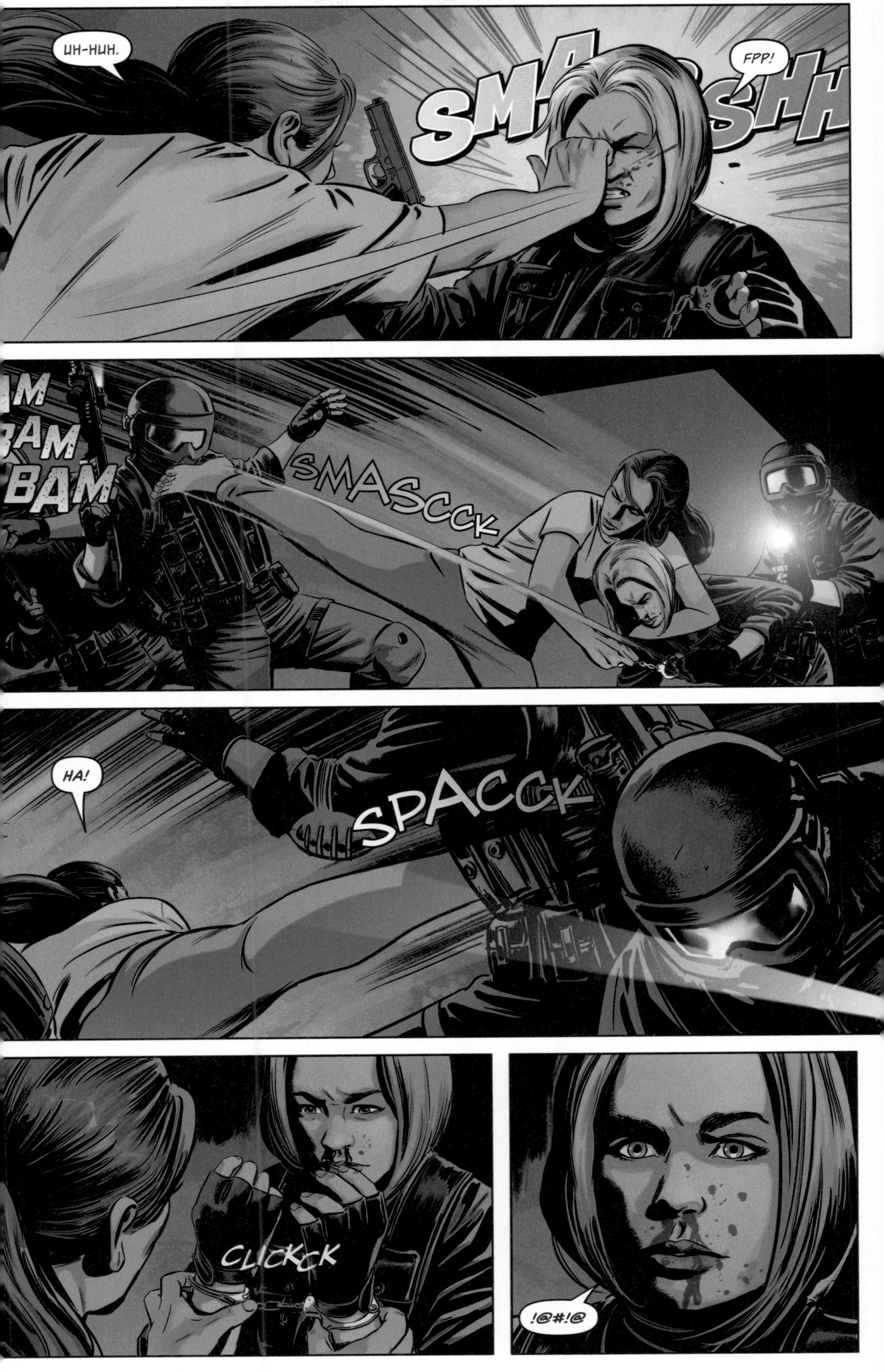
UH-HUH.
FPP!
BAM
BAM
SMASCCK
HA!
SPACCK
CLICKCK
!@#!@

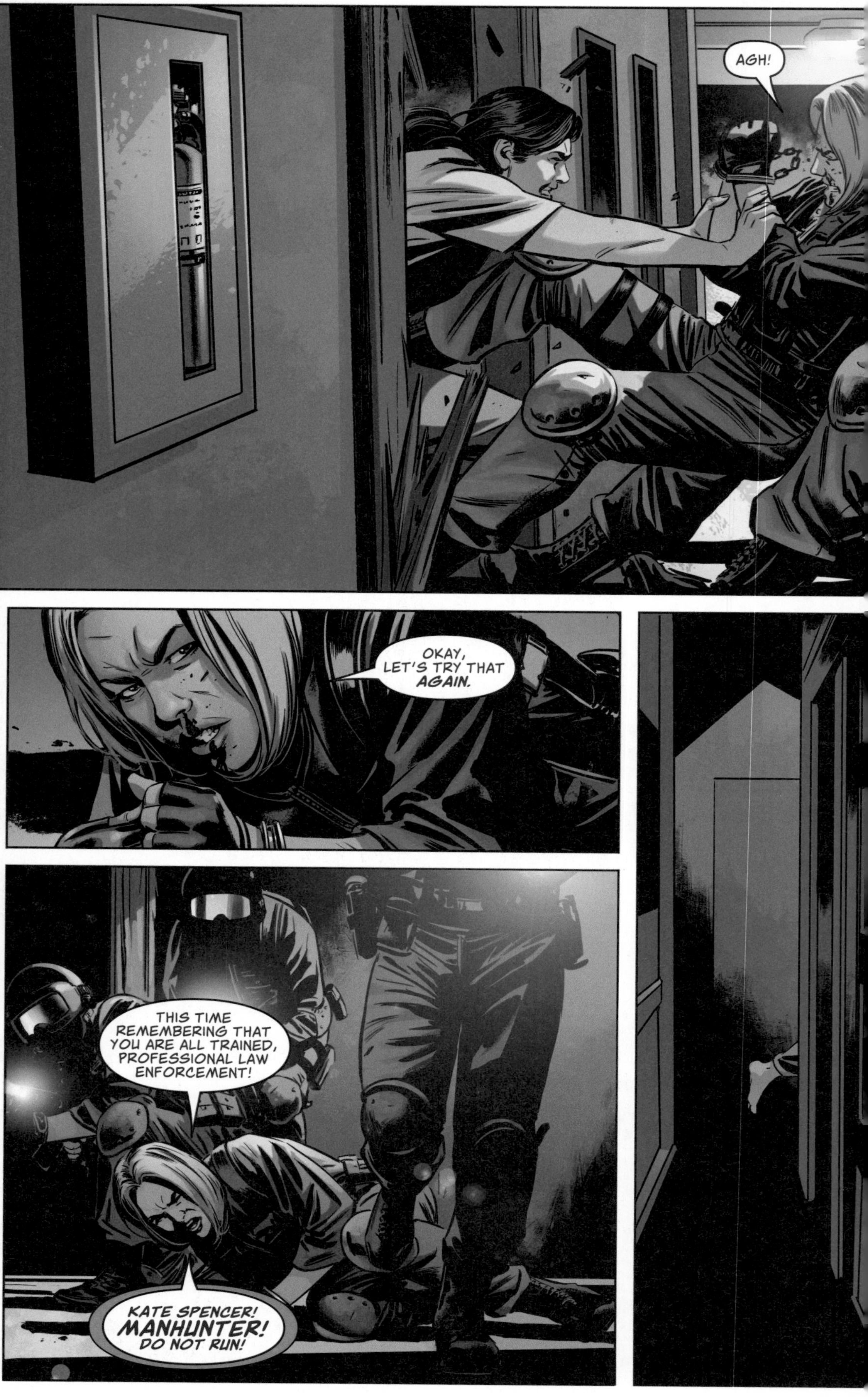
AGH!
OKAY, LET'S TRY THAT AGAIN.
THIS TIME REMEMBERING THAT YOU ARE ALL TRAINED, PROFESSIONAL LAW ENFORCEMENT!
KATE SPENCER! MANHUNTER! DO NOT RUN!

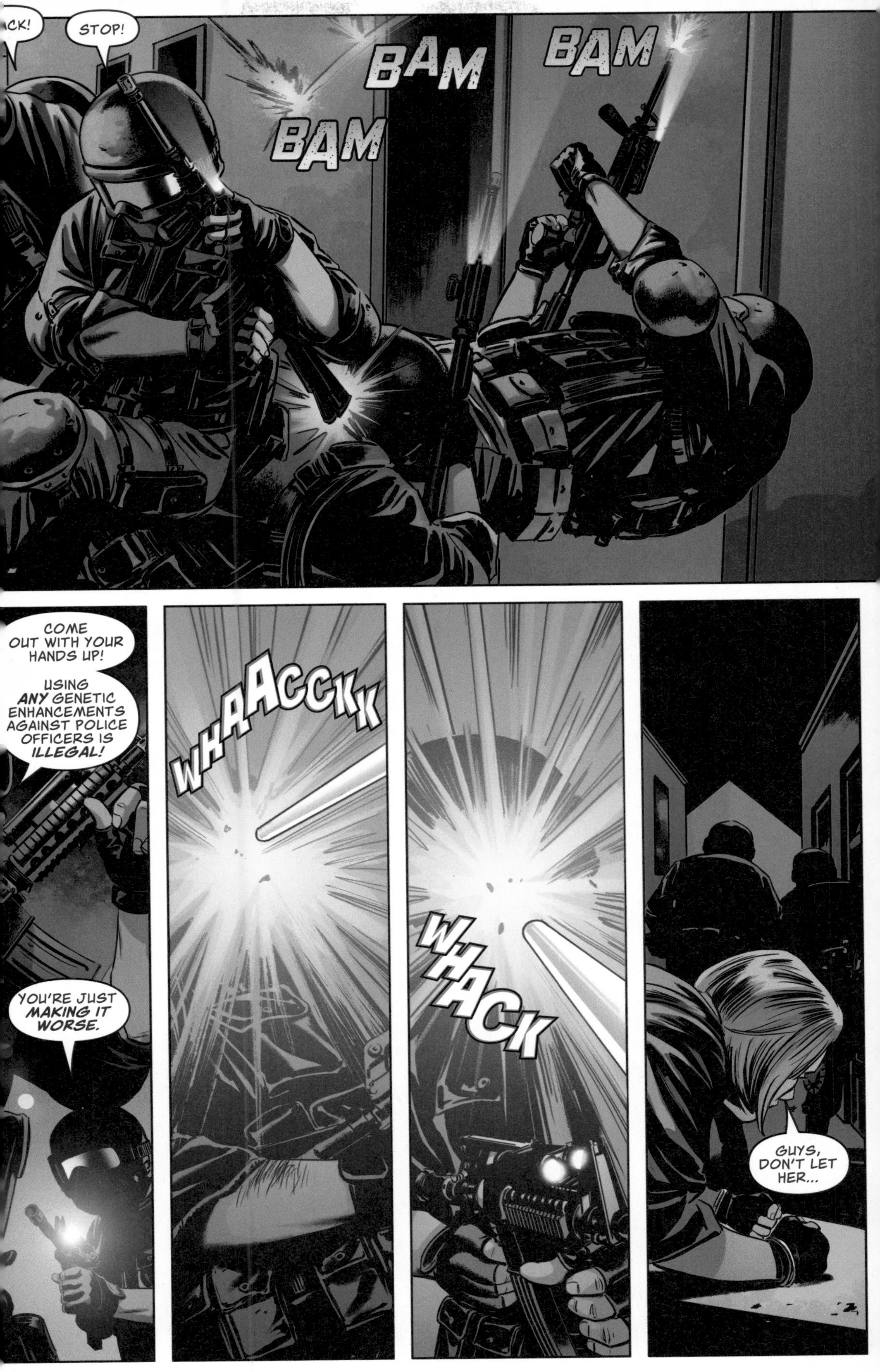
CK!
STOP!
BAM
BAM
BAM
COME OUT WITH YOUR HANDS UP!
USING ANY GENETIC ENHANCEMENTS AGAINST POLICE OFFICERS IS ILLEGAL!
YOU'RE JUST MAKING IT WORSE.
WHAACCKKK
WHACK
GUYS, DON'T LET HER...

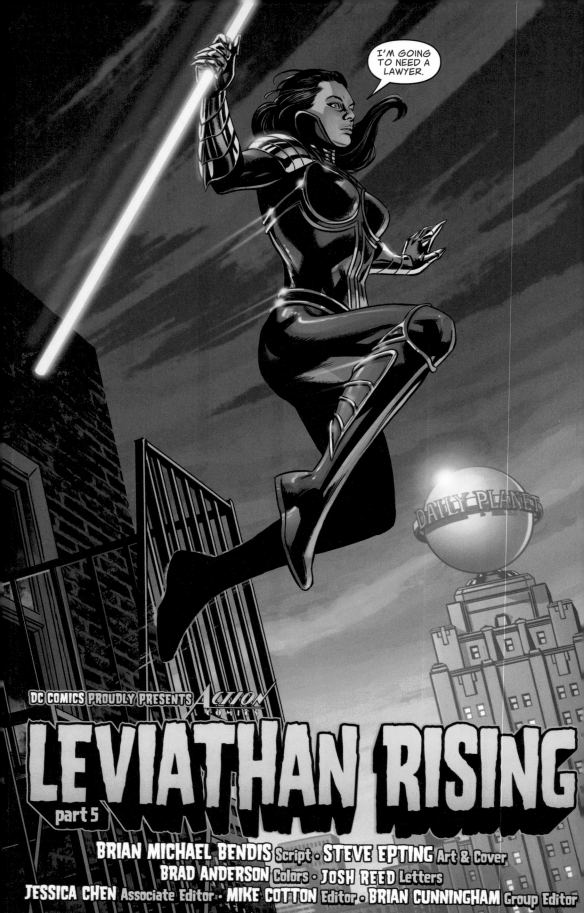

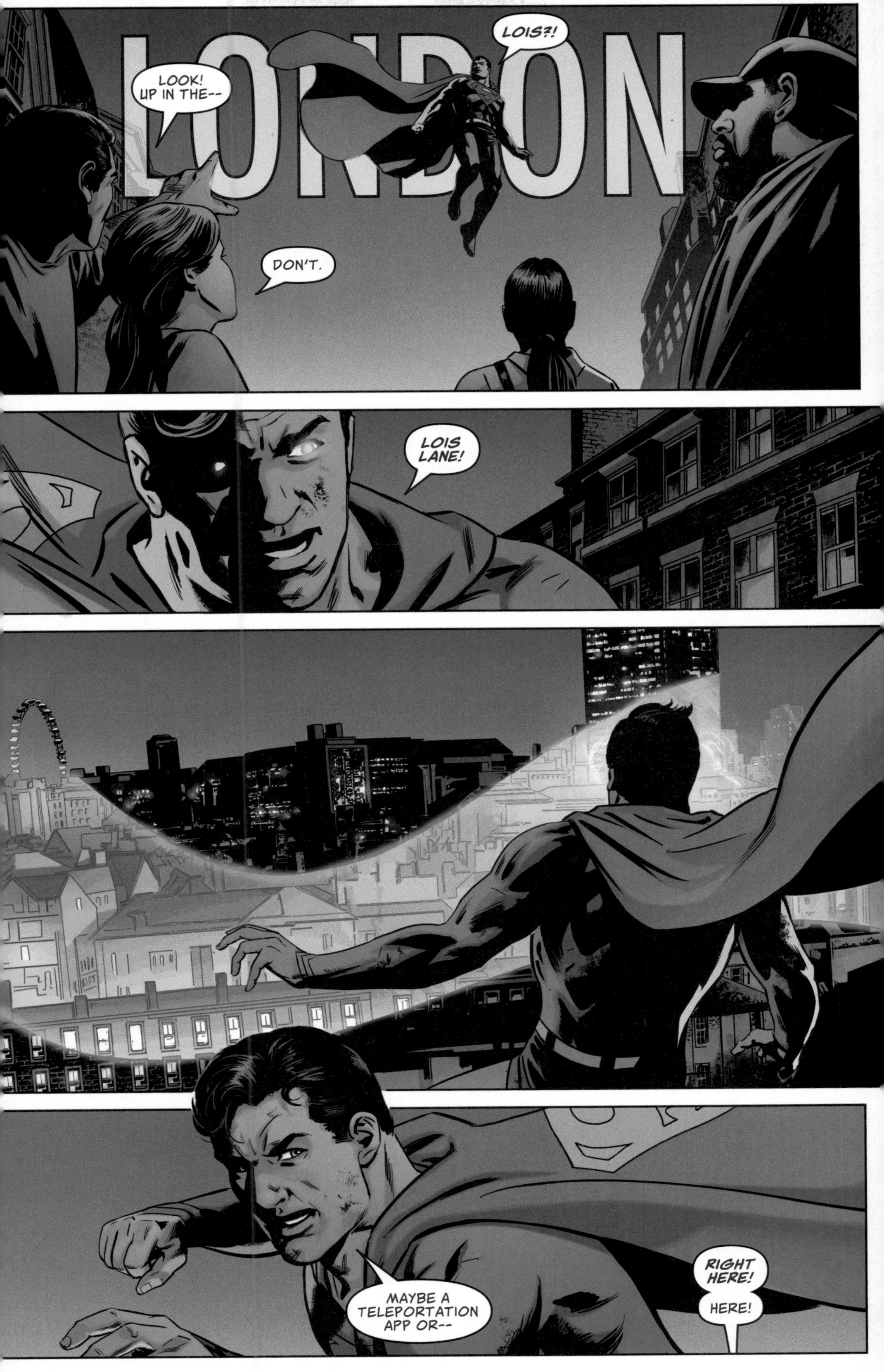
LONDON
LOIS?!
LOOK! UP IN THE--
DON'T.
LOIS LANE!
MAYBE A TELEPORTATION APP OR--
RIGHT HERE!
HERE!

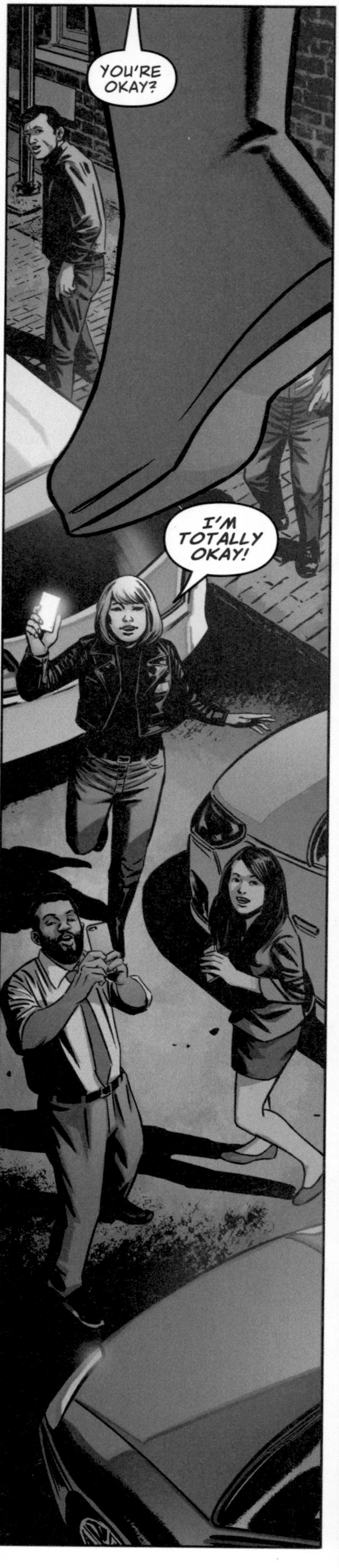
YOU'RE OKAY?
I'M TOTALLY OKAY!
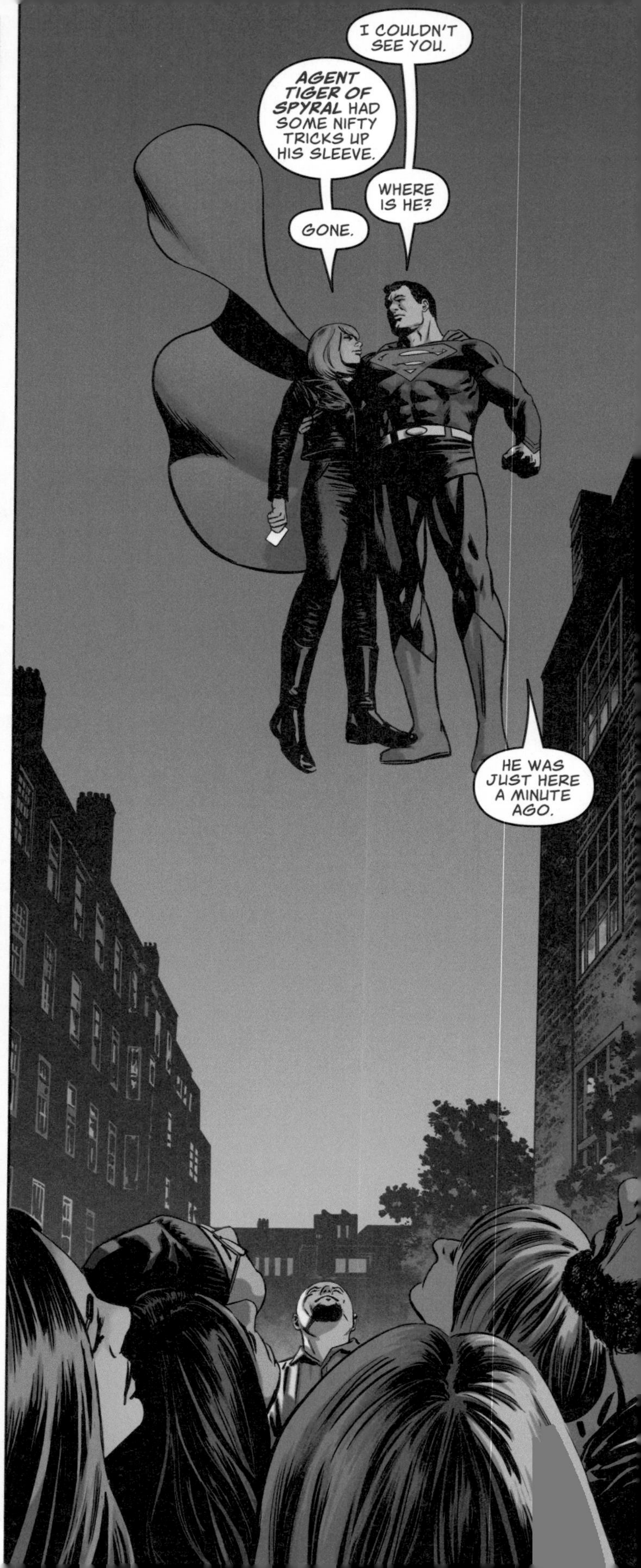
I COULDN'T SEE YOU.
AGENT TIGER OF SPYRAL HAD SOME NIFTY TRICKS UP HIS SLEEVE.
WHERE IS HE?
GONE.
HE WAS JUST HERE A MINUTE AGO.

WHAT-- WHAT IS THIS?

SPYRAL CAMOUFLAGE TECH.

WE'LL BE INVISIBLE FOR ABOUT TWENTY SECONDS.

LET'S GO!

I MEANT: WHERE ARE YOU *TAKING* ME?

THERE'S A BACK ALLEY EXIT THAT LEADS TO THE FISH MARKET ROOFTOP?

YOU AND--AND YOUR FRIEND *SUPERMAN* CAN TAKE IT FROM THERE.

WHO IS BEHIND THIS?

YOU COME AT ME IN DISGUISE AND *DEMAND ANSWERS?*

YOU AND *SUPERMAN?*

MY NAME IS LOIS LANE.

I'M A REPORTER FOR THE *DAILY PLANET.*

#$#$@!

YOU'RE-- YOU'RE LOIS LANE?

TELL ME WHAT HAPPENED TO YOU.

BOOM

BOOM

OKAY, LOOKS LIKE SUPERMAN GOT LEVIATHAN'S ATTACK AWAY FROM US IN TIME.

YOU'RE SAFE.

SAFE?

YOU'RE OUT OF YOUR BLOODY MIND.

WHAT IS IT?

HERE.

IT'S EVERYTHING.

EVERY SECRET.

EVERY NAME.

THE STORY OF SPYRAL.

WHICH, I HAD JUST DISCOVERED--JUST MOMENTS BEFORE MEETING YOU...

INCLUDES THEIR DARKEST SECRETS...

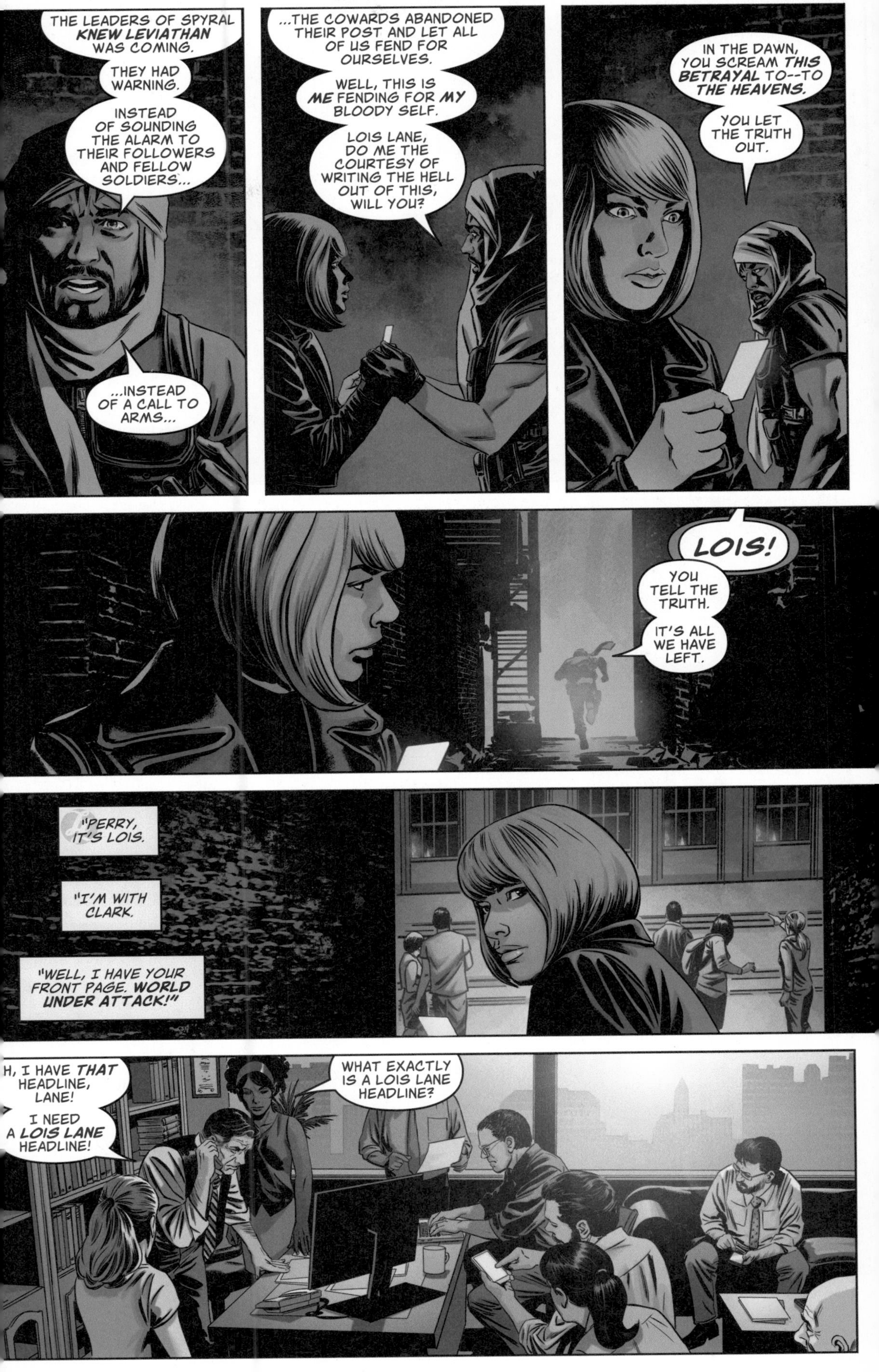
THE LEADERS OF SPYRAL KNEW LEVIATHAN WAS COMING.
THEY HAD WARNING.
INSTEAD OF SOUNDING THE ALARM TO THEIR FOLLOWERS AND FELLOW SOLDIERS...
...INSTEAD OF A CALL TO ARMS...
...THE COWARDS ABANDONED THEIR POST AND LET ALL OF US FEND FOR OURSELVES.
WELL, THIS IS ME FENDING FOR MY BLOODY SELF.
LOIS LANE, DO ME THE COURTESY OF WRITING THE HELL OUT OF THIS, WILL YOU?
IN THE DAWN, YOU SCREAM THIS BETRAYAL TO--TO THE HEAVENS.
YOU LET THE TRUTH OUT.
LOIS!
YOU TELL THE TRUTH.
IT'S ALL WE HAVE LEFT.
"PERRY, IT'S LOIS.
"I'M WITH CLARK.
"WELL, I HAVE YOUR FRONT PAGE. WORLD UNDER ATTACK!"
H, I HAVE THAT HEADLINE, LANE!
I NEED A LOIS LANE HEADLINE!
WHAT EXACTLY IS A LOIS LANE HEADLINE?

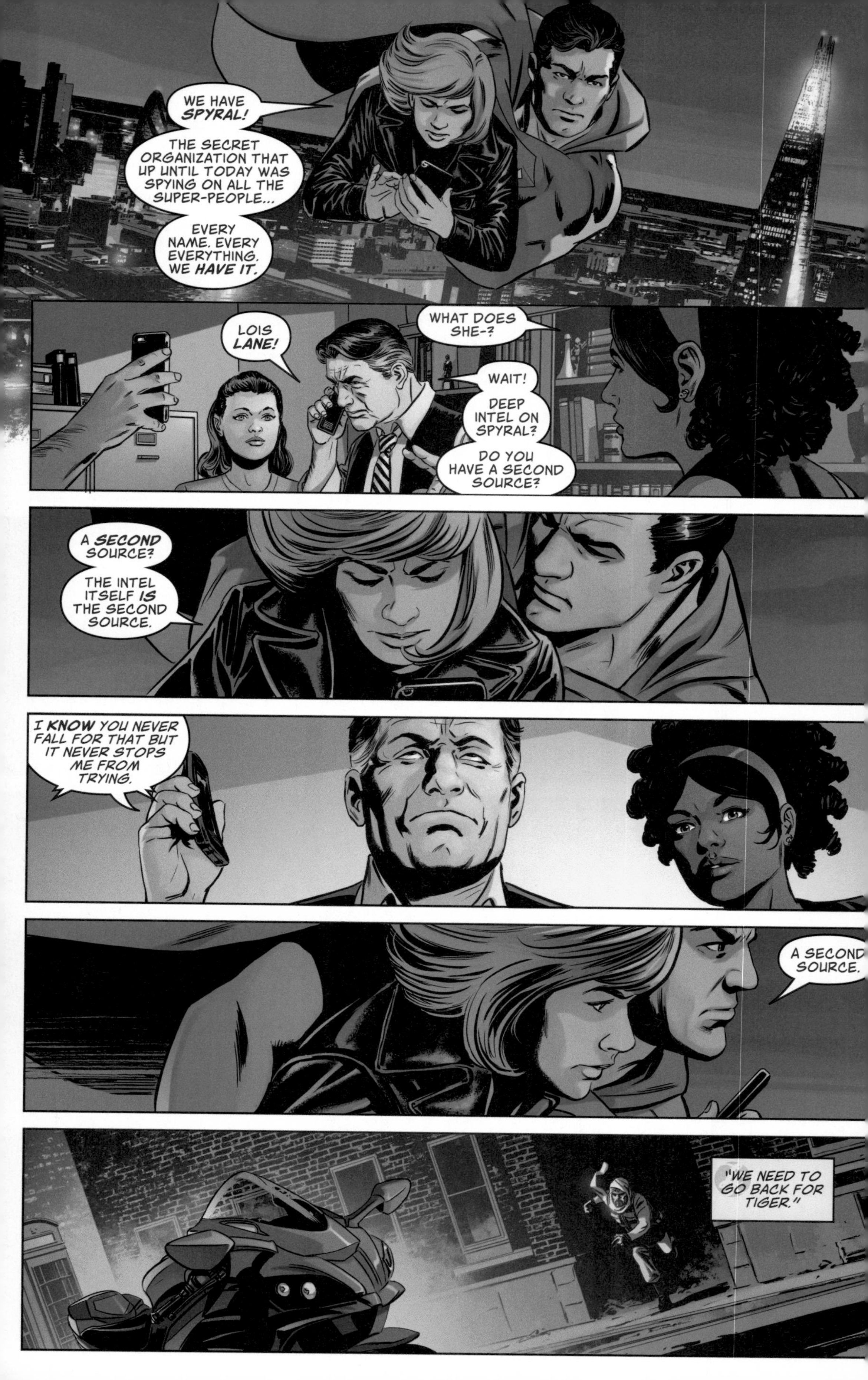
WE HAVE SPYRAL!
THE SECRET ORGANIZATION THAT UP UNTIL TODAY WAS SPYING ON ALL THE SUPER-PEOPLE...
EVERY NAME. EVERY EVERYTHING. WE HAVE IT.
LOIS LANE!
WHAT DOES SHE-?
WAIT!
DEEP INTEL ON SPYRAL?
DO YOU HAVE A SECOND SOURCE?
A SECOND SOURCE?
THE INTEL ITSELF IS THE SECOND SOURCE.
I KNOW YOU NEVER FALL FOR THAT BUT IT NEVER STOPS ME FROM TRYING.
A SECOND SOURCE.
"WE NEED TO GO BACK FOR TIGER."

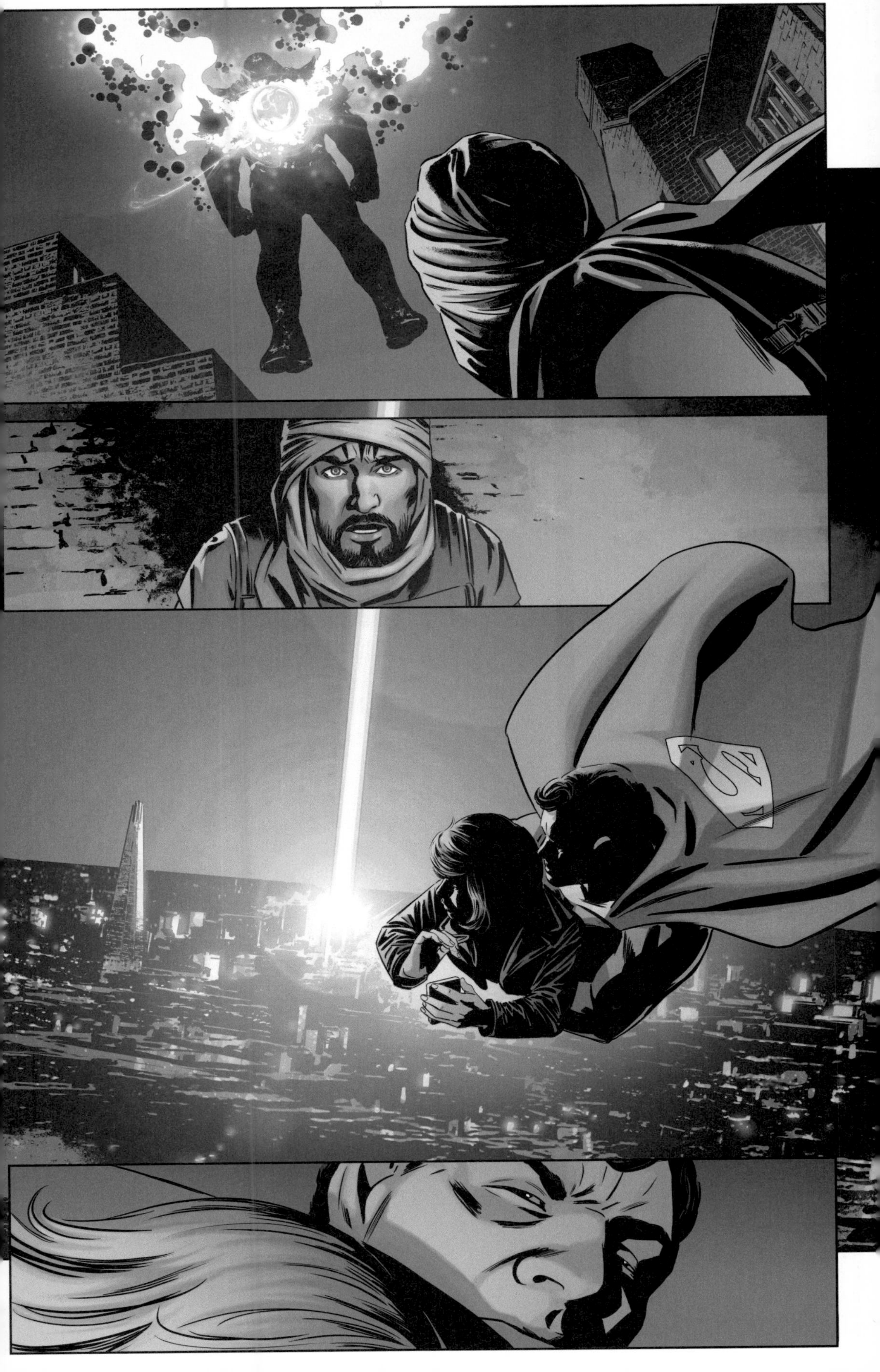

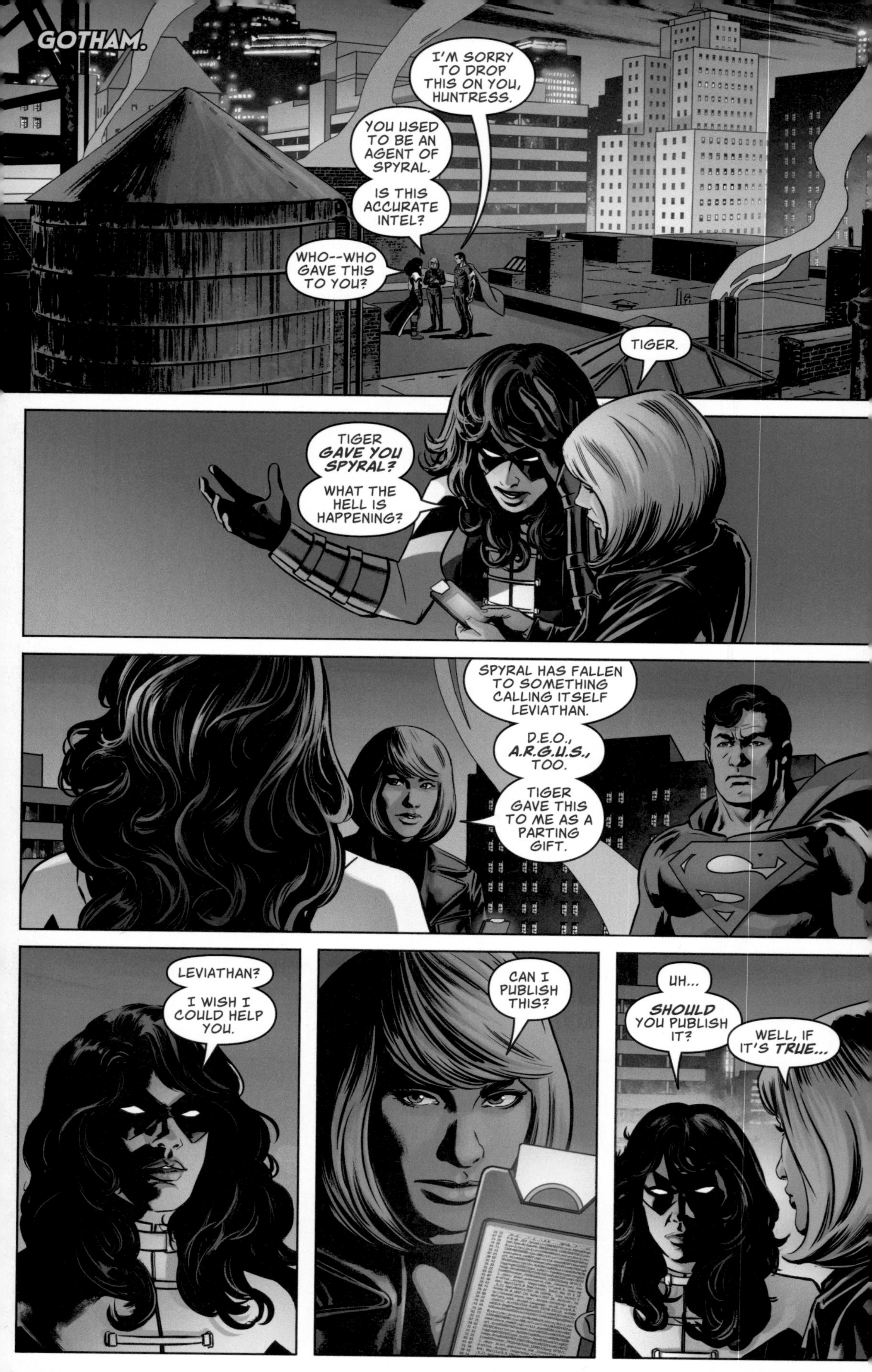
GOTHAM.
I'M SORRY TO DROP THIS ON YOU, HUNTRESS.
YOU USED TO BE AN AGENT OF SPYRAL.
IS THIS ACCURATE INTEL?
WHO--WHO GAVE THIS TO YOU?
TIGER.
TIGER GAVE YOU SPYRAL?
WHAT THE HELL IS HAPPENING?
SPYRAL HAS FALLEN TO SOMETHING CALLING ITSELF LEVIATHAN.
D.E.O., A.R.G.U.S., TOO.
TIGER GAVE THIS TO ME AS A PARTING GIFT.
LEVIATHAN?
I WISH I COULD HELP YOU.
CAN I PUBLISH THIS?
UH...
SHOULD YOU PUBLISH IT?
WELL, IF IT'S TRUE...

LEVIATHAN. TALIA AL GHUL?

IT JUST DOESN'T MAKE ANY TALIA SENSE?

YOU'LL LET US KNOW IF YOU HEAR *ANYTHING.*

THE WORLD WILL *TILT OFF ITS AXIS* IF YOU PUBLISH THAT.

THAT DESCRIBES A WORLD MOST DON'T KNOW EVEN EXISTS.

I JUST SPENT THE NIGHT IN LONDON *DEALING* WITH THE FIRST WAVE...

...PEOPLE ARE GETTING HURT.

THE REASONS NEED TO BE KNOWN. THE TRUTH NEEDS TO BE HEARD.

ALL THESE TENTPOLES OF OUR INTELLIGENCE COMMUNITY HAVE FALLEN IN A DAY?

WHAT HAPPENS IN THE MORNING?

I NEED TO GET AMANDA WALLER'S EYES ON THIS.

AMANDA WALLER?

WHERE IS *SHE* IN ALL THIS?

SAFE AT OUR PLACE.

YOU LEFT AMANDA WALLER ALONE IN YOUR HOUSE?

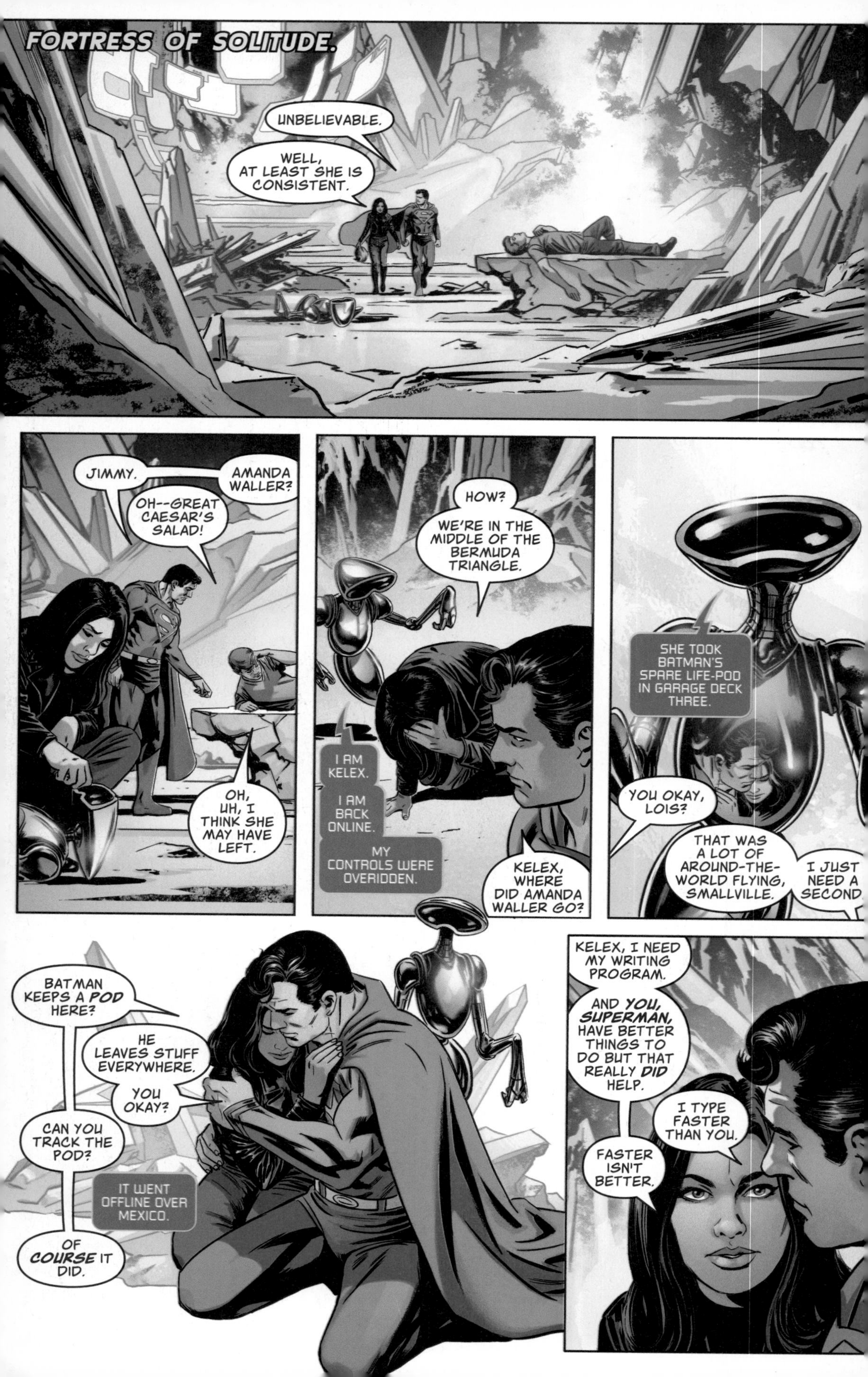
FORTRESS OF SOLITUDE.
UNBELIEVABLE.
WELL, AT LEAST SHE IS CONSISTENT.
JIMMY.
AMANDA WALLER?
OH--GREAT CAESAR'S SALAD!
OH, UH, I THINK SHE MAY HAVE LEFT.
HOW?
WE'RE IN THE MIDDLE OF THE BERMUDA TRIANGLE.
I AM KELEX.
I AM BACK ONLINE.
MY CONTROLS WERE OVERIDDEN.
KELEX, WHERE DID AMANDA WALLER GO?
SHE TOOK BATMAN'S SPARE LIFE-POD IN GARAGE DECK THREE.
YOU OKAY, LOIS?
THAT WAS A LOT OF AROUND-THE-WORLD FLYING, SMALLVILLE.
I JUST NEED A SECOND.
BATMAN KEEPS A POD HERE?
HE LEAVES STUFF EVERYWHERE.
YOU OKAY?
CAN YOU TRACK THE POD?
IT WENT OFFLINE OVER MEXICO.
OF COURSE IT DID.
KELEX, I NEED MY WRITING PROGRAM.
AND YOU, SUPERMAN, HAVE BETTER THINGS TO DO BUT THAT REALLY DID HELP.
I TYPE FASTER THAN YOU.
FASTER ISN'T BETTER.

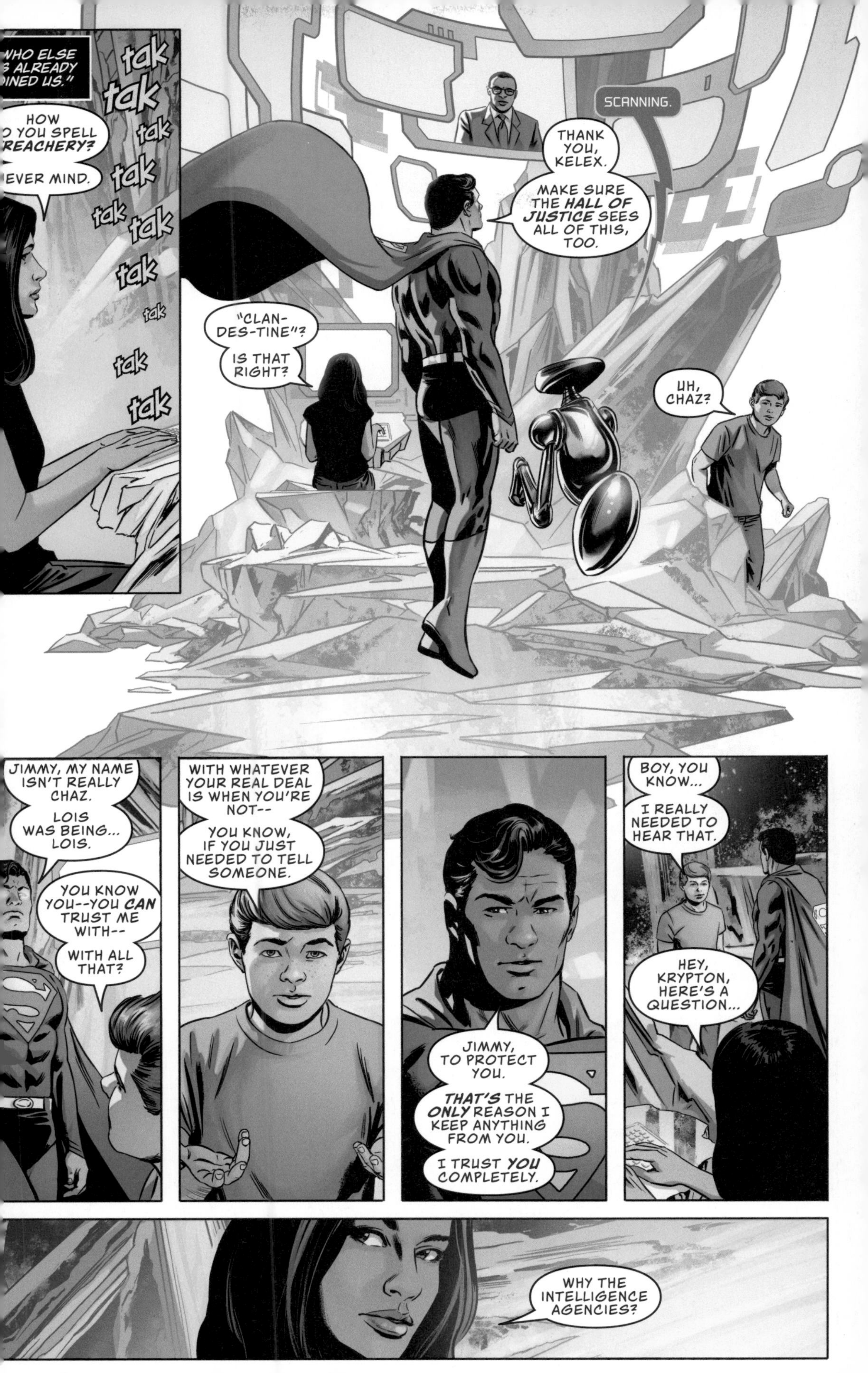

WHO ELSE
S ALREADY
OINED US."
tak tak tak tak tak tak tak tak tak tak
HOW
O YOU SPELL
REACHERY?
EVER MIND.
SCANNING.
THANK YOU, KELEX.
MAKE SURE THE HALL OF JUSTICE SEES ALL OF THIS, TOO.
"CLAN-DES-TINE"?
IS THAT RIGHT?
UH, CHAZ?
JIMMY, MY NAME ISN'T REALLY CHAZ.
LOIS WAS BEING... LOIS.
YOU KNOW YOU--YOU CAN TRUST ME WITH--
WITH ALL THAT?
WITH WHATEVER YOUR REAL DEAL IS WHEN YOU'RE NOT--
YOU KNOW, IF YOU JUST NEEDED TO TELL SOMEONE.
JIMMY, TO PROTECT YOU.
THAT'S THE ONLY REASON I KEEP ANYTHING FROM YOU.
I TRUST YOU COMPLETELY.
BOY, YOU KNOW...
I REALLY NEEDED TO HEAR THAT.
HEY, KRYPTON, HERE'S A QUESTION...
WHY THE INTELLIGENCE AGENCIES?

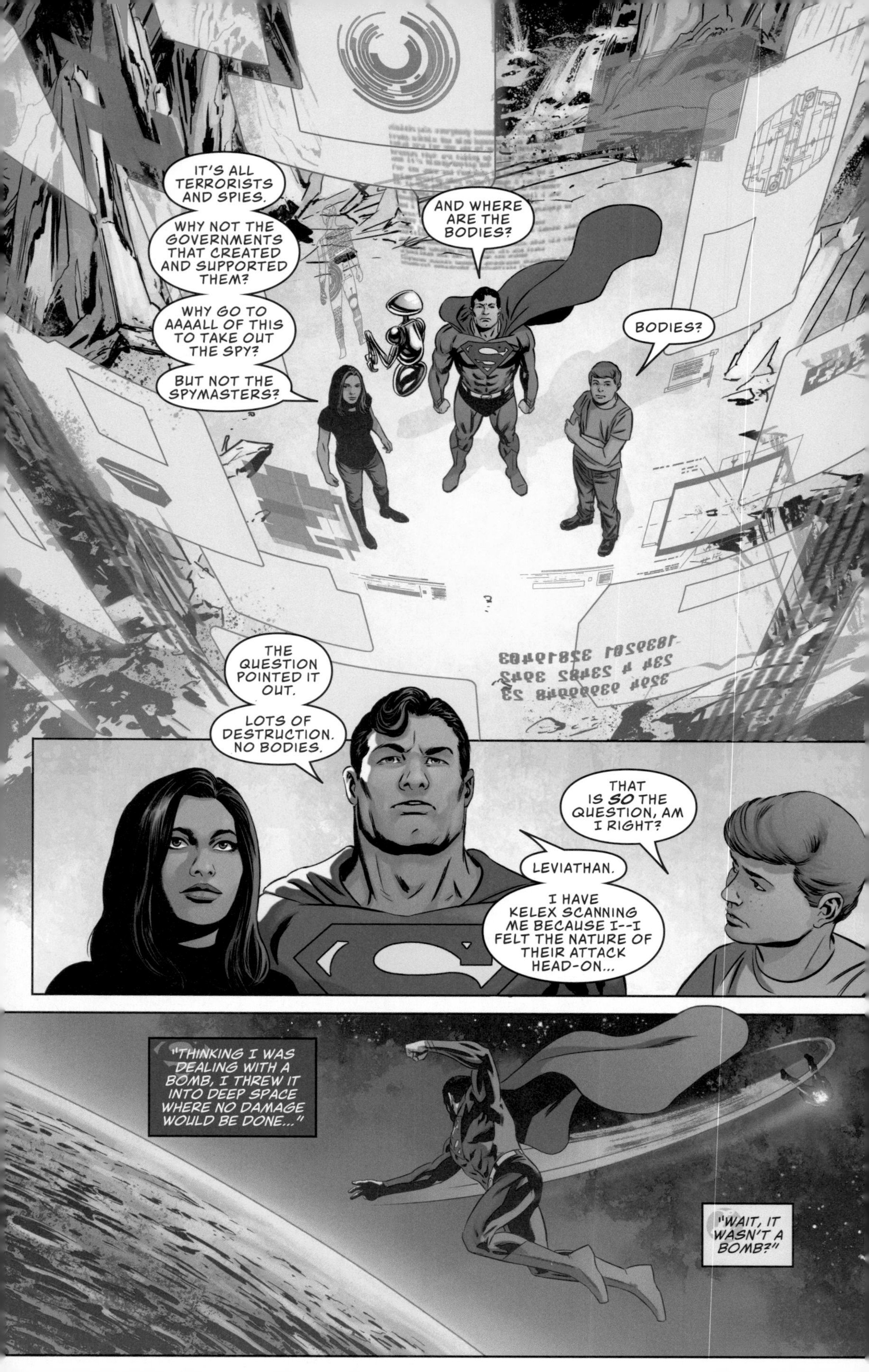
IT'S ALL TERRORISTS AND SPIES.
WHY NOT THE GOVERNMENTS THAT CREATED AND SUPPORTED THEM?
WHY GO TO AAAALL OF THIS TO TAKE OUT THE SPY?
BUT NOT THE SPYMASTERS?
AND WHERE ARE THE BODIES?
BODIES?
THE QUESTION POINTED IT OUT.
LOTS OF DESTRUCTION. NO BODIES.
THAT IS SO THE QUESTION, AM I RIGHT?
LEVIATHAN.
I HAVE KELEX SCANNING ME BECAUSE I--I FELT THE NATURE OF THEIR ATTACK HEAD-ON...
"THINKING I WAS DEALING WITH A BOMB, I THREW IT INTO DEEP SPACE WHERE NO DAMAGE WOULD BE DONE..."
"WAIT, IT WASN'T A BOMB?"

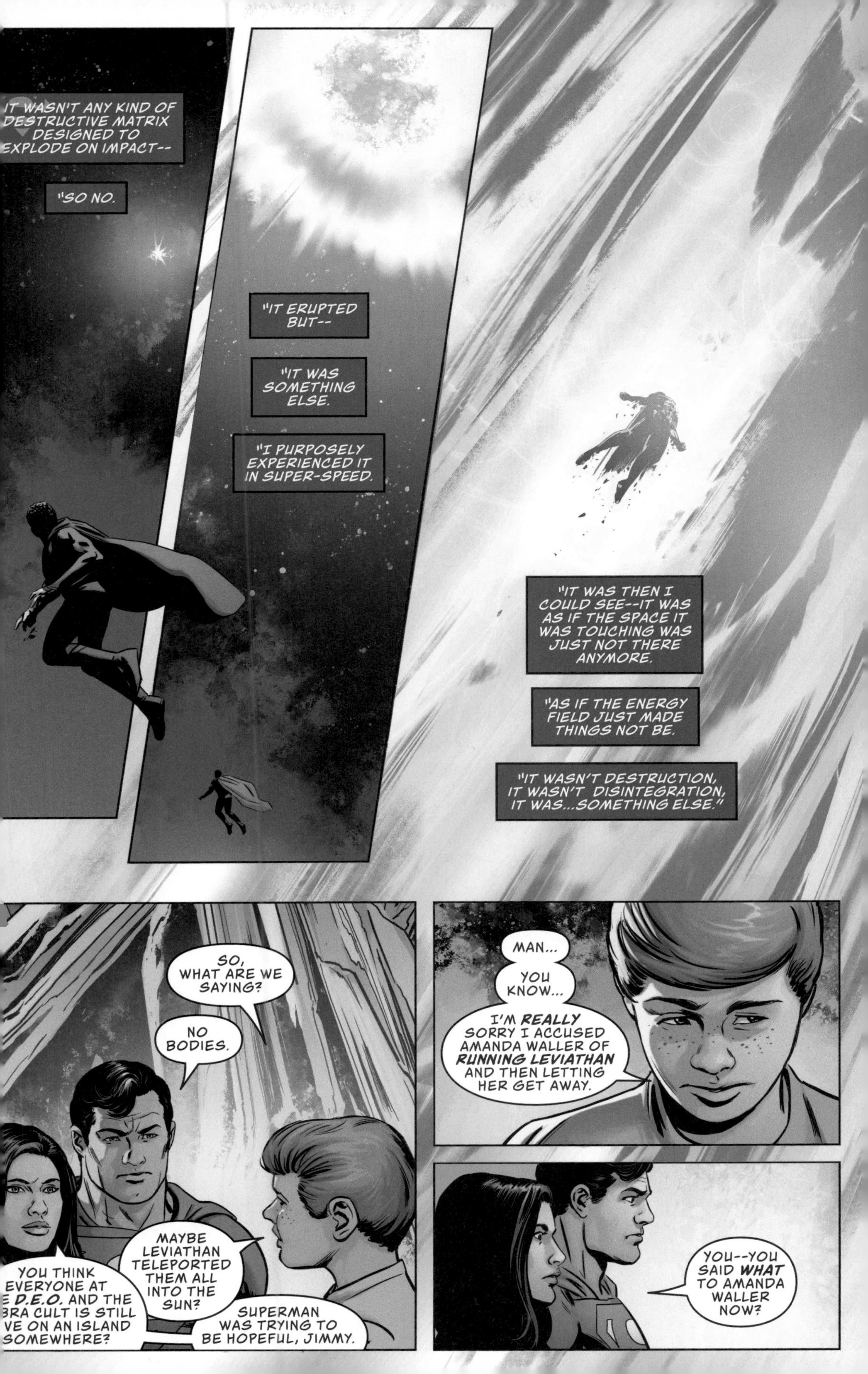

IT WASN'T ANY KIND OF DESTRUCTIVE MATRIX DESIGNED TO EXPLODE ON IMPACT--
"SO NO.
"IT ERUPTED BUT--
"IT WAS SOMETHING ELSE.
"I PURPOSELY EXPERIENCED IT IN SUPER-SPEED.
"IT WAS THEN I COULD SEE--IT WAS AS IF THE SPACE IT WAS TOUCHING WAS JUST NOT THERE ANYMORE.
"AS IF THE ENERGY FIELD JUST MADE THINGS NOT BE.
"IT WASN'T DESTRUCTION, IT WASN'T DISINTEGRATION, IT WAS...SOMETHING ELSE."
SO, WHAT ARE WE SAYING?
NO BODIES.
YOU THINK EVERYONE AT E *D.E.O.* AND THE BRA CULT IS STILL VE ON AN ISLAND SOMEWHERE?
MAYBE LEVIATHAN TELEPORTED THEM ALL INTO THE SUN?
SUPERMAN WAS TRYING TO BE HOPEFUL, JIMMY.
MAN...
YOU KNOW...
I'M ***REALLY*** SORRY I ACCUSED AMANDA WALLER OF ***RUNNING LEVIATHAN*** AND THEN LETTING HER GET AWAY.
YOU--YOU SAID ***WHAT*** TO AMANDA WALLER NOW?

I TOTALLY PAPPED HER.

YOU SAID TO THE LEADER OF *A.R.G.U.S.* AND *SUICIDE SQUAD,* "YOU'RE *LEVIATHAN,"* AND TOOK *THAT* PIC?

YES.

AND THEN SHE *PUNCHED* YOU, STOLE BATMAN'S WHATEVER AND IS NOW ON THE LAM.

I FEEL BAD. I MADE HER ANGRY.

NOT AS ANGRY AS SHE'S GOING TO BE WHEN SHE SEES *THIS* ON THE COVER OF THE *PLANET* TOMORROW.

SHE DIDN'T TAKE YOUR CAMERA?

SHE DID.

IT ALL GOES TO THE CLOUD OR WHATEVER.

I'M A PROFESSIONAL WAR CORRESPONDENT, DUH.

SIDEBAR, SUPERMAN.

YOUR FATHER IS FINE. I KEEP CHECKING.

YES.

THIS IS FRONT PAGE.

BUT THIS DOESN'T MAKE *HER* LEVIATHAN.

NO, IT MAKES HER SOMEONE WHO RAN AWAY IN A VIOLENT OUTBURST WHEN ASKED.

WE'D REPORT THIS IF IT DIDN'T HAPPEN HERE.

AMANDA WALLER CAME TO SUPERMAN FOR HELP AS THE WORLD FELL AND *THIS* IS THE FALLOUT...

WE REPORT THE TRUTH, NO MATTER WHAT.

SHE COULD COME AFTER US WITH HER TRUTH...ABOUT YOU.

THE ONLY TRUTH THAT MATTERS IS...

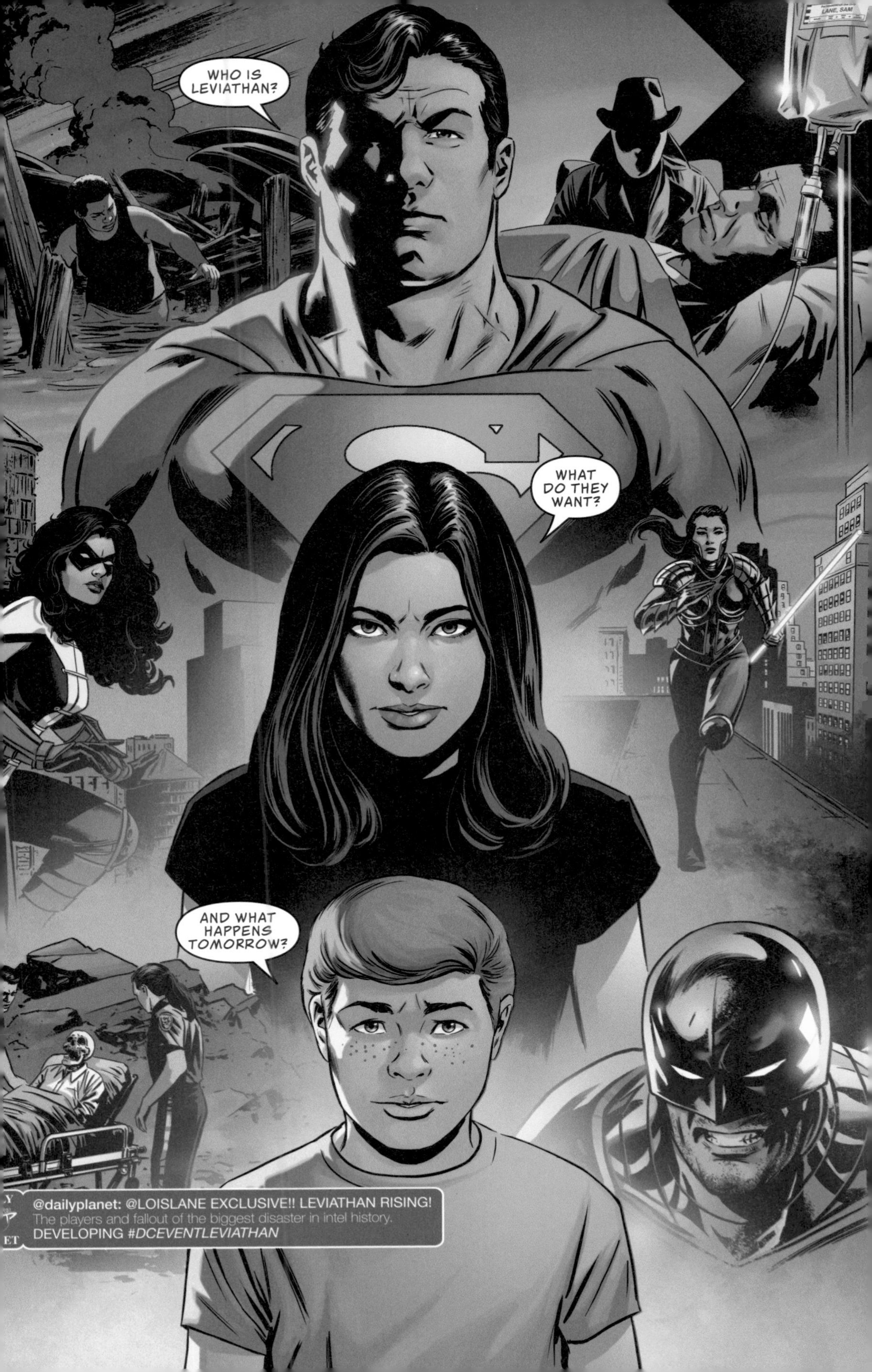
WHO IS LEVIATHAN?
LANE, SAM
WHAT DO THEY WANT?
AND WHAT HAPPENS TOMORROW?
@dailyplanet: @LOISLANE EXCLUSIVE!! LEVIATHAN RISING!
The players and fallout of the biggest disaster in intel history.
DEVELOPING #DCEVENTLEVIATHAN

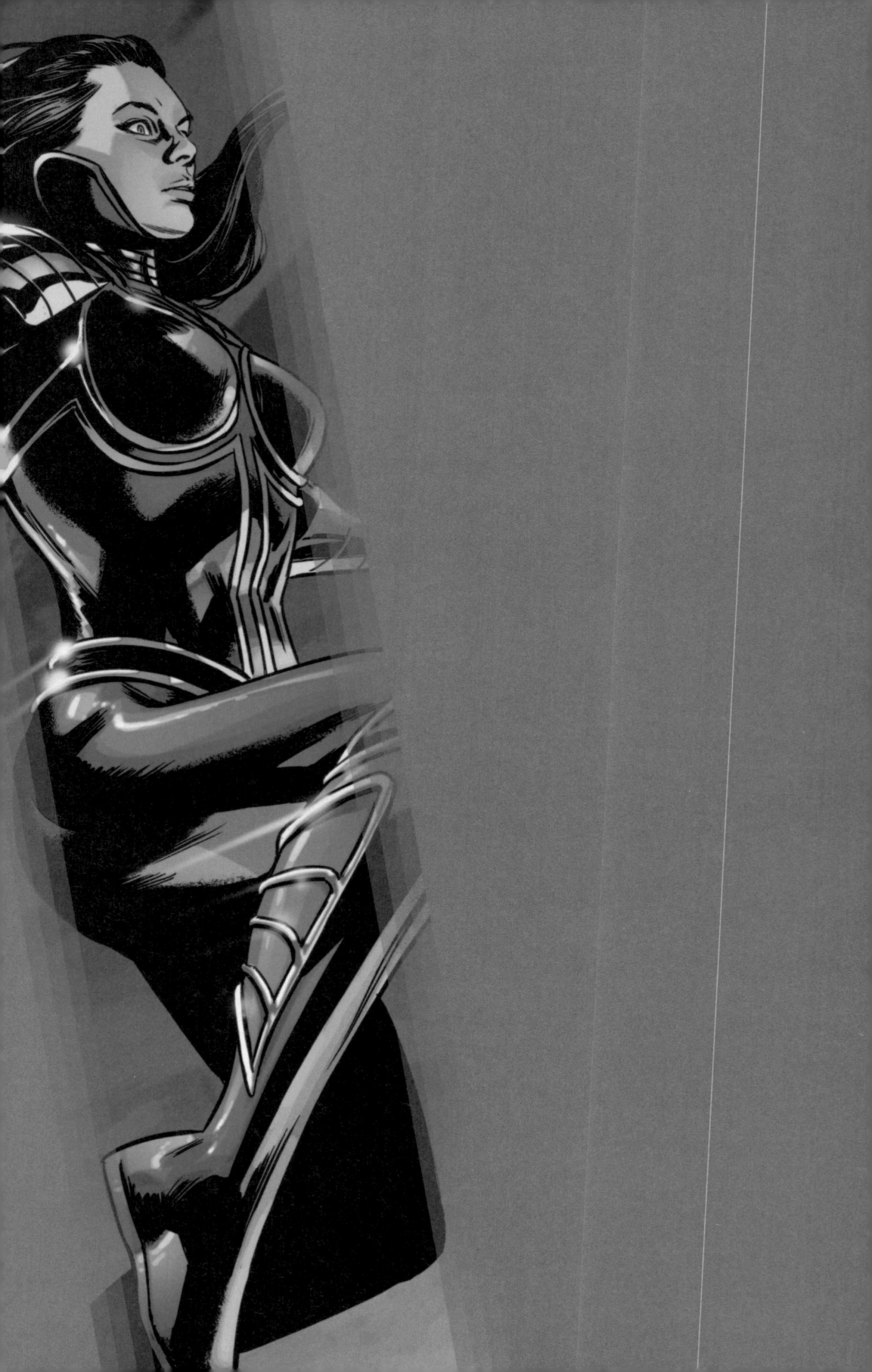

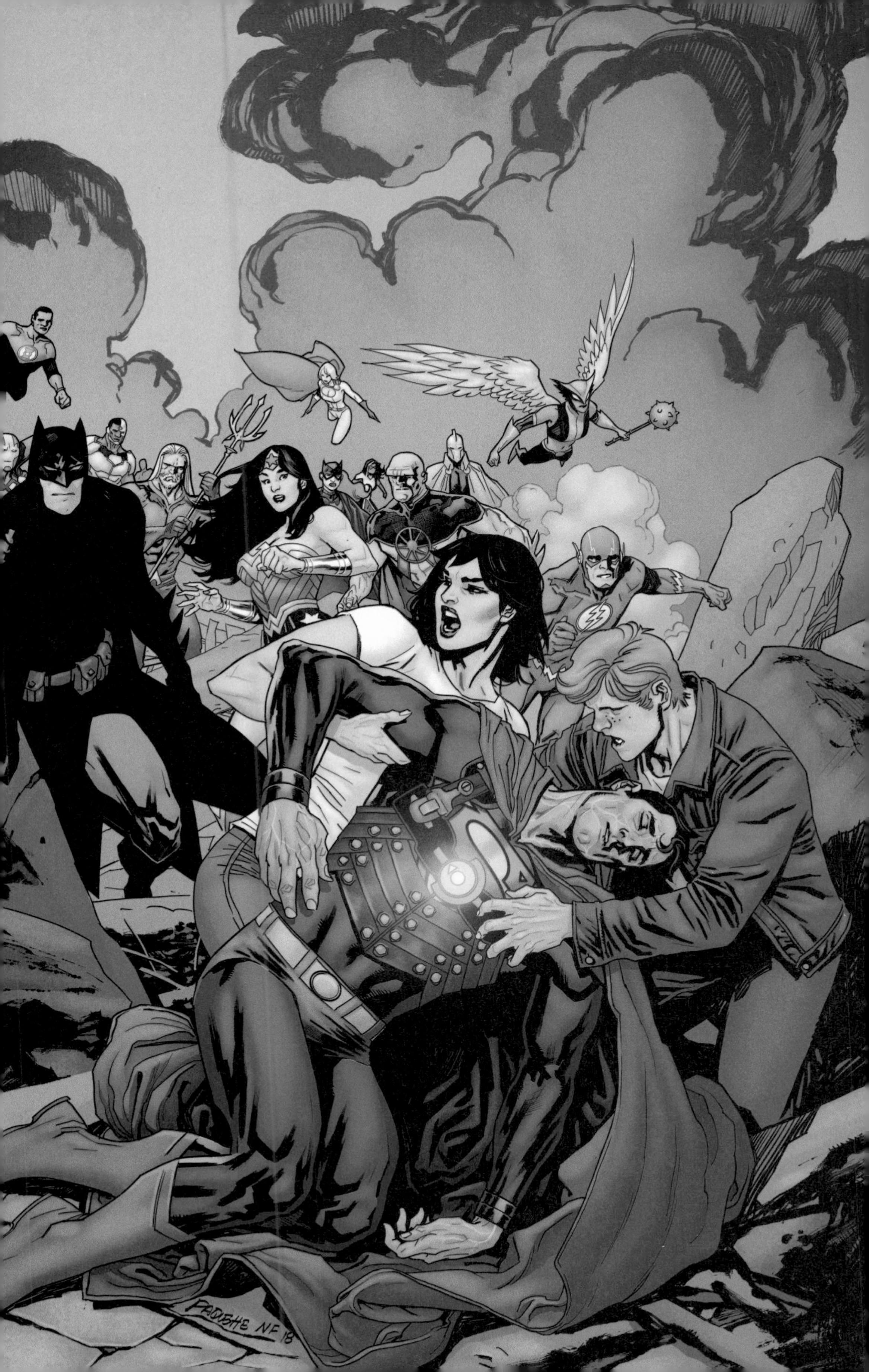

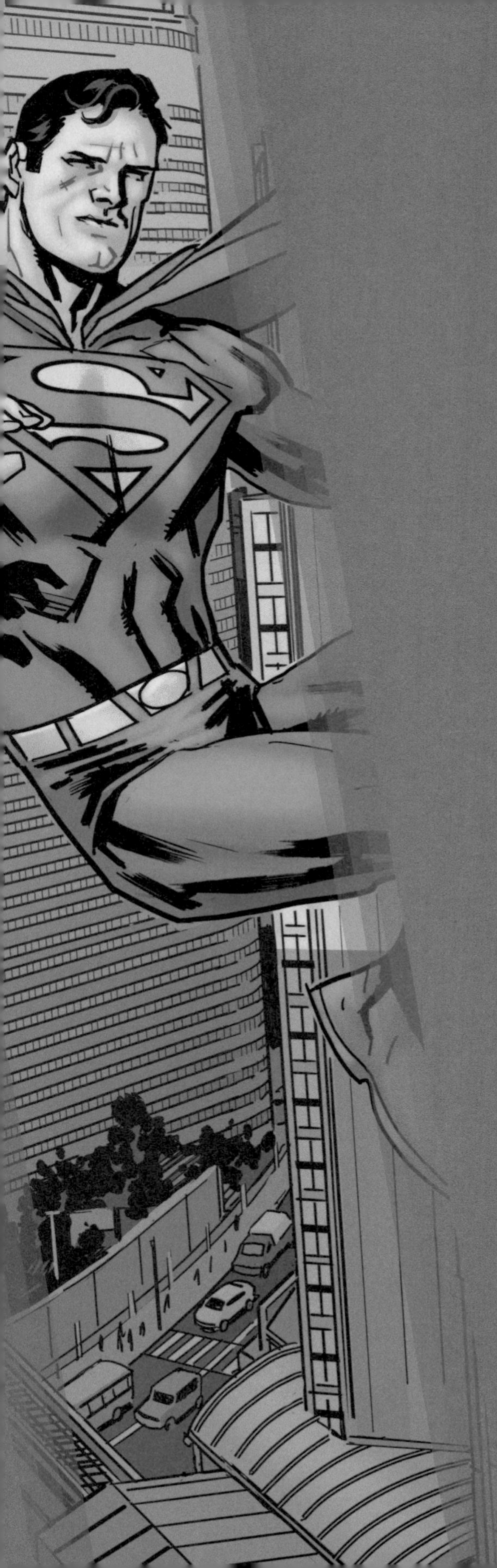

DC COMICS PRESENTS:
LEVIATHAN RISING

BRIAN MICHAEL BENDIS
writer

YANICK PAQUETTE
artist

NATHAN FAIRBAIRN
colorist

DAVE SHARPE
ALW'S TROY PETERI
letterers

YANICK PAQUETTE
and NATHAN FAIRBAIRN
cover

JESSICA CHEN
associate editor

MIKE COTTON
editor

BRIAN CUNNINGHAM
group editor

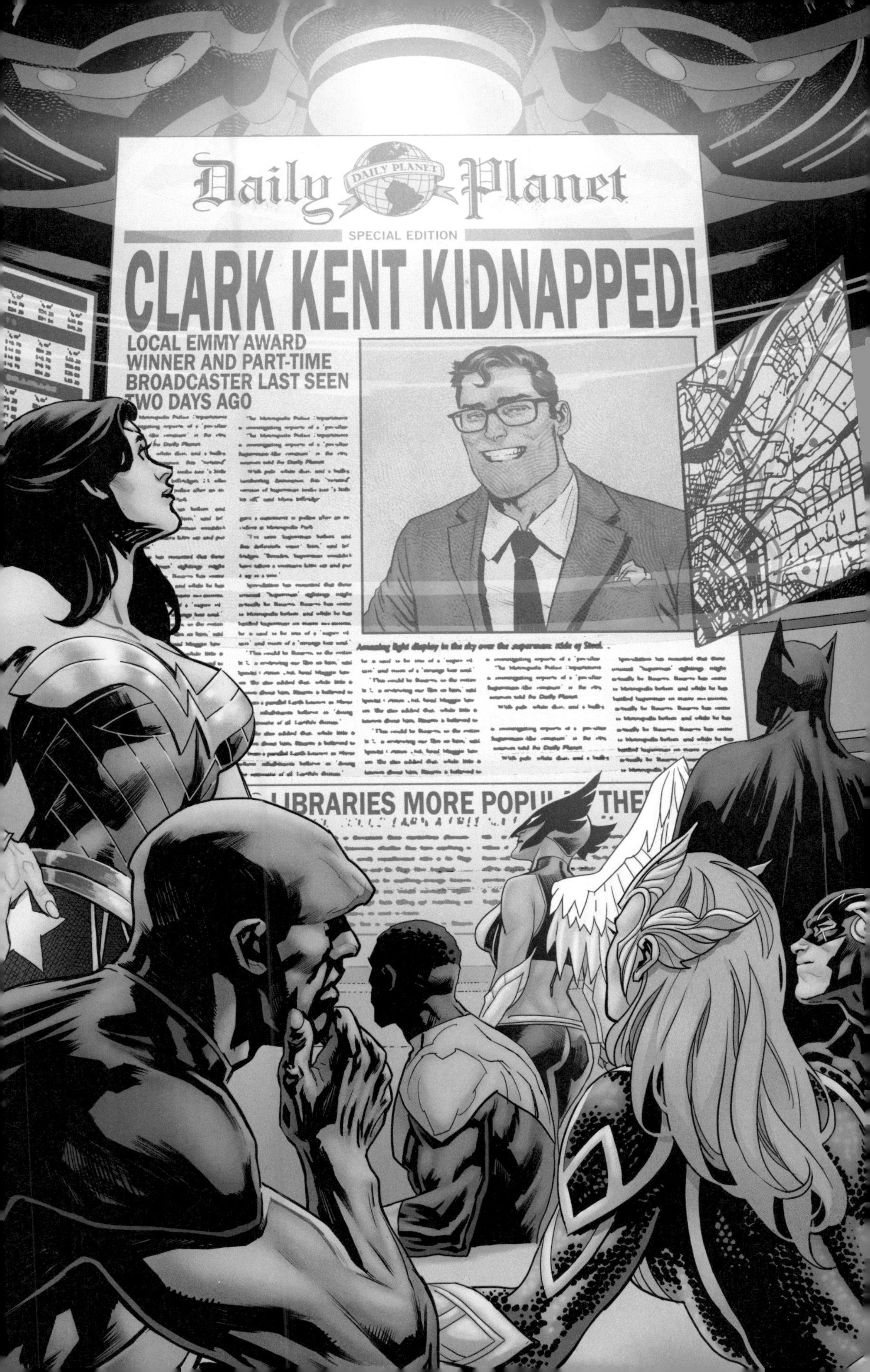
Daily Planet
DAILY PLANET
SPECIAL EDITION
CLARK KENT KIDNAPPED!
LOCAL EMMY AWARD WINNER AND PART-TIME BROADCASTER LAST SEEN TWO DAYS AGO
LIBRARIES MORE POPU
THE

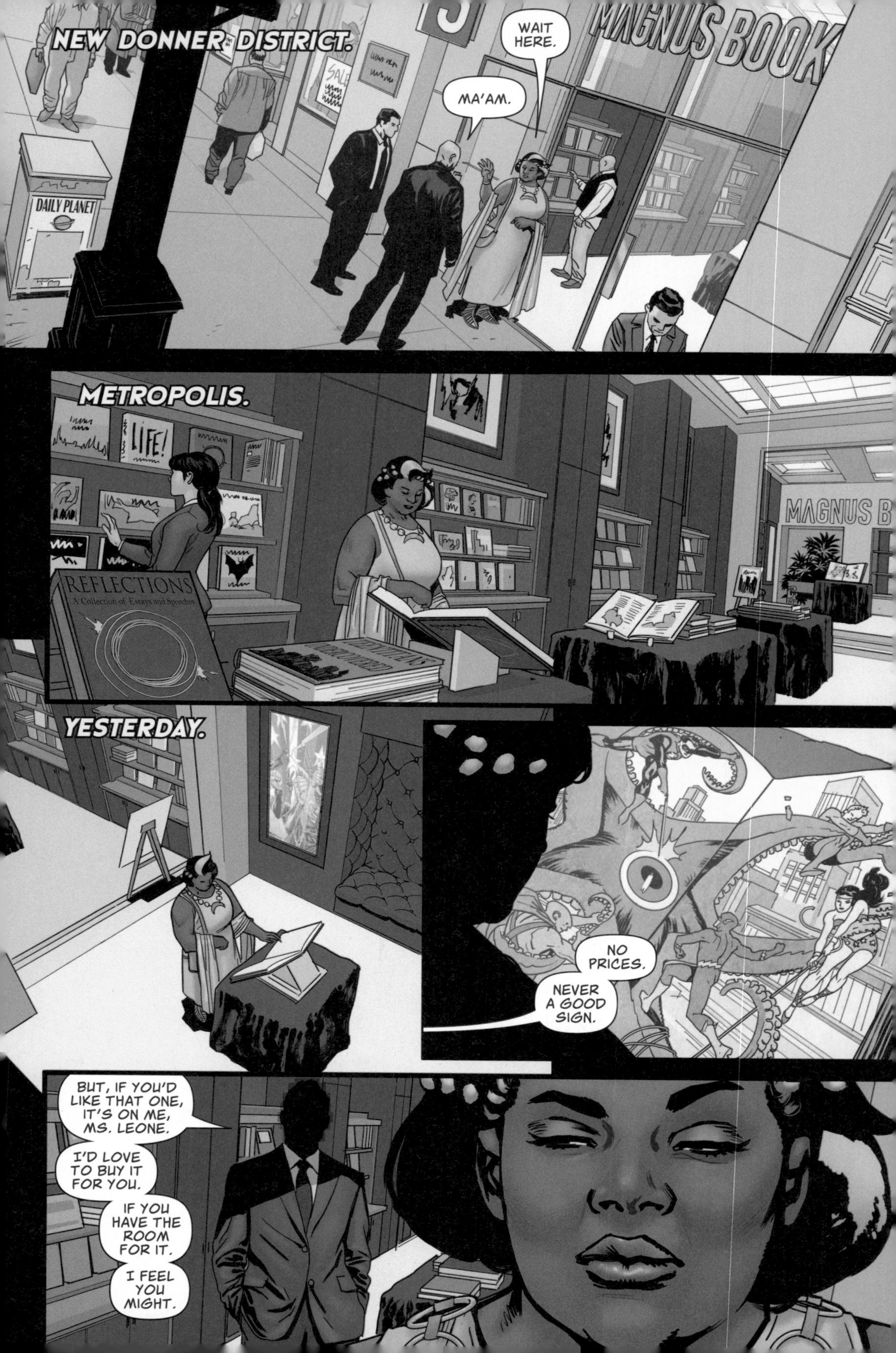
NEW DONNER DISTRICT.
MAGNUS BOOK
DAILY PLANET
WAIT HERE.
MA'AM.
METROPOLIS.
LIFE!
REFLECTIONS
A Collection of Essays and Speeches
MAGNUS B
YESTERDAY.
NO PRICES.
NEVER A GOOD SIGN.
BUT, IF YOU'D LIKE THAT ONE, IT'S ON ME, MS. LEONE.
I'D LOVE TO BUY IT FOR YOU.
IF YOU HAVE THE ROOM FOR IT.
I FEEL YOU MIGHT.

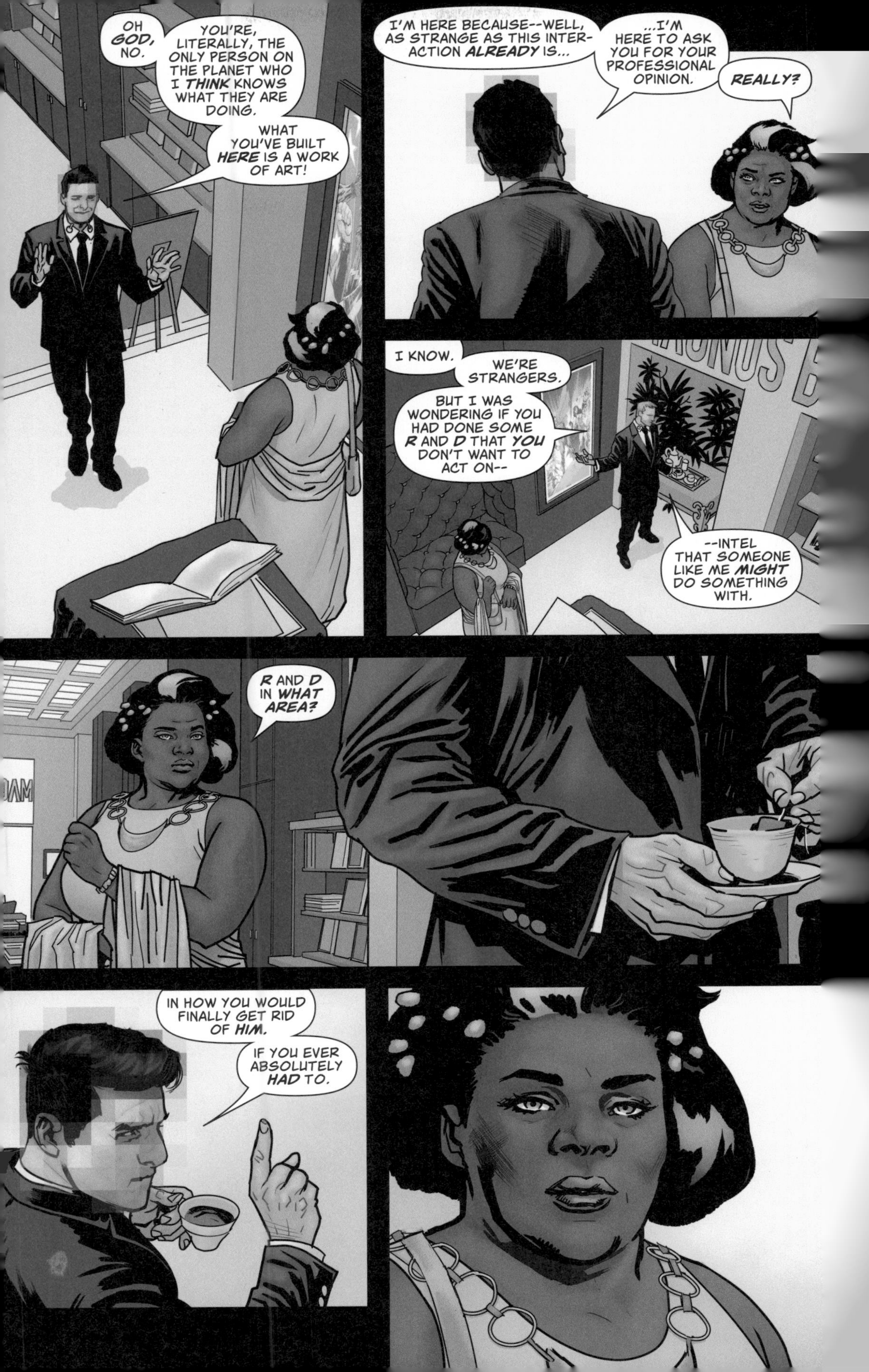

OH GOD, NO.
YOU'RE, LITERALLY, THE ONLY PERSON ON THE PLANET WHO I THINK KNOWS WHAT THEY ARE DOING.
WHAT YOU'VE BUILT HERE IS A WORK OF ART!
I'M HERE BECAUSE--WELL, AS STRANGE AS THIS INTERACTION ALREADY IS...
...I'M HERE TO ASK YOU FOR YOUR PROFESSIONAL OPINION.
REALLY?
I KNOW.
WE'RE STRANGERS.
BUT I WAS WONDERING IF YOU HAD DONE SOME R AND D THAT YOU DON'T WANT TO ACT ON--
--INTEL THAT SOMEONE LIKE ME MIGHT DO SOMETHING WITH.
R AND D IN WHAT AREA?
IN HOW YOU WOULD FINALLY GET RID OF HIM.
IF YOU EVER ABSOLUTELY HAD TO.

"IT'S NOT HARD TO FIND THE THINGS THAT HE CARES ABOUT.

"OR HOW TO TAKE THEM AWAY FROM HIM.

"PICK ONE...

"...WATCH *HOW FAST* THE LITTLE BROKEN BOY WILL CRUMBLE."

"YOU'RE TALKING ABOUT THAT REPORTER, LOI--"

I NEED LOIS *LANE*!

"AND THE ANSWER IS NO.

"NOT *HER*.

"*EVERYONE* HAS TRIED *THAT*."

I NEED LOIS LANE!

LOIS LANE WOULD HAVE BROKEN THIS STORY AND WE'D BE HOME FOR SHABBAT DINNER!

YOU KNOW, MR. WHITE...

...IT REALLY ISN'T HELPFUL TO US THAT YOU KEEP WISHING OUT LOUD THAT WE *WERE ALL LOIS LANE.*

WE HAVE A SOURCE THAT SAYS THE MAIN BUSINESSES OF LEXCORP ARE ABOUT TO FILE FOR CHAPTER 11 AND WE WOULD LIKE--

THEY WOULDN'T HAVE HUNG UP ON LOIS LANE.

OF *COURSE* THEY WOULD HAVE.

KENT!

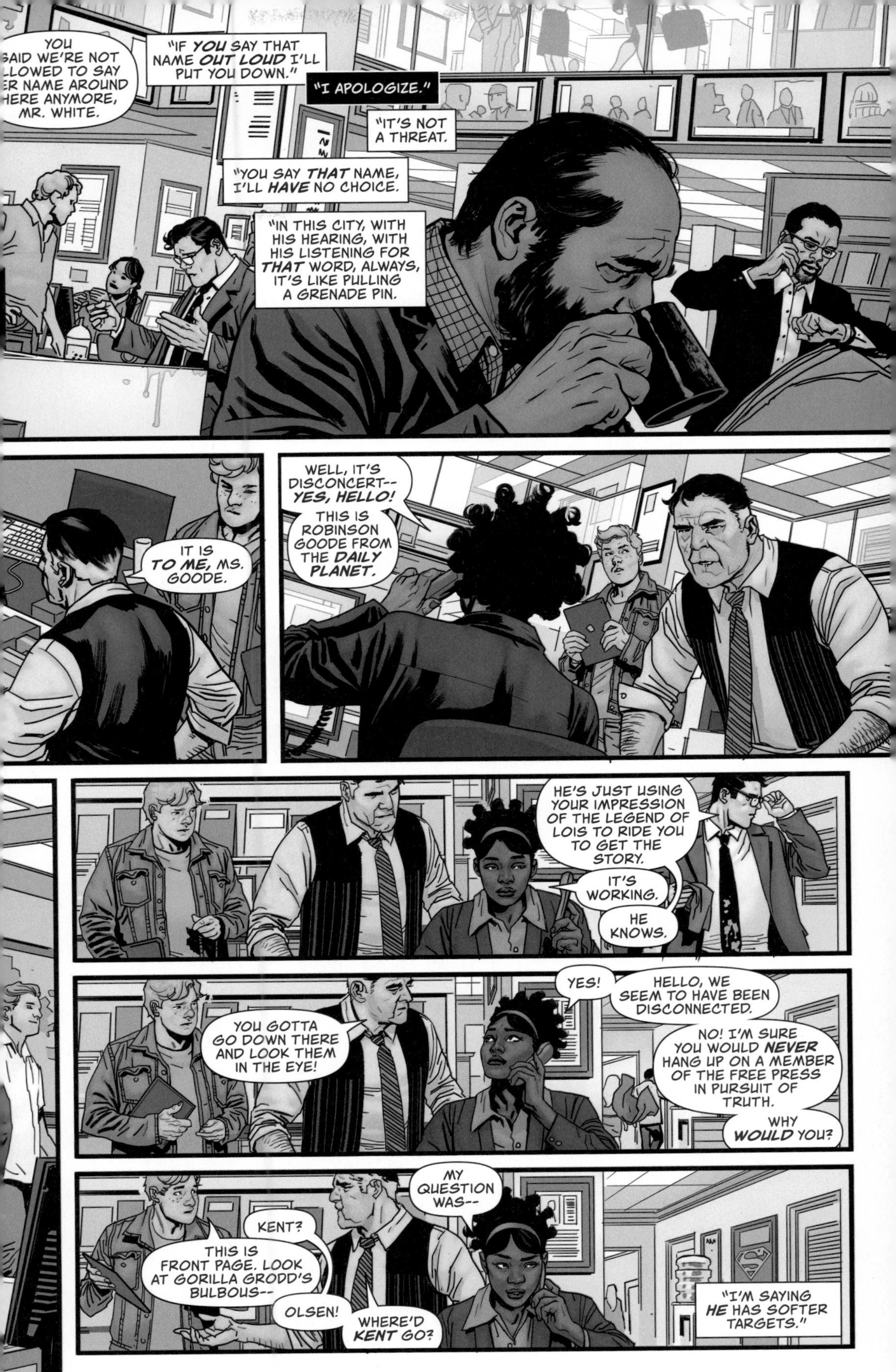

YOU
SAID WE'RE NOT
LLOWED TO SAY
ER NAME AROUND
HERE ANYMORE,
MR. WHITE.
"IF *YOU* SAY THAT NAME *OUT LOUD* I'LL PUT YOU DOWN."
"I APOLOGIZE."
"IT'S NOT A THREAT.
"YOU SAY *THAT* NAME, I'LL *HAVE* NO CHOICE.
"IN THIS CITY, WITH HIS HEARING, WITH HIS LISTENING FOR *THAT* WORD, ALWAYS, IT'S LIKE PULLING A GRENADE PIN.
IT IS *TO ME,* MS. GOODE.
WELL, IT'S DISCONCERT-- *YES, HELLO!*
THIS IS ROBINSON GOODE FROM THE *DAILY PLANET.*
HE'S JUST USING YOUR IMPRESSION OF THE LEGEND OF LOIS TO RIDE YOU TO GET THE STORY.
IT'S WORKING.
HE KNOWS.
YOU GOTTA GO DOWN THERE AND LOOK THEM IN THE EYE!
YES!
HELLO, WE SEEM TO HAVE BEEN DISCONNECTED.
NO! I'M SURE YOU WOULD *NEVER* HANG UP ON A MEMBER OF THE FREE PRESS IN PURSUIT OF TRUTH.
WHY *WOULD* YOU?
MY QUESTION WAS--
KENT?
THIS IS FRONT PAGE. LOOK AT GORILLA GRODD'S BULBOUS--
OLSEN!
WHERE'D *KENT* GO?
"I'M SAYING *HE* HAS SOFTER TARGETS."

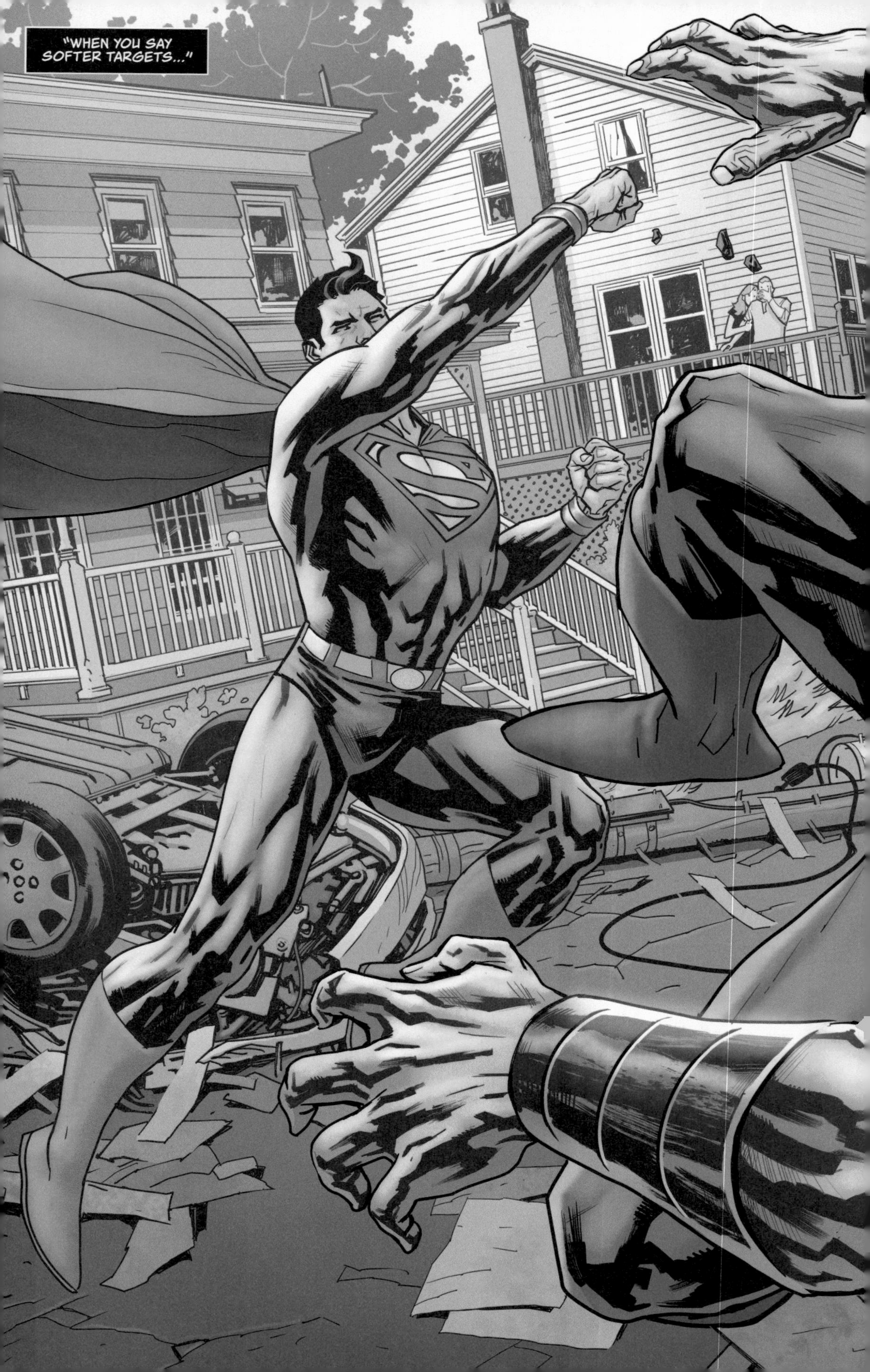
"WHEN YOU SAY SOFTER TARGETS..."

ND THEY'RE HIDING IN OUR PARTMENT?

BACK IN ETROPOLIS.

RIGHT NOW.

LOOKING TO KIDNAP *YOU?*

"*THAT* PART WAS CLEAR."

NOT *ME?*

HUH.

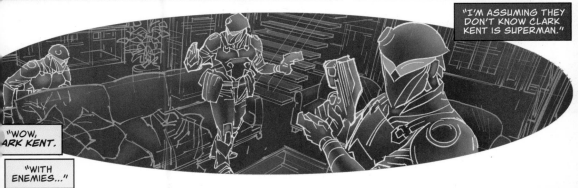

"I'M ASSUMING THEY DON'T KNOW CLARK KENT IS SUPERMAN."

"WOW, ARK KENT.

"WITH ENEMIES..."

CLARK KENT S A LAW-ABIDING CITIZEN, WHO--

THAT HATCHET PIECE ON *YOUNG JUSTICE.*

S.T.A.R. LABS EXPOSÉ.

HATCHET PIECE? THOSE KIDS NEED A LESSON IN CLEANING UP AFTER--

OH, YES.

THEY *MIGHT* HAVE A BEEF WITH ME.

LET'S CALL THE POLICE.

LET'S CALL METROPOLIS SPECIAL FORCES--GIVE MAGGIE SAWYER A THRILL.

ACTUALLY, I'M THINKING ABOUT GOING ALONG WITH IT.

WHAT?

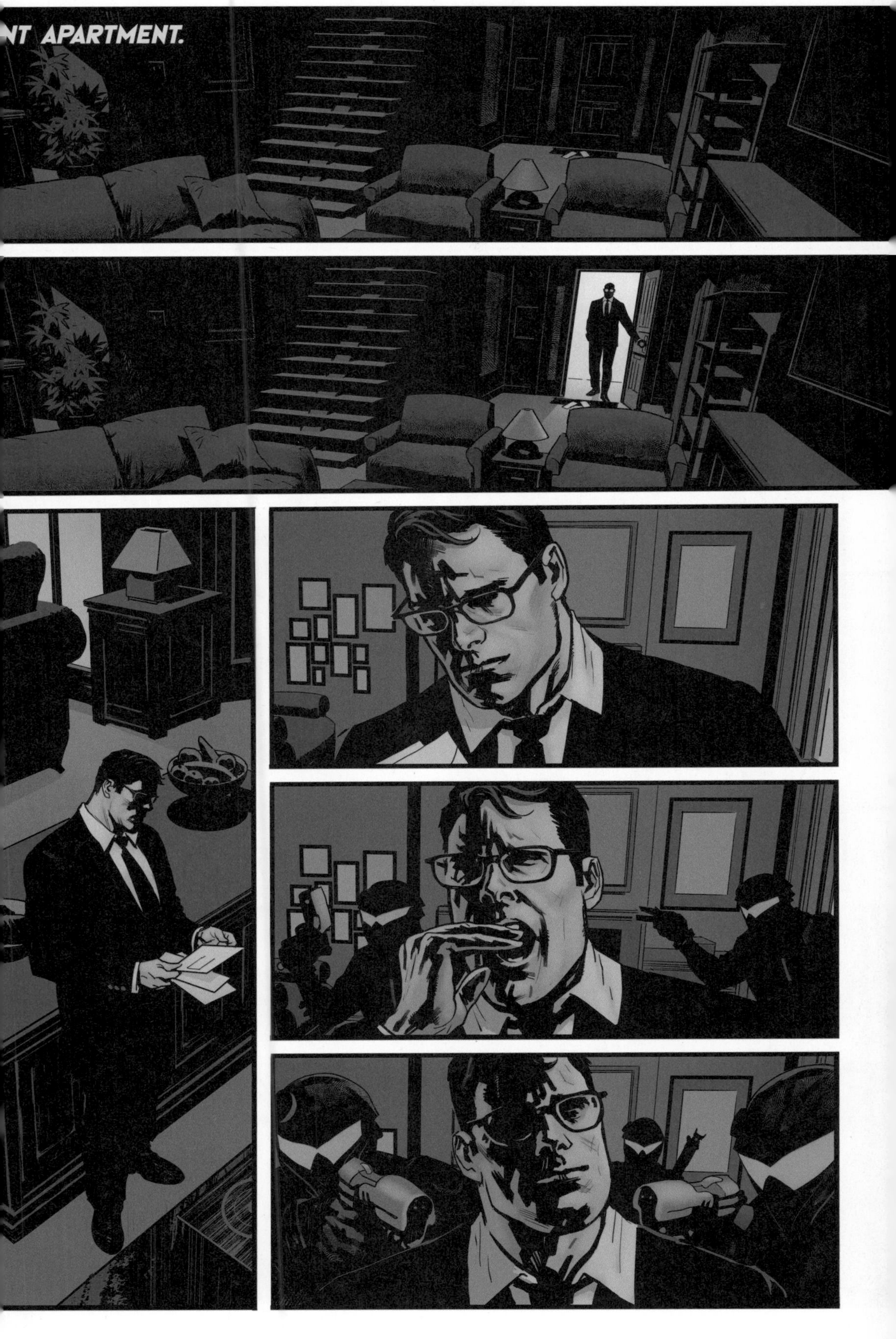
NT APARTMENT.

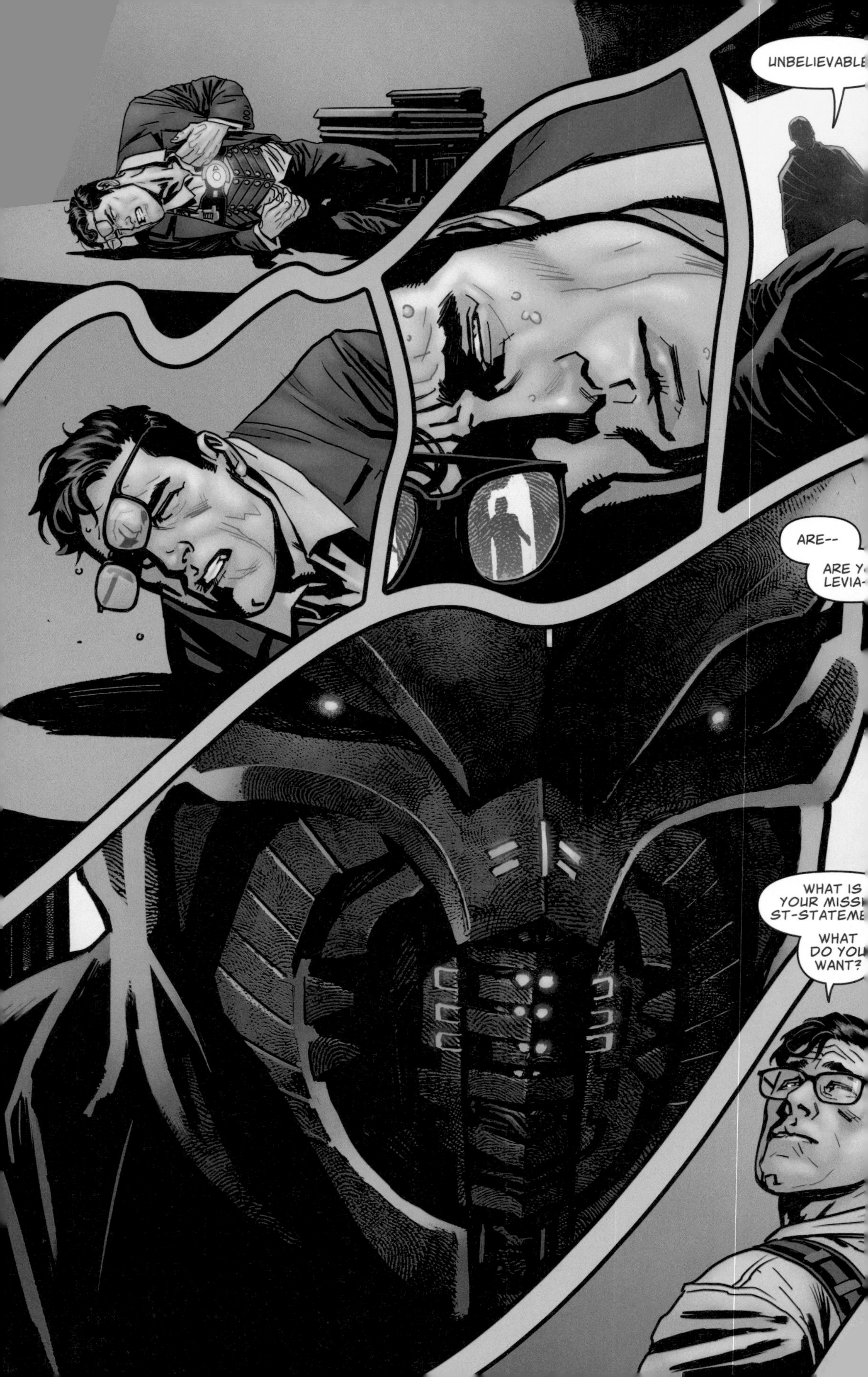
UNBELIEVABLE
ARE--
ARE Y
LEVIA-
WHAT IS
YOUR MISS
ST-STATEME
WHAT
DO YOU
WANT?

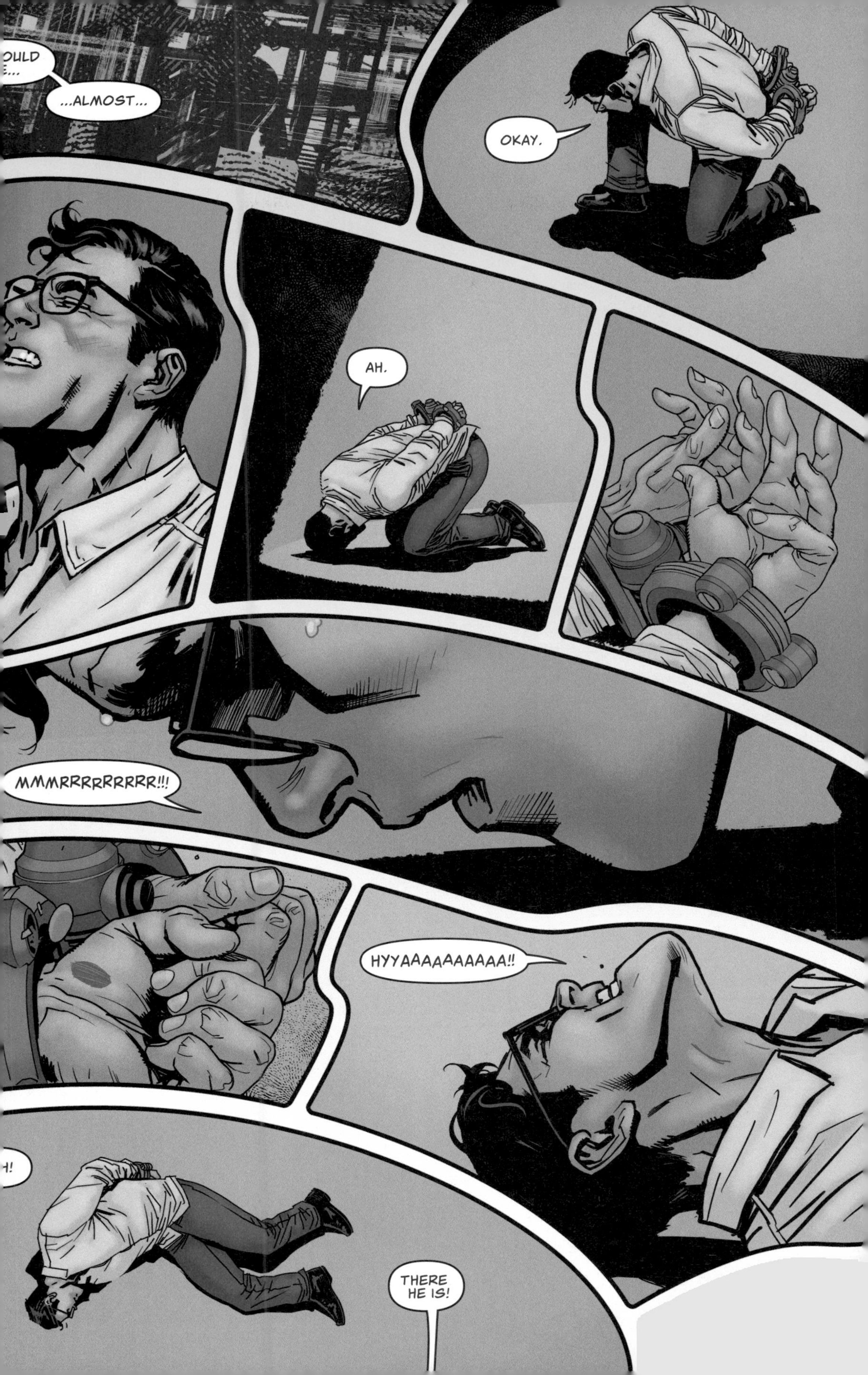
OULD
E...
...ALMOST...
OKAY.
AH.
MMMRRRRRRRRR!!!
HYYAAAAAAAAAA!!
H!
THERE
HE IS!

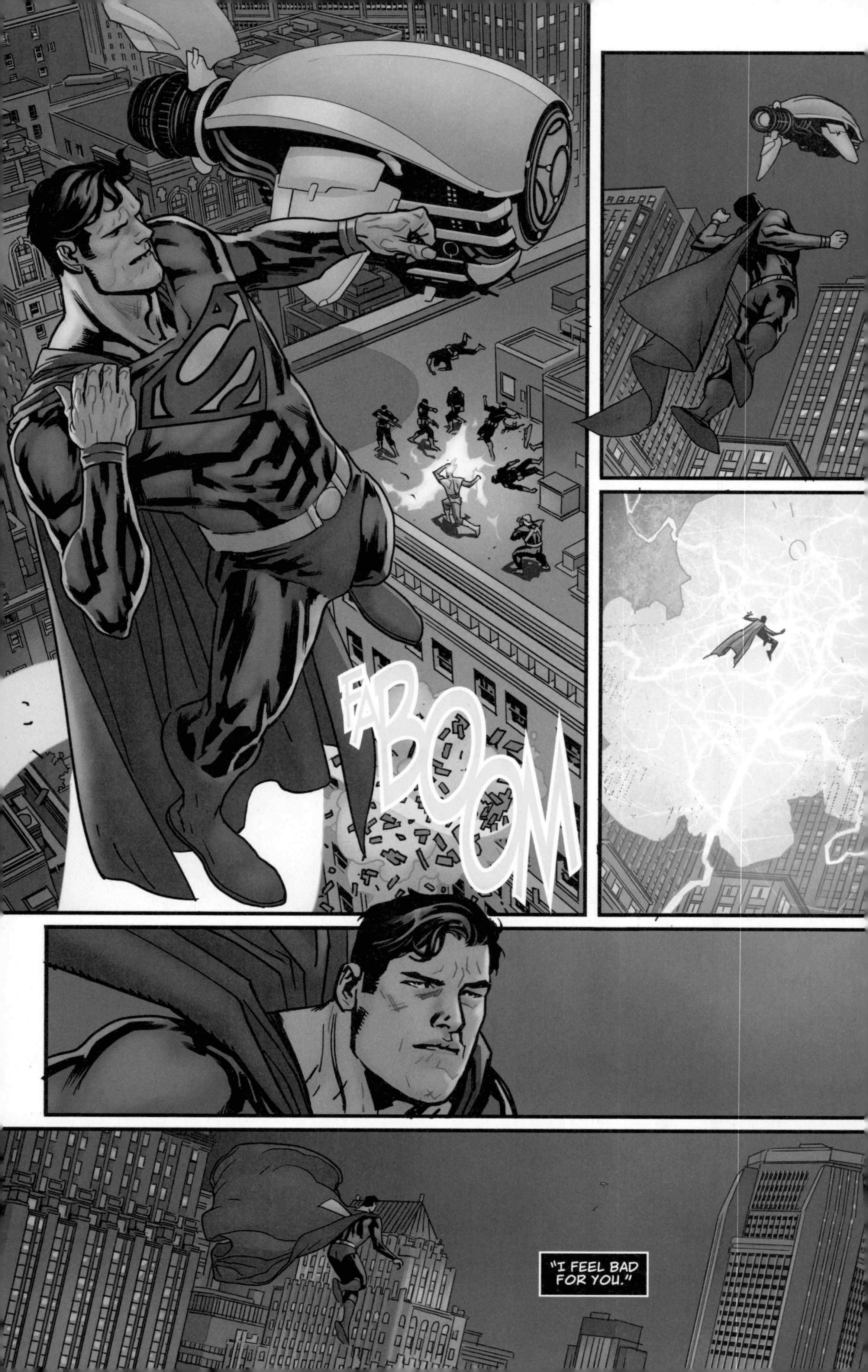
FABOOOM
"I FEEL BAD FOR YOU."

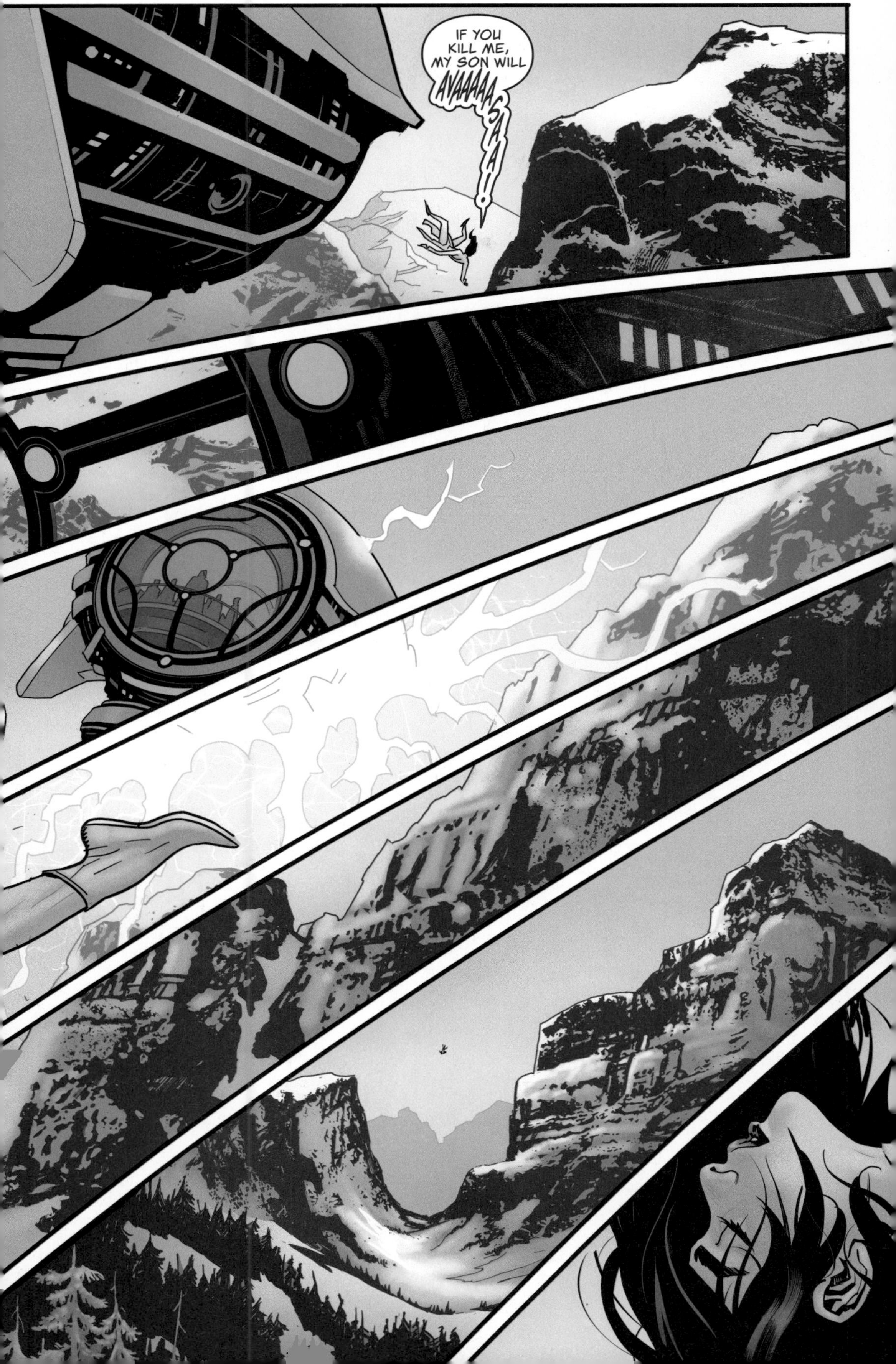
IF YOU KILL ME, MY SON WILL
AVAAAAASAA!

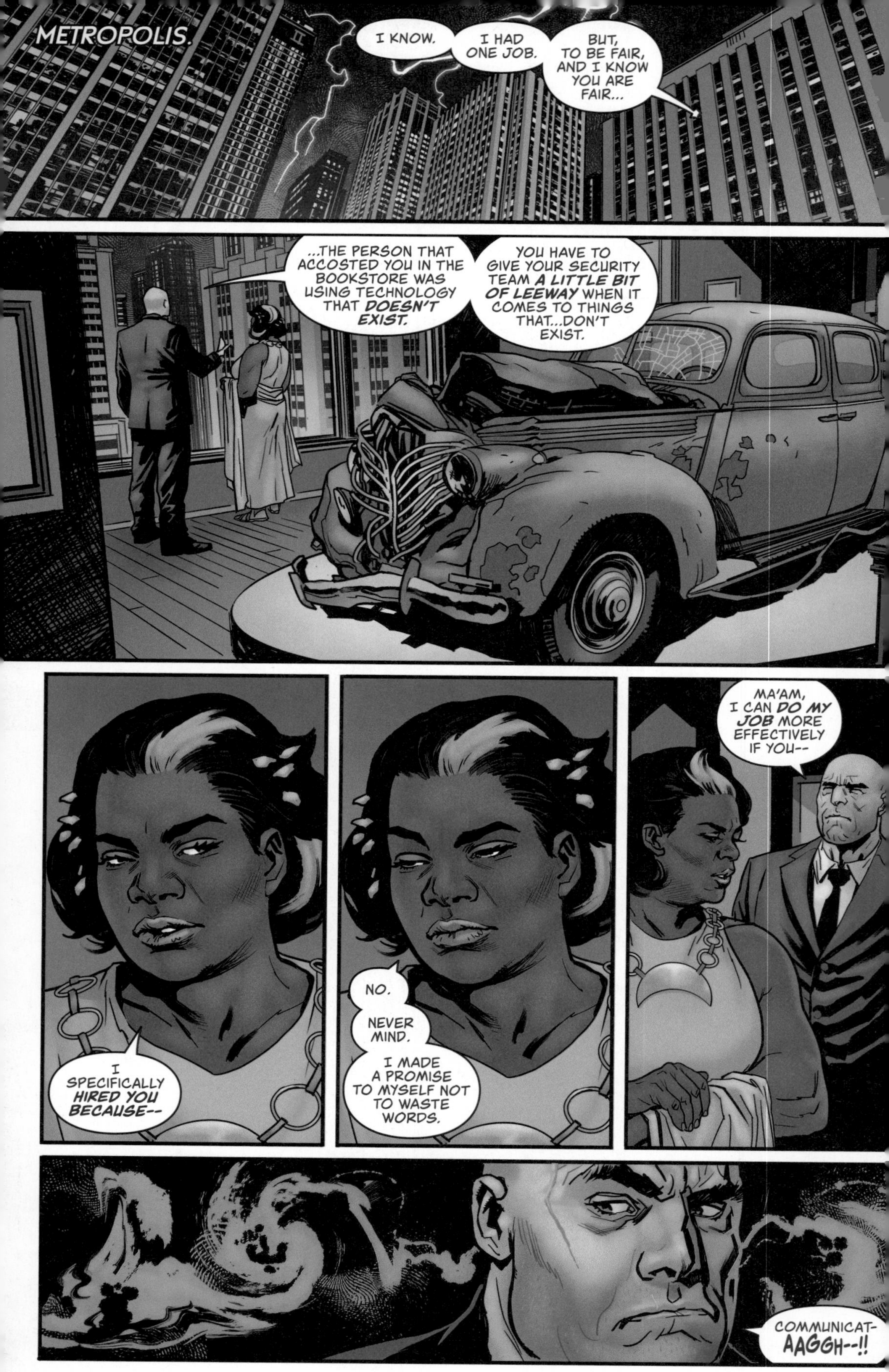
METROPOLIS.
I KNOW.
I HAD ONE JOB.
BUT, TO BE FAIR, AND I KNOW YOU ARE FAIR...
...THE PERSON THAT ACCOSTED YOU IN THE BOOKSTORE WAS USING TECHNOLOGY THAT DOESN'T EXIST.
YOU HAVE TO GIVE YOUR SECURITY TEAM A LITTLE BIT OF LEEWAY WHEN IT COMES TO THINGS THAT...DON'T EXIST.
I SPECIFICALLY HIRED YOU BECAUSE--
NO.
NEVER MIND.
I MADE A PROMISE TO MYSELF NOT TO WASTE WORDS.
MA'AM, I CAN DO MY JOB MORE EFFECTIVELY IF YOU--
COMMUNICAT-AAGGH--!!

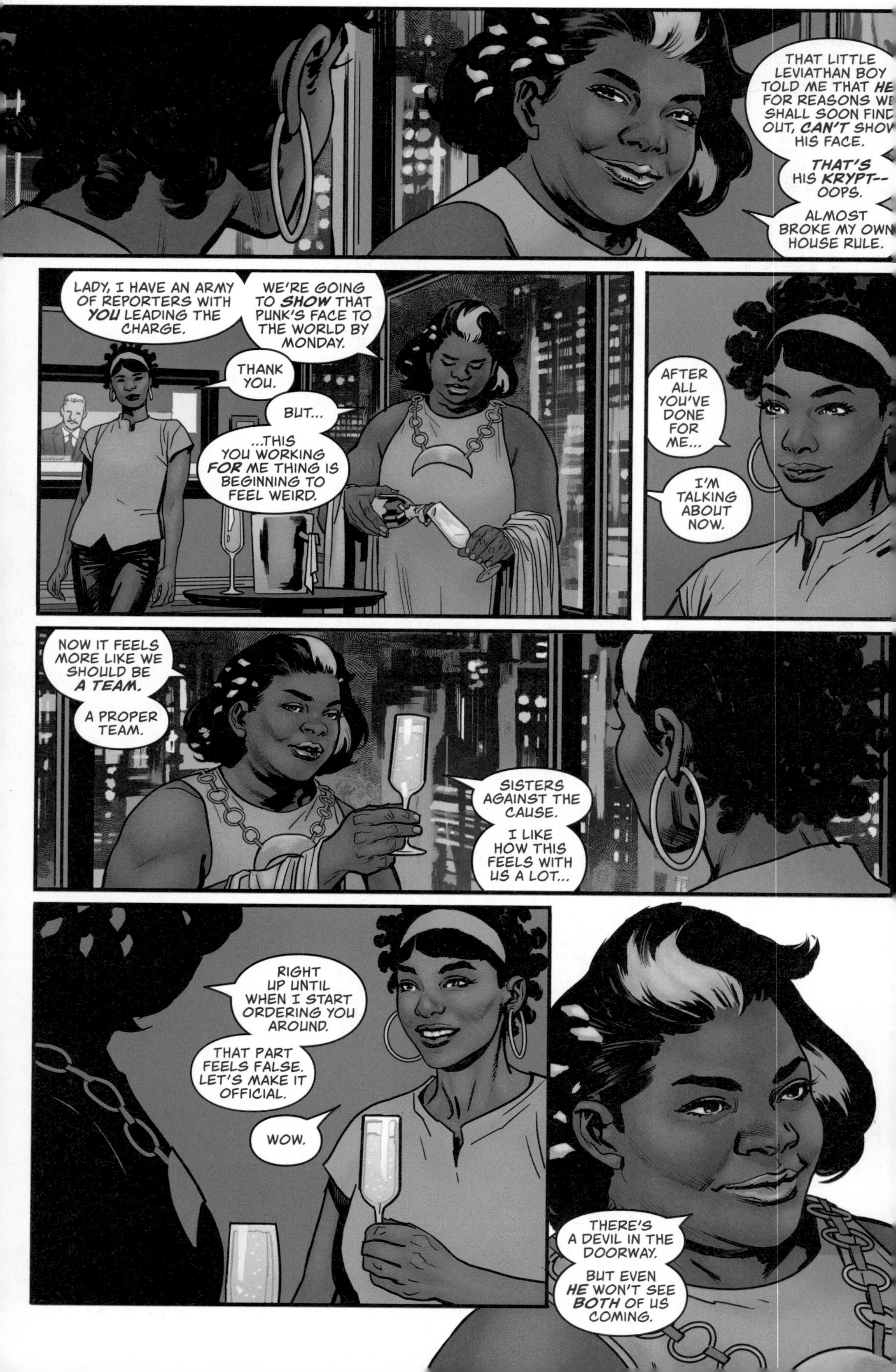

THAT LITTLE LEVIATHAN BOY TOLD ME THAT HE, FOR REASONS WE SHALL SOON FIND OUT, CAN'T SHOW HIS FACE.
THAT'S HIS KRYPT-- OOPS.
ALMOST BROKE MY OWN HOUSE RULE.
LADY, I HAVE AN ARMY OF REPORTERS WITH YOU LEADING THE CHARGE.
WE'RE GOING TO SHOW THAT PUNK'S FACE TO THE WORLD BY MONDAY.
THANK YOU.
BUT...
...THIS YOU WORKING FOR ME THING IS BEGINNING TO FEEL WEIRD.
AFTER ALL YOU'VE DONE FOR ME...
I'M TALKING ABOUT NOW.
NOW IT FEELS MORE LIKE WE SHOULD BE A TEAM.
A PROPER TEAM.
SISTERS AGAINST THE CAUSE.
I LIKE HOW THIS FEELS WITH US A LOT...
RIGHT UP UNTIL WHEN I START ORDERING YOU AROUND.
THAT PART FEELS FALSE. LET'S MAKE IT OFFICIAL.
WOW.
THERE'S A DEVIL IN THE DOORWAY.
BUT EVEN HE WON'T SEE BOTH OF US COMING.

VARIANT COVER GALLERY

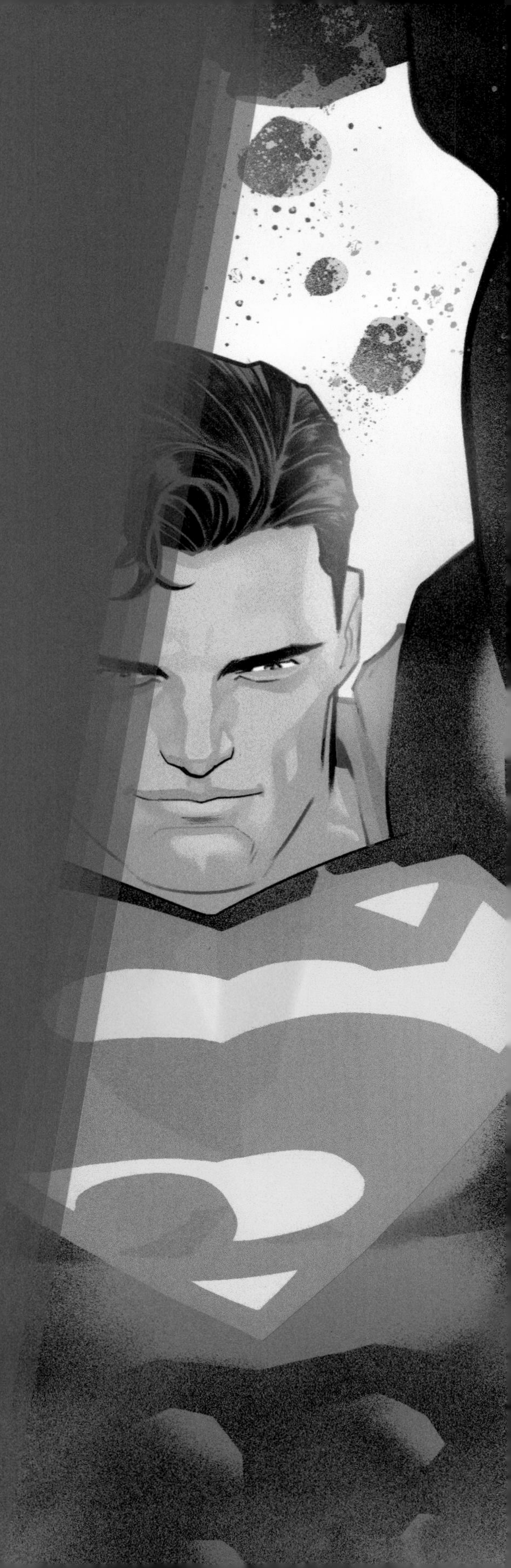

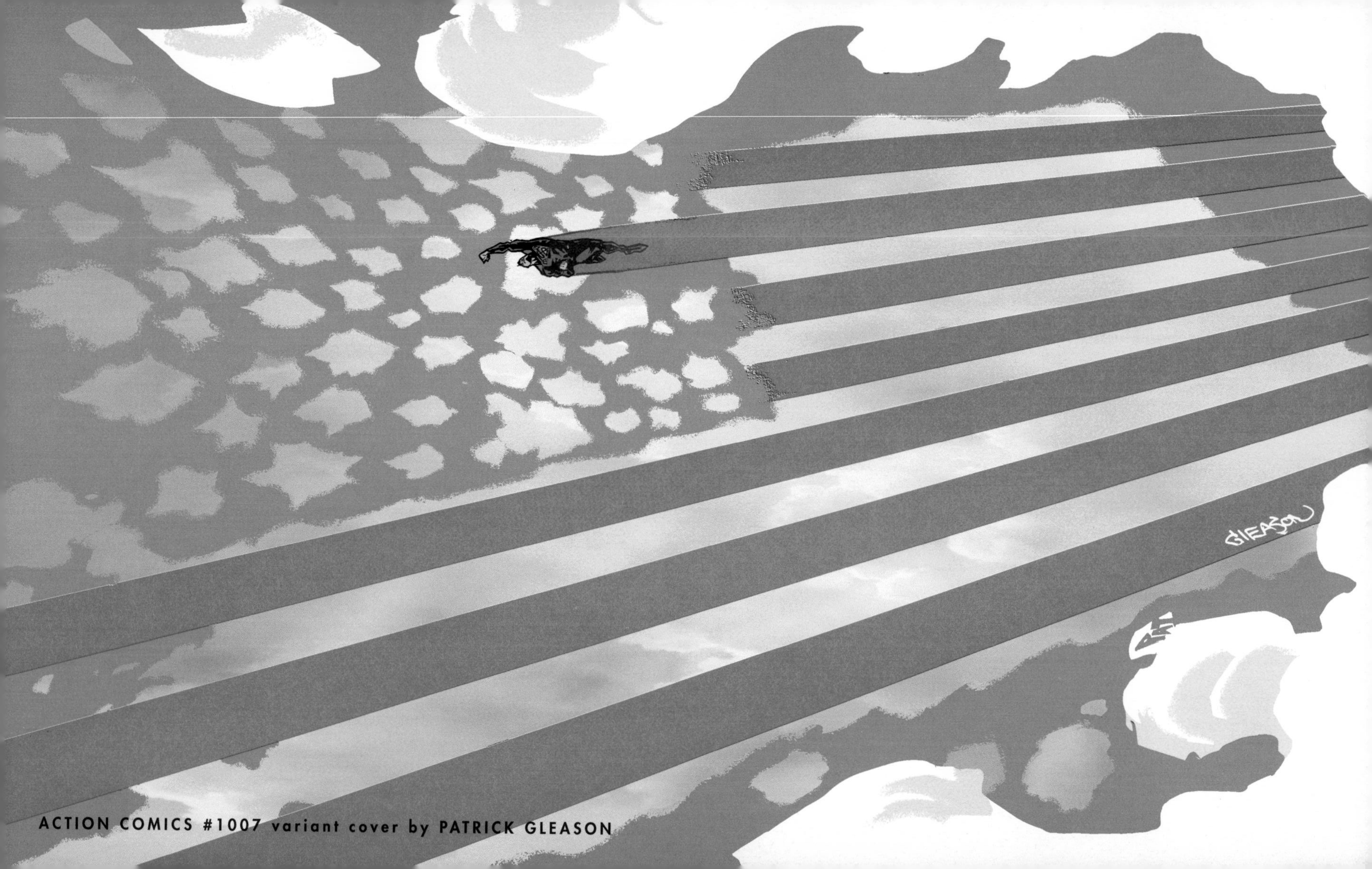
GLEASON

ACTION COMICS #1007 variant cover by PATRICK GLEASON

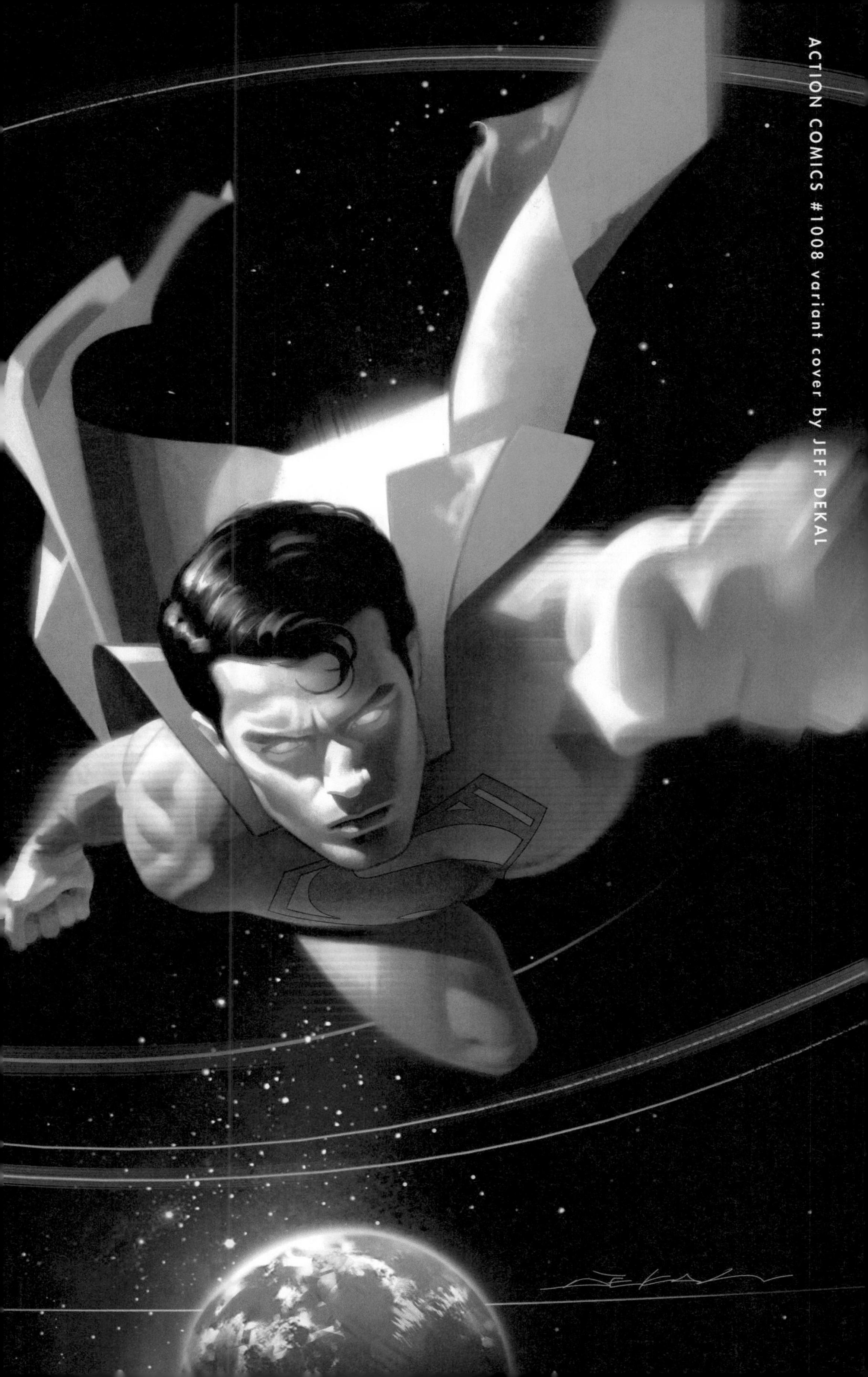

ACTION COMICS #1008 variant cover by JEFF DEKAL

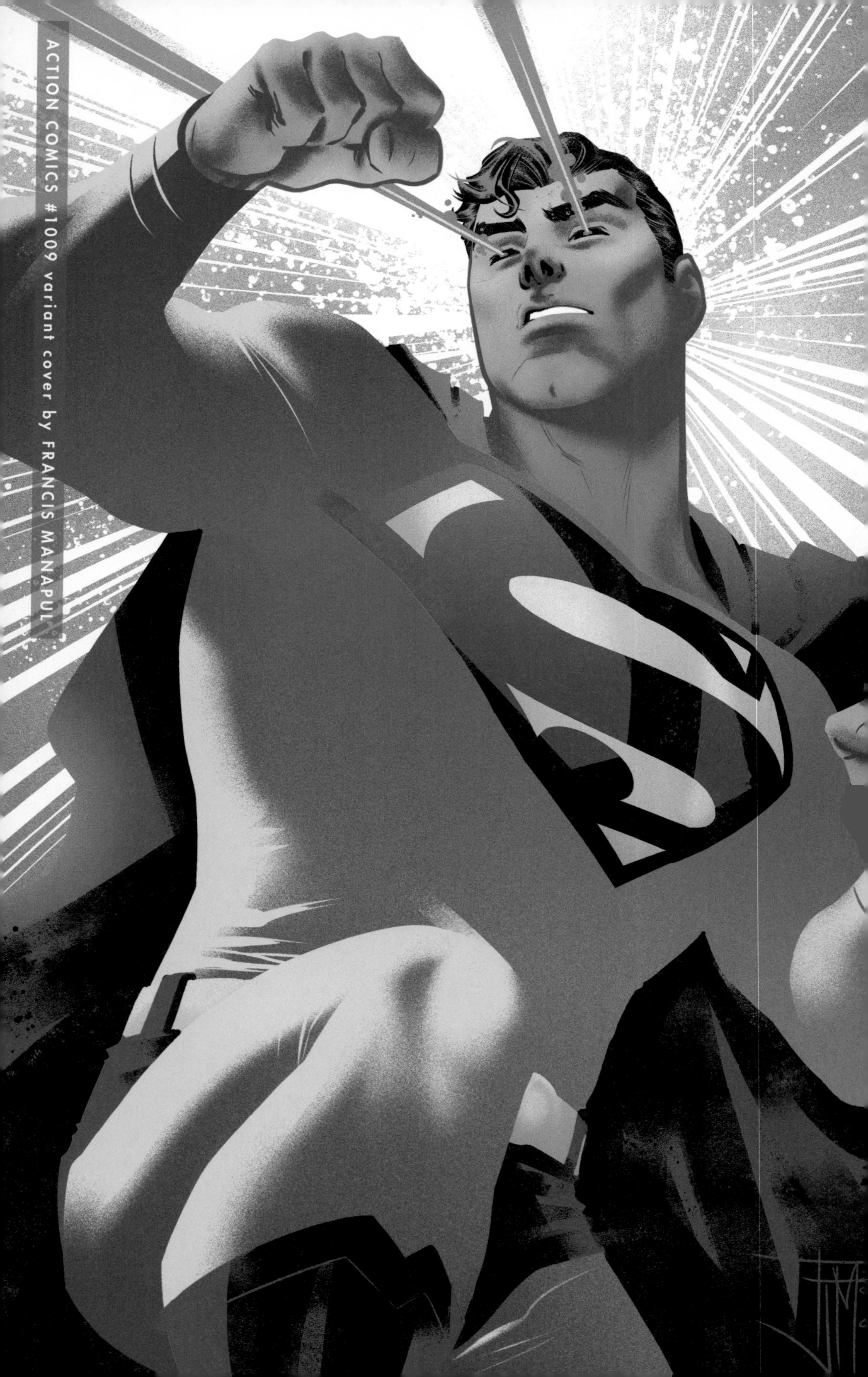

ACTION COMICS #1009 variant cover by FRANCIS MANAPUL

ACTION COMICS #1010 variant cover by FRANCIS MANAPUL

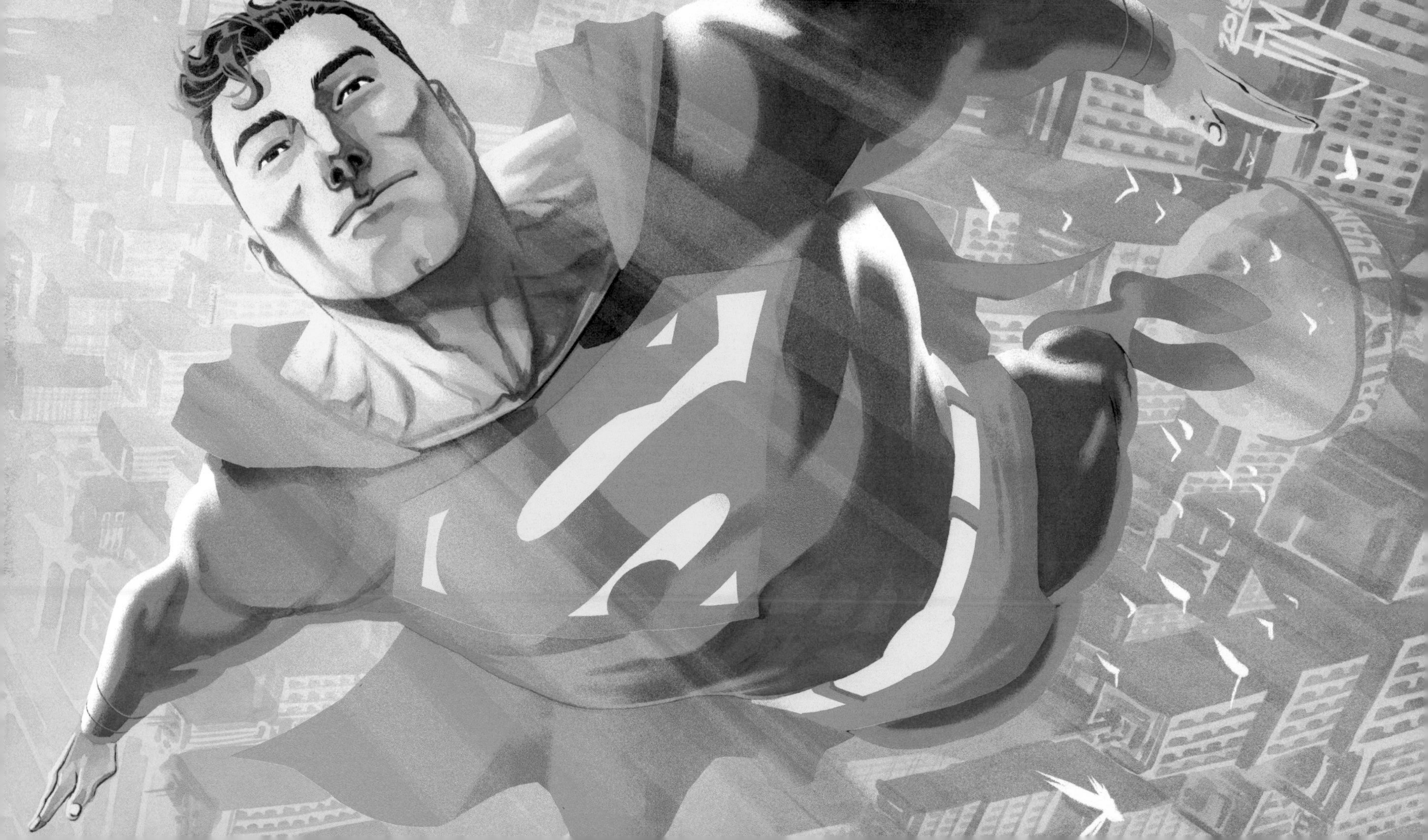

2018
DAILY PLANET

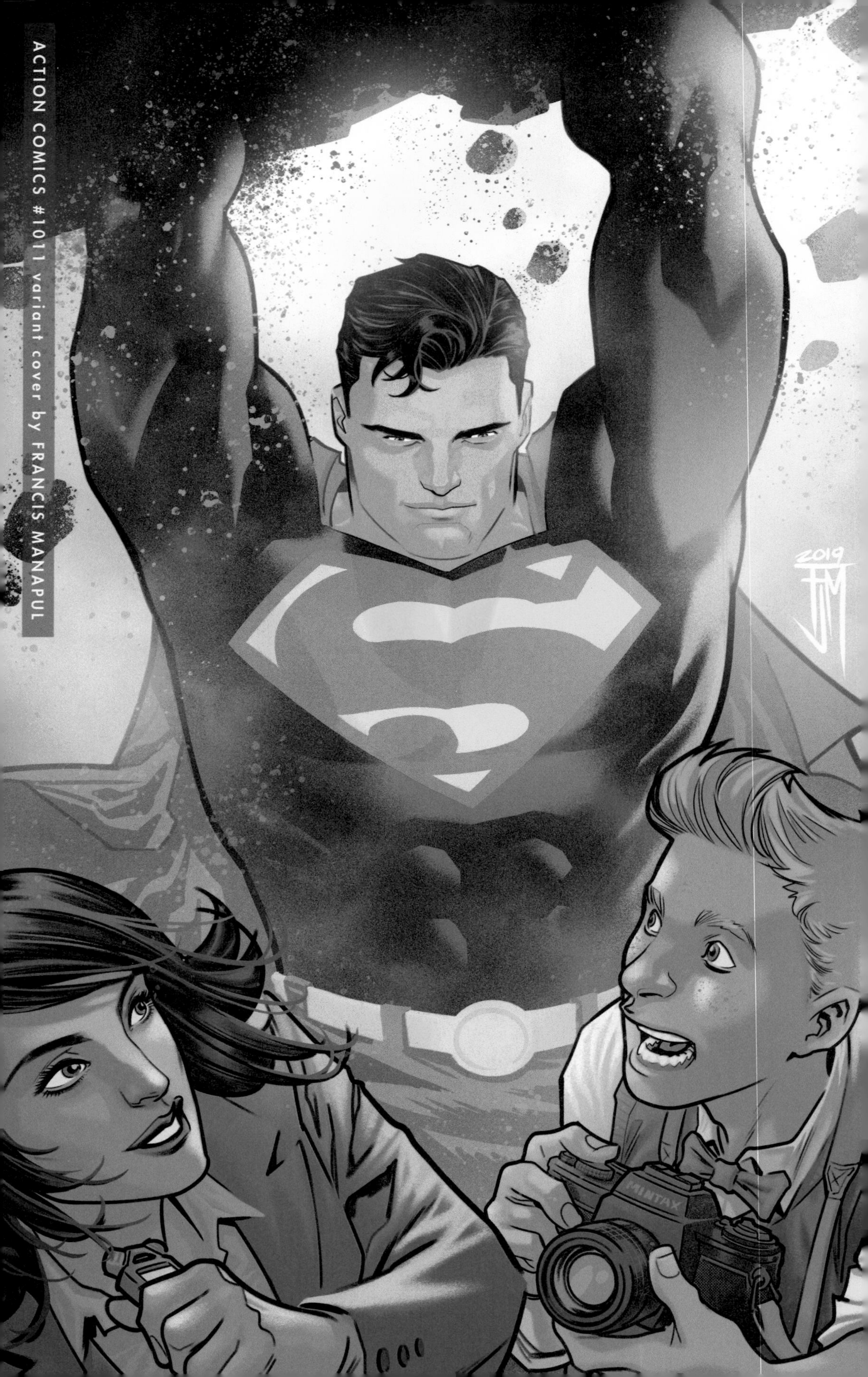

ACTION COMICS #1011 variant cover by FRANCIS MANAPUL

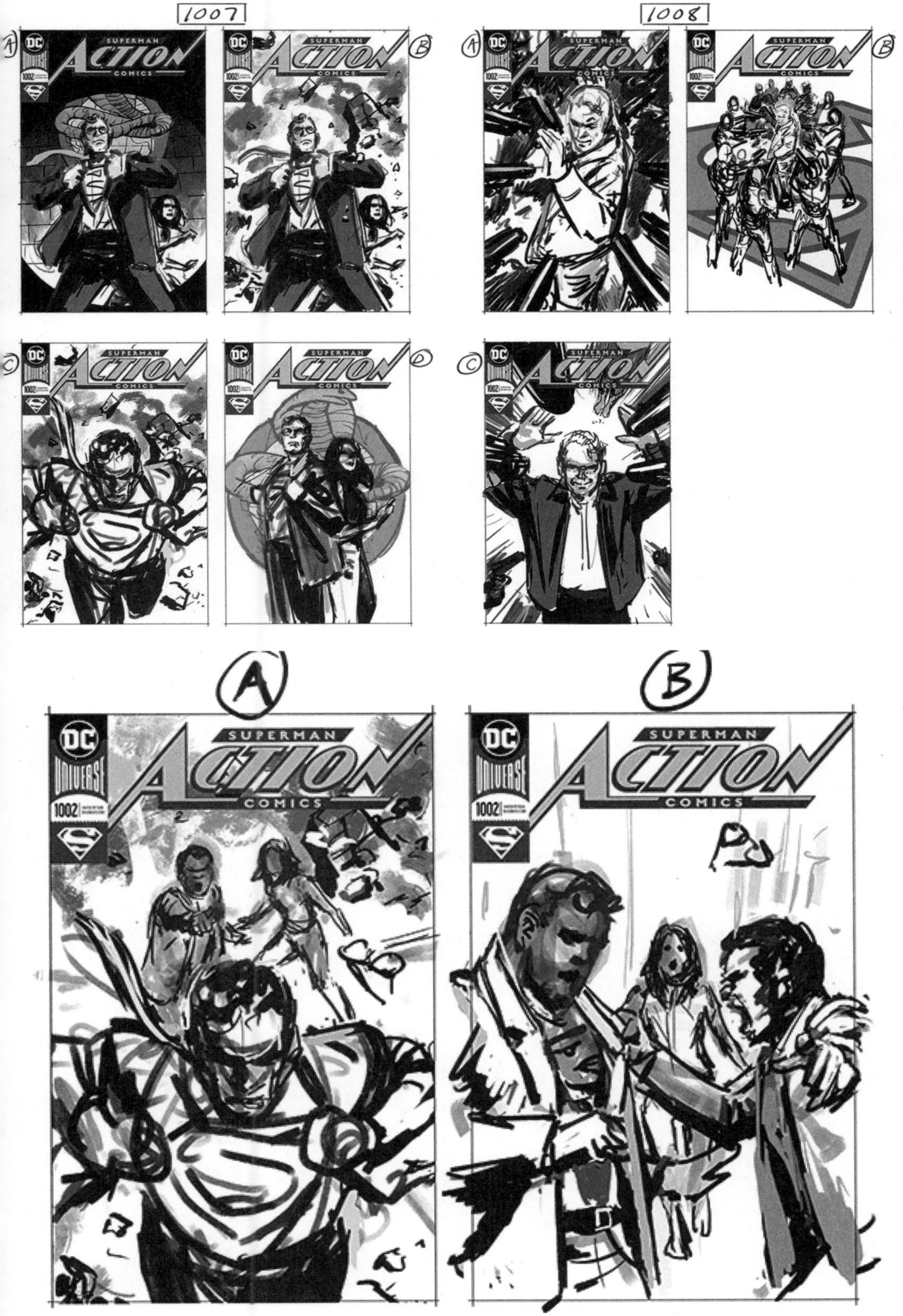
1007
1008
A
B

Cover sketches for ACTION COMICS #1007-1009 by STEVE EPTING

Ⓐ

Ⓑ

Cover sketches for ACTION COMICS #1010-1011 by STEVE EPTING

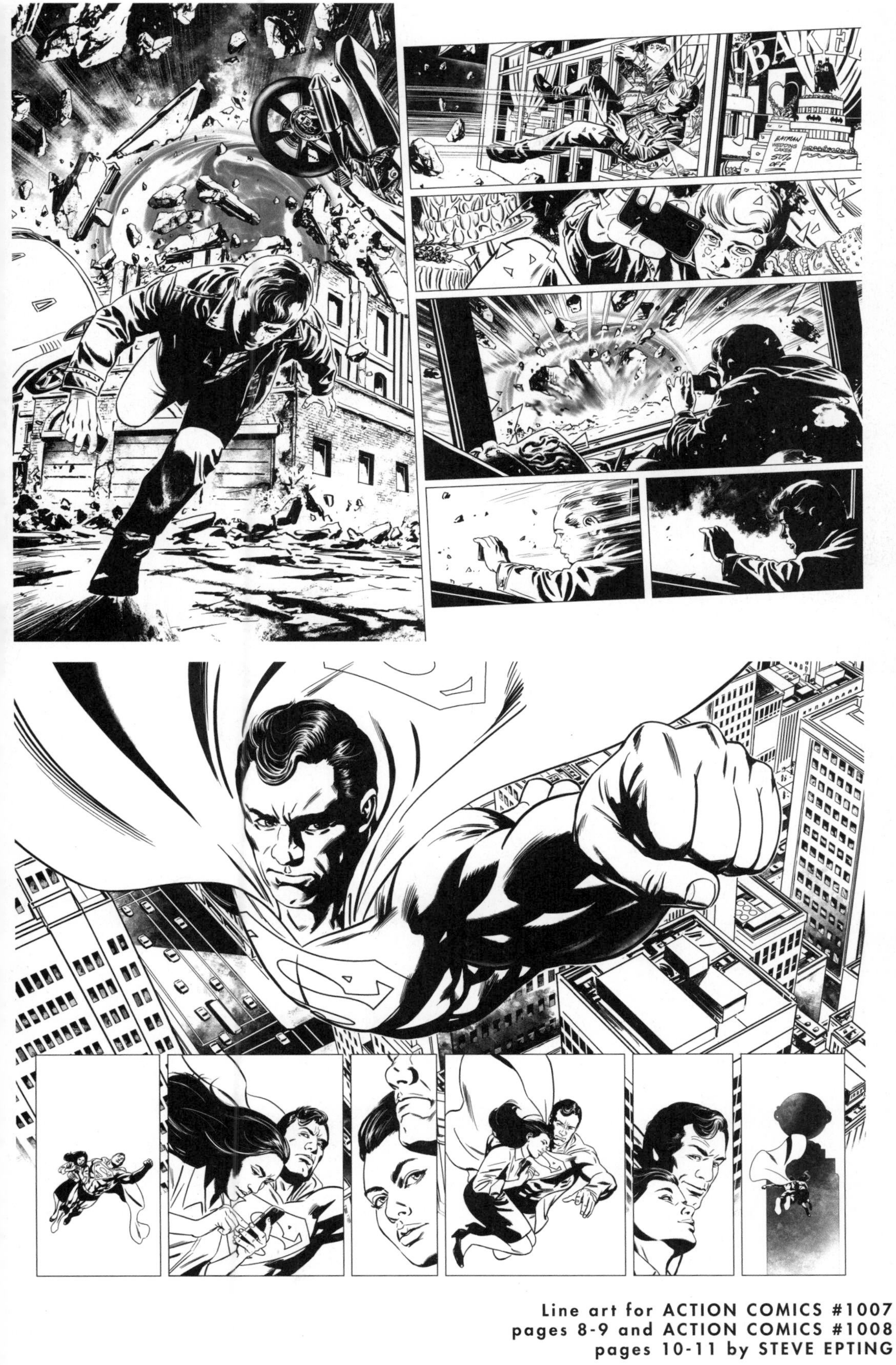
BAKE
BATMAN WEDDING CAKES 50% OFF

Line art for ACTION COMICS #1007 pages 8-9 and ACTION COMICS #1008 pages 10-11 by STEVE EPTING

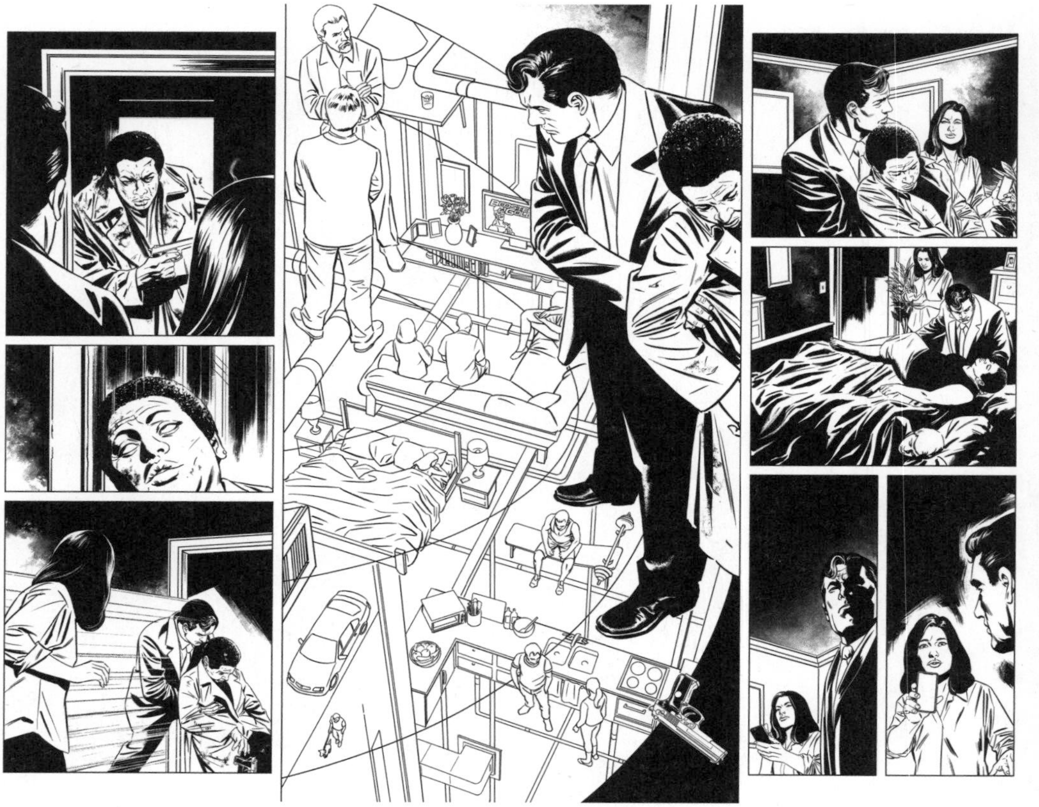

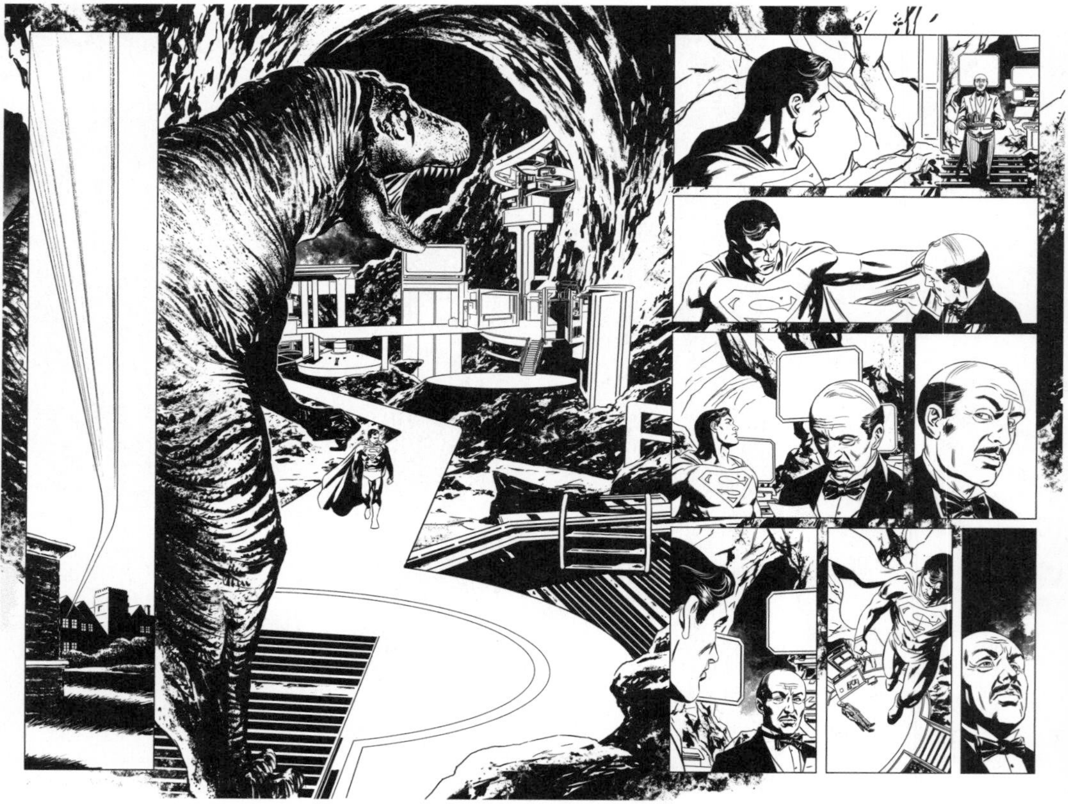

Line art for ACTION COMICS #1009
pages 4-5 and 16-17 by STEVE EPTING

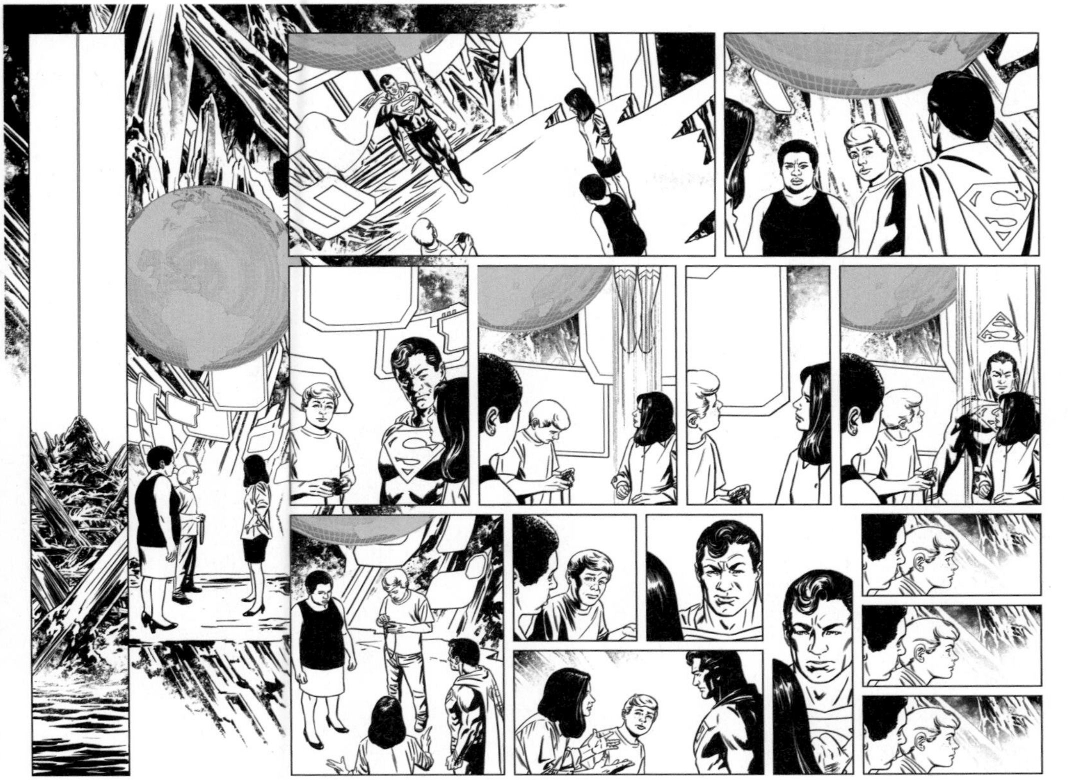

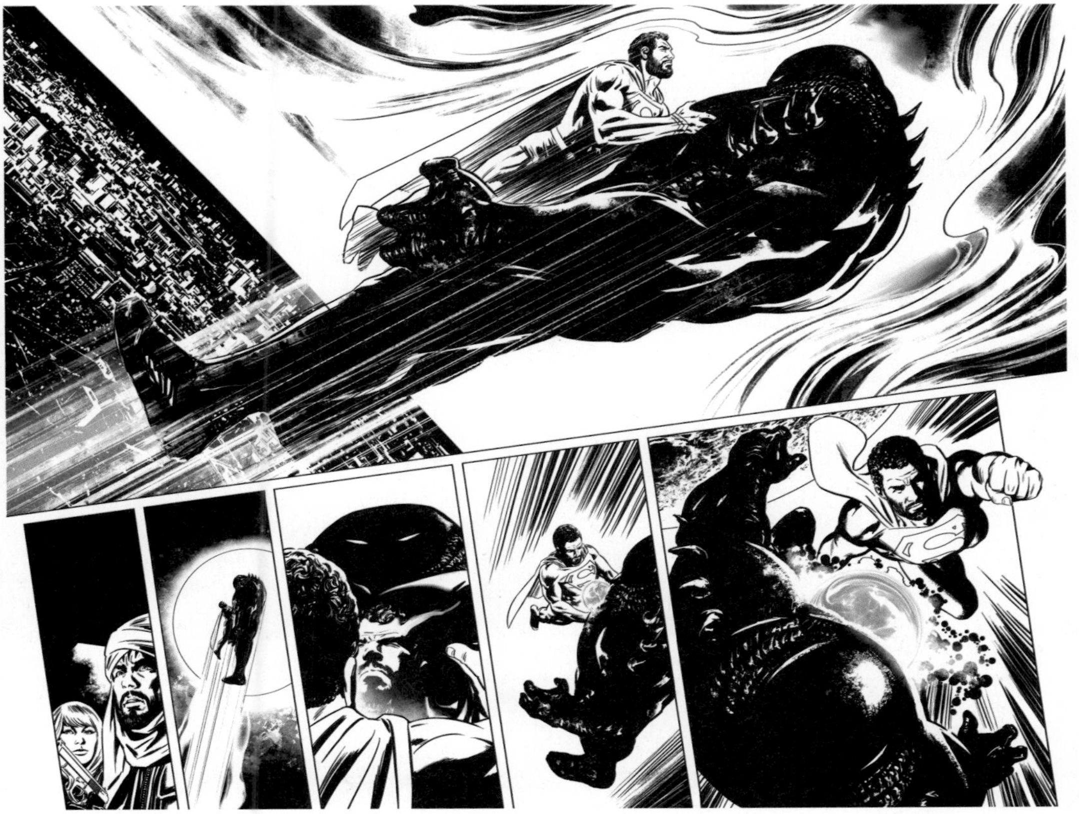

Line art for ACTION COMICS #1009 pages 20-21 and
ACTION COMICS #1010 pages 18-19 by STEVE EPTING

DC UNIVERSE REBIRTH
SUPERMAN
VOL. 1: SON OF SUPERMAN
PETER J. TOMASI with PATRICK GLEASON, DOUG MAHNKE & JORGE JIMENEZ

SUPERGIRL VOL. 1: REIGN OF THE SUPERMEN

ACTION COMICS VOL. 1: PATH OF DOOM

BATMAN VOL. 1: I AM GOTHAM

Get more DC graphic novels wherever comics and books are sold!

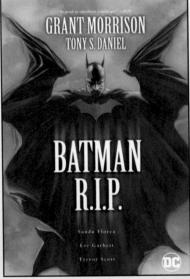

"ACTION COMICS has successfully carved its own territory and continued exploring Morrison's familiar themes about heroism and ideas." – **IGN**

THE #1 NEW YORK TIMES BESTSELLER
THE NEW 52!
SUPERMAN
ACTION COMICS
VOLUME 1
SUPERMAN AND THE MEN OF STEEL
"BELIEVE THE HYPE: GRANT MORRISON WENT AND WROTE THE SINGLE BEST ISSUE OF SUPERMAN THESE EYES HAVE EVER READ."
— USA TODAY
GRANT MORRISON RAGS MORALES ANDY KUBER

SUPERMAN: ACTION COMICS

VOL. 1: SUPERMAN AND THE MEN OF STEEL

GRANT MORRISON
with RAGS MORALES

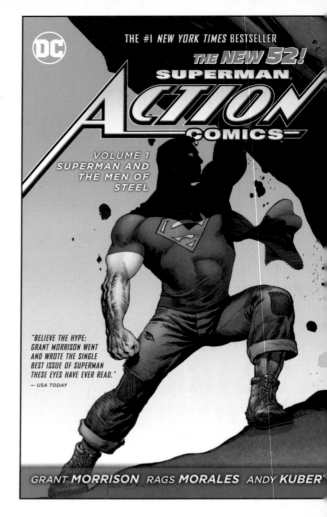

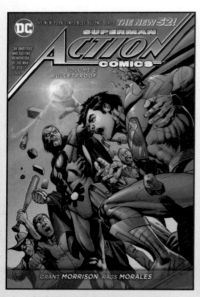

THE NEW YORK TIMES BEST-SELLING SERIES THE NEW 52!
SUPERMAN
ACTION COMICS
VOLUME 2
BULLETPROOF
GRANT MORRISON RAGS MORALES

SUPERMAN: ACTION COMICS VOL. 2: BULLETPROOF

THE NEW 52!
SUPERMAN
ACTION COMICS
GRANT MORRISON RAGS MORALES BRAD WALKER

SUPERMAN: ACTION COMICS VOL. 3: AT THE END OF DAYS

READ THE ENTIRE E

SUPERMAN: ACTION COMICS V
HY

SUPERMAN: ACTION COMICS V
WHAT LIES BEN

SUPERMAN: ACTION COMICS V
SUPERI

SUPERMAN: ACTION COMICS V
UNDER THE

SUPERMAN: ACTION COMICS V
T

SUPERMAN: ACTION COMICS V
LAST

Get more DC graphic novels wherever comics and books are sold!